2. Right now I'm in class. I (*sit*) _I'm sitting_ at my desk. I usually (*sit*)
I sat at the same desk in class every day.

3. Ali (*speak*) _speak_ Arabic. Arabic is his native language, but
right now he (*speak*) _is speaking_ English.

4. Our teacher (*stand up, not*) _She not standing_ right now. She (*sit*) _sits_
sits on the corner of her desk.

5. It's 6:00 p.m. Mary is at home. She (*eat*) _is eats_ dinner. She
always (*eat*) _eating_ dinner with her family around six o'clock.

6. Alice (*take, not*) _doesn't Takes_ the bus to school every day. She
usually (*walk*) _walks_ instead.

7. It (*rain, not*) _isn't raining_ right now. The sun (*shine*) _is shining_

8. It's 7:30 a.m. and the Wilsons are in their kitchen. Mrs. Wilson (*sit*) _sits_
around at the breakfast table. She (*read*) _____
the morning paper. She (*read*) _reads_ the newspaper every
morning. Mr. Wilson (*pour*) _pours_ a cup of coffee. He (*drink*)
is drinking two cups of coffee every morning before he (*go*) _____
_____ to work. There is a cartoon on TV, but the children
(*watch, not*) _____ it. They (*play*) _____ with
their toys instead. They usually (*watch*) _____ cartoons in the
morning, but this morning they (*pay, not*) _____ any attention
to the TV. Mr. and Mrs. Wilson (*watch, not*) _aren't watching_ the TV
either. They (*like, not*) _don't like_ to watch cartoons.

EXERCISE 3—ORAL (BOOKS CLOSED): Practice using *the present progressive.* Practice using your classmates' names.

(To the teacher: On note cards, write instructions of actions to be performed. Pass the note cards out to the class. Ask Student A to perform the action on his or her card, and then ask Student B to describe the action. B should use A's name.)

Example:	stand up
Teacher:	Someone's card says, "Stand up." Would that person please stand up?
Student A:	(Student A stands up.)
Teacher:	Who is standing up?
Student B:	Maria is standing up.

(After going through all of the actions, collect and redistribute the cards. Ask Student A to perform the action on his or her card (without your naming it). Ask Student B to describe the action.)

Teacher:	Please perform the action on your card.
Student A:	(Student A scratches her hand.)
Teacher:	What is Maria doing?
Student B:	She's scratching her hand.

(Below are suggestions for actions. To make sure that the students understand the vocabulary in the instructions on their note cards, you may wish to perform all of the actions first yourself. Also, if you wish, some of the instructions can require the use of things you bring to class: He is smelling a rose. She is hammering a nail. He is eating a piece of candy.)

1. stand up
2. smile
3. whistle
4. open or close the door
5. hum   *pujand*
6. bite your fingernails
7. read your grammar book
8. erase the board
9. look at the ceiling
10. hold your pen in your left hand
11. rub your palms together
12. kick your desk
13. knock on the door
14. sit on the floor
15. shake hands with somebody
16. look at your watch
17. count aloud the number of people in the room
18. scratch your head

(As a variation, ask two or more students to perform an action simultaneously in order to practice plural forms.)

Claire
krascav.

EXERCISE 4—ORAL: Describe *your* daily activities by making sentences with frequency adverbs.

FREQUENCY ADVERBS:*

100%   **always**
↑   **usually**
       often
       sometimes
       seldom
↓   **rarely**
0%   **never**

Example: eat breakfast
Student A: I usually eat breakfast.
Student B: I never eat breakfast.
Student C: I always eat breakfast.
Etc.†

1. eat breakfast
2. drink coffee in the morning
3. drink more than two cups of coffee in the morning
4. drink tea in the morning
5. drink orange juice in the morning
6. drink tomato juice in the morning
7. drink milk in the morning
8. put sugar in your coffee
9. have a sandwich for lunch
10. eat dinner around six o'clock
11. come to class
12. get to class on time
13. walk to school
14. take a bus to school
15. take a taxi to school
16. drive to school
17. ride a bike to school
18. watch TV in the evening
19. study at the library
20. do your homework

EXERCISE 5—ORAL (BOOKS CLOSED):   Answer the questions.

WHAT ARE SOME THINGS YOU . . .

1. always do every day?

WHAT ARE SOME THINGS YOUR ROOMMATE/MOTHER/FATHER/ HUSBAND/WIFE/FRIEND . . .

1. always does?

---
*See Chart 6–7, MIDSENTENCE ADVERBS, in Chapter 6 for more information about frequency adverbs.
†*To the teacher: Ask for responses from three or four students for each item.*

2. usually do every day?

3. often do?

4. sometimes do?

5. seldom do?

6. rarely do?

7. never do?

2. usually does?

3. often does?

4. sometimes does?

5. seldom does?

6. rarely does?

7. never does?

EXERCISE 6—ORAL (BOOKS CLOSED):   Practice using the simple present.

(To the teacher: Beginning with the time they get up until the time they go to bed, get your students to talk about their daily activities. Develop and complete a brief conversation with Student A, and then ask Student B to tell the class about Student A. Then repeat the process with a different Student A and a different Student B. Tell Student B to say final -s loudly and clearly.)

Example: from 6:00 a.m. to 9:00 a.m.

T: Tell us about your daily activities from the time you get up until 9:00 a.m. What are some of the things you usually do?

A: I get up at seven.

T: Always?

A: Usually. I put on my clothes. I eat breakfast.

T: Do you always eat breakfast?

A: Yes.

T: What do you usually have for breakfast?

A: Bread and cheese and coffee. Sometimes I have an egg.

T: Do you ever have cereal for breakfast?

A: No, I don't.

T: Can you tell us about (. . .)? What does he/she usually do in the morning?

B: He/She usually gets up at seven. He/She puts on his/her clothes. He/She eats breakfast.

T: Always?

B: Yes. He/She always eats breakfast. He/She usually has bread and cheese and coffee for breakfast, but sometimes he/she has an egg. He/She never has cereal for breakfast.

1. from 6:00 a.m. to 9:00 a.m.
2. from 9:00 a.m. to noon
3. from noon to 3:00 p.m.
4. from 3:00 p.m. to 6:00 p.m.
5. from 6:00 p.m. until you go to bed

1-2   NONPROGRESSIVE VERBS

(a) I **hear** a bird. It is singing.	Some verbs are not used in the present progressive.
	CORRECT: *I hear a bird.* (*right now*)
(b) I'm hungry. I **want** a sandwich.	INCORRECT: *I am hearing a bird.*

NONPROGRESSIVE VERBS		
be	*hear*	*prefer*
believe	*know*	*see*
belong	*like*	*think* (meaning *believe*)†
hate	*love*	*understand*
have (meaning *possess*)*	*need*	*want*

*When **have** expresses possession, it is not used in the present progressive: *Tom has a car.* In certain idiomatic expressions (e.g., *have a good time*), **have** can be used in the present progressive: *I'm having a good time.*

†When **think** means *believe*, it is nonprogressive: *I think that grammar is easy.* However, when **think** expresses thoughts that are going through a person's mind, it can be used in the present progressive: *I'm thinking about grammar right now.*

EXERCISE 7:   Complete the sentences with the words in parentheses. Use *the simple present* or *the present progressive*.

1. Right now Yoko (*read*) _____is reading_____ an article in the newspaper, but
   she (*understand, not*) __doesn't understand__ it. Some of the vocabulary (*be*)
   _____is_____ too difficult for her.

2. Right now I (*look*) __I'm looking__ at the board. I (*see*) __seen__
   some words on the board.

3. I (*need*) __need__ to call my parents today and tell them about
   my new apartment. They can't call me because they (*know, not*) __don't know__,
   __know__ my new telephone number.

4. This tea is good. I (*like*) __like__ it. What kind is it? I (*prefer*)
   __I prefer__ tea to coffee. How about you?

5. Sam is at the library. He (*sit*) __is sitting__ at a table. He (*write*)
   __writing__ a composition. He (*use*) __is useing__ a dictionary
   to look up the spelling of some words. The dictionary (*belong, not*) __dosen't__
   __belong__ to him. It (*belong*) __belongs__ to his
   roommate. Sam (*look*) __looks__ up words in the dictionary because
   he (*want*) __wants__ to make sure that he doesn't misspell any
   words.

6. Right now the children (*be*) __are__ at the beach. They (*have*)
   __are haven__ a good time. They (*have*) __have__ a beach
   ball, and they (*play*) __are playing__ catch with it. They (*like*)_____
   __like__ to play catch. Their parents (*sunbathe*) __are__
   __sunbathering__. They (*try*) __try__ to get a tan. They
   (*listen*) __are listening__ to some music on a transistor radio. They also
   (*hear*) __hear__ the sound of sea gulls and the sound of the
   waves.

7. Right now I (*think*) __I'm thinking__ about sea gulls and waves.

8. I (*think*) __I think__ that sea gulls are beautiful birds.

EXERCISE 8:   Complete the following dialogues by using the words in parentheses.
Also give short answers to the questions as necessary. Use *the simple present* or
the present progressive.

1. A: (*Mary, have*) __Does Mary have__ a bicycle?

B: Yes, _____*she does.*_____ . She (*have*) _____*has*_____

_____ a ten-speed bike.

2. A: (*it, rain*) _____*It's raining*_____ right now?

   B: No, it _____*is't doesen*_____ . At least, I (*think, not*) _____*No I don't think,*_____ _____*so*_____ so.

3. A: (*you, like*) _____*do you like*_____ sour oranges?

   B: No, I _____*don't*_____ . I (*like*) _____*I like*_____

   sweet ones.

4. A: (*your friends, write*) _____*yes they do*_____ a lot of letters?

   B: Yes, _____*they do*_____ . I (*get*) _____*I get*_____

   lots of letters all the time.

5. A: (*the students, take*) _____*are the studen*_____ a test in class right now?

   B: No, _____*they aren't*_____ . They (*do*) _____*are doing*_____

   an exercise.

6. A: (*you, know*) _____*do you know*_____ Tom Adams?

   B: No, _____*I don't*_____ . I've never met him.

7. A: (*your desk, have*) _____*does your desk (have)*_____ any drawers?

   B: Yes, _____*it does*_____ . It (*have*) _____*It has*_____

   six drawers.

8. A: (*Jean, study*) _____*Is jean, study*_____ at the library this evening?

   B: No, _____*she doesn't*_____ . She (*be*) _____*She is he*_____

   at the student union. She (*play*) _____*She is playin*_____ pool with

   her boyfriend.

A: (*Jean, play*) _does Jean play_ pool every evening?

B: No, _She doesn't_ . She usually (*study*) _She does usually studys_ at the library.

A: (*she, be*) _Is she been_ a good pool player?

B: Yes, _she does_ . She (*play*) _she plays_ pool a lot.

A: (*you, know*) _do you know_ how to play pool?

B: Yes, _I know_ . But I (*be, not*) _I not been_ very good.

EXERCISE 9:   Complete the sentences by using the words in parentheses. Use *the simple present* or *the present progressive.* Some of the sentences are negative. Some of the sentences are questions. Supply the short answer to a question if necessary.

1. A: Where are the children?
    B: In the living room.

    A: What are they doing? (*they, watch*) _are they_ TV?

    B: No, _They aren't_ . They (*play*) _are playing_ a game.

2. A: Shhhh. I (*hear*) _I hear_ a noise. (*you, hear*) _do you hear_ it too?

    B: Yes, _I do_ . I wonder what it is.

3. A: My sister (*have*) _My sister has_ a new car. She bought it last month.

    B: (*you, have*) _do you have_ a car?

    A: No, _I don't_ . Do you?
    B: No, but I have a ten-speed bike.

4. A: Shhhh.

    B: Why? (*the baby, sleep*) _Is the baby ? sleeping_

    A: Uh-huh. She (*take*) _She takeing_ her afternoon nap.

    B: Okay, I'll talk softly. I (*want, not*) _I not want_ to wake her up.

5. A: Ron, (*be*) _is this Ron_ this your hat?

B: No, _It doesn't_ . It (belong, not) _it not belong_ to me.

Maybe it (belong) _it belongs_ to Howard. Why don't you ask him about it?

A: Okay.

6. A: Johnny, (you, listen) _are you listening_ to me?

B: Of course I am, Mom. You (want) _do you want_ me to take out the garbage. Right?

A: Right! And right now!

7. A: What (you, think) _I think_ about every night before you fall asleep?

B: I (think) _I'm thinking_ about all of the pleasant things that happened during the day. I (think, not) _I not think_ about my problems.

8. A: A penny for your thoughts!

B: Huh?

A: What (you, think) _do you think_ about right now?

B: I (think) _I think_ about English grammar. I (think, not) _I'm not thinking_ about anything else.

A: I (believe, not) _I not believe_ you!

B: But it's true.

9. A: (you, know) _do you know_ any tongue-twisters?

B: Yes, _I know_ . Here's one: She sells sea shells down by the seashore.

A: That (be) _Is that_ hard to say! Can you say this: Sue wears cheap shoes to zoos to look at sheep.

B: That (make, not) _That not make_ any sense.

A: I (know) _I know_ .

10. A: (you, see) _do you see_ that man over there?

B: Which man? The man in the brown jacket?

A: No, I (talk) _I talk_ about the man who (wear) _who is wearing_ the blue shirt.

B: Oh, that man.

A: (you, know) _do you know_ him?

B: No, I (think, not) _I not think_ so.

A: I (know, not) _I not know_ him either.

EXERCISE 10—WRITTEN: Write about your classmates' immediate activities.

(To the teacher: Divide the class into two groups, I and II. Ask Group I to do any-thing they feel like doing (stand up, talk, look out the window, etc.). Ask Group II to describe in writing the immediate activities of the students in Group I (e.g., Ali is talking to Ricardo. Yoko is scratching her chin. Spyros is leaning against the wall.) It is helpful to encourage Group I to do interesting or unusual things.
*   Later, reverse the roles of Group I and II, with Group II acting and Group I writing.)*

EXERCISE 11—ORAL: Use the following prepositional expressions of place in sen-tences. Talk about things and people in the classroom. Perform actions to demon-strate the meaning of the expressions if necessary.

Example:	on (the) top of
Responses:	My book is on (the) top of my desk.
	My pen is on (the) top of my book.
	My hand is on (the) top of my head.

1. on (the) top of
2. above
3. under/below
4. next to/beside
5. against
6. in front of
7. in back of/behind
8. between
9. among
10. in
11. on

12. next to
13. across from
14. near/close to
15. far away from
16. in the front of
17. in the middle of
18. in the back of
19. at the top of
20. at the bottom of
21. in the corner of
22. on the corner of

EXERCISE 12—PREPOSITIONS: Complete the sentences with prepositions. This exercise contains prepositions that follow adjectives. (See Appendix 4 for a list of preposition combinations.)

1. Mr. Porter is nice _____to_____ everyone.

2. Kathy was absent _____from_____ class yesterday.

3. Jack's thermos bottle is full _Full up_ coffee.

4. I'm angry _with_ Tom.

5. I'm mad _with_ Tom.

6. Are you afraid _of_ dogs?

7. Sometimes people aren't kind _to_ animals.

8. One inch is equal _To_ 2.54 centimeters.

9. I'm thirsty _For_ a big glass of ice water.

10. Joe has good manners. He's always polite _To_ everyone.

11. I'm not familiar _with_ that book. Who wrote it?

12. Are you ready _For_ the test?

13. I don't understand that sentence. It isn't clear _To_ me.

14. Mark Twain is famous _For_ his novels about life on the Mississippi in the nineteenth century.

15. I'm hungry _For_ some chocolate ice cream.

16. Our daughter graduated from the university. We're very proud _at_ her.

17. A lot of sugar isn't good _For_ you. Sugar is especially bad _For_ your teeth.

18. Who was responsible _For_ the accident?

19. My coat is similar _to_ yours, but different _From_ Al's.

20. Some people aren't friendly _with_ _To_ strangers.

chapter 2

Past Time

2-1 EXPRESSING PAST TIME: THE SIMPLE PAST

(a)	Mary **walked** downtown yesterday.	The simple past is used to talk about activities or situations that began and ended in the past (e.g., *yesterday, last night, two days ago*).
(b)	I **slept** for eight hours last night.	
(c)	Bob **stayed** home yesterday morning.	Most simple past verbs are formed by adding *-ed* to a verb. See Appendix 2 for the spelling of verbs that end in *-ed*.
(d)	Our plane **arrived** on time.	
(e)	Jack **studied** last night.	
(f)	I **ate** breakfast this morning.	Some verbs have irregular past forms. See Appendix 1 for a list of irregular verbs.
(g)	Sue **took** a taxi to the airport.	
(h)	The phone **rang** while I was in the shower.	

FORMS OF THE SIMPLE PAST

STATEMENT	I You He She **worked** yesterday. It We They	QUESTION	**Did** I you he she **work** yesterday? it we they

Phora = 522·25-32.

Beatriz

NEGATIVE	I You He She } **did not (didn't) work** yesterday. It We They	SHORT ANSWER	Yes, { I you he she } **did.** it we they
			No, { I you he she } **didn't.** it we they

EXERCISE 1—ORAL (BOOKS CLOSED):   Answer the questions. Use *the simple present* or *the simple past.*

1. What are some things you usually do every morning?
   What are some things you did yesterday (OR: this) morning?
2. What do you usually do in the evening?
   What did you do last night?
3. What do we usually do in this class?
   What did we do in this class yesterday?
4. What do you usually do after this class?
   What did you do after class yesterday?
5. What did you do two days ago? Last week? Last month? Last year?
6. Take out a piece of paper. Write what you did (your activities) yesterday.
   Write as fast as you can.

EXERCISE 2—IRREGULAR VERBS: Complete the sentences by using *the simple past* of the given verbs. *Use each verb only one time.* All of the verbs have irregular past forms.*

begin	*go*	*read*
cut	*hold*	*shake*
✔*drink*	*keep*	*shut*
eat	*lose*	*speak*
find	*meet*	*spend*

─────────────
*See Appendix 1 for a list of irregular verbs.

1. Sue _____ drank _____ a cup of coffee before class this morning.

2. We _____ ate _____ dinner at a Mexican restaurant last night.

3. When it _____ began _____ to rain yesterday afternoon, I _____ shut _____ all of the windows in the apartment.

4. Bob hurt his finger when he was fixing his dinner last night. He accidental-ly _____ cut _____ it with a sharp knife.

5. I don't have any money in my pocket at all. I _____ spent _____ my last dime yesterday. I'm flat broke.

6. Mary didn't throw her old shoes away. She _____ kept _____ them.

7. I _____ read _____ an interesting article in the newspaper yesterday.

8. Jack _____ lost _____ his pocketknife at the park yesterday. This morn-ing he _____ went _____ back to the park to look for it. Finally he _____ found _____ it in the grass. He was glad to have it back again.

9. Peter was nervous when he _____ held _____ his baby in his arms for the first time.

10. I _____ met _____ Sue's parents when they visited her. She introduced me to them.

11. Yesterday I called Marvin on the phone. He wasn't home, so I _____ spoke _____ to his sister.

12. When I introduced Tom to Bob, they _____ shook _____ hands.

EXERCISE 3—IRREGULAR VERBS: Complete the sentences by using the *simple past* of the given verbs. *Use each verb only one time.* All of the verbs have irregular past forms.

bite	feel	leave
draw	forget	lend
✓ drive	get	ride
fall	hear	steal
feed	hurt	take

1. Mary walked to school today. Sue _____ drove _____ her car. Alice _____ rode _____ her bicycle. Sandy _____ took _____ the bus.

2. When Alan slipped on the icy sidewalk yesterday, he _fall_ down and _hurt_ his back. His back is very painful today.

3. I didn't have any money yesterday, so my roommate _lent_ me five bucks.

4. The children had a good time at the park yesterday. They _fed_ the ducks small pieces of bread.

5. Alice called the police yesterday because someone _stole_ her bicycle while she was in the library studying. She's very angry.

6. Dick _left_ his apartment in a hurry this morning because he was late for school. That's why he _forgot_ to bring his books to class.

7. The children _took_ pictures in art class yesterday.

8. I have a cold. Yesterday I _felt_ terrible, but I'm feeling better today.

9. Last night I _heard_ a strange noise in the house around 2:00 a.m., so I _took_ up to investigate.

10. My dog isn't very friendly. Yesterday she _bit_ my neighbor's leg. Luckily, however, my dog is very old and doesn't have sharp teeth.

EXERCISE 4—IRREGULAR VERBS: Complete the sentences by using *the simple past* of the given verbs. *Use each verb only one time.* All of the verbs have irregular past forms.

break	dig	teach
bring	freeze	think
buy	ring	wake
catch	rise	wear
come	sleep	write

1. I dropped my favorite vase. It fell to the floor and _broke_ into a hundred pieces.

2. When I went shopping yesterday, I _bought_ some light bulbs and a cooking pot.

3. Alex _brought_ his books to class this morning. He didn't forget them.

4. My brother and his wife ___came___ to our apartment for dinner last night.

5. Last night around midnight, when I was sound asleep, the telephone ___rang___. It ___woke___ me up.

6. The sun ___rose___ at 6:04 this morning.

7. I ___wrote___ a letter to my folks after I finished studying yesterday evening.

8. Ms. Manning ___taught___ chemistry at the local high school last year.

9. The police ___caught___ the bank robbers. The robbers are in jail now.

10. Last night I had a good night's sleep. I ___slept___ for nine hours.

11. Today Paul is wearing slacks and a sports jacket, but yesterday he ___wore___ jeans and a sweatshirt to class.

12. It was really cold yesterday. The temperature was around −3 °F./ −20 °C. I nearly ___froze___ to death when I walked home!

13. I ___thought___ about going to Florida for my vacation, but I finally decided to go to Puerto Rico.

14. My dog ___made___ a hole in the yard and buried his bone.

EXERCISE 5: All of the following sentences are inaccurate. Correct them by (a) writing a negative sentence with **don't**, **doesn't**, or **didn't**, and (b) writing an affirmative sentence.

1. Thomas Edison invented the telephone.

   (a) _Thomas Edison didn't invent the telephone._

   (b) _Alexander Graham Bell invented the telephone._

2. Rocks float.

   (a) _Rocks don't float._

   (b) _They sink._ sank sunk

3. Wood sinks.

   (a) _____

   (b) _____

4. I stay home every day.

   (a) _I don't stay home every day._

   (b) _But my brother stayed home all day_

5. I stayed home all day yesterday.

   (a) _I didn't stay home yesterday_

   (b) _My brother stayed home all day_

6. Spiders have six legs.

   (a) _____

   (b) _____

7. I took a taxi to school today.

   (a) _____

   (b) _____

8. This book has 289 pages.

   (a) _this book doesen't have 289 pages_

   (b) _this book has 300 pages_

9. I got up at 4:30 this morning.

   (a) _____

   (b) _____

10. Our teacher wrote *Romeo and Juliet*.

   (a) _____

   (b) _____

EXERCISE 6: Complete the following dialogues. Use the words in parentheses. Give short answers to questions where necessary.

1. A: (*you, go*) <u>Did you go</u> to class yesterday?

    B: No, <u>I didn't</u> . I (*stay*) <u>stayed</u> home because I
    (*feel, not*) <u>didn't feel</u> good.

2. A: (*you, sleep*) _____ well last night?

    B: Yes, _____ . I (*sleep*) _____ very well.

3. A: (*Tom's plane, arrive*) _____ on time yesterday?

    B: Yes, _____ . It (*get in*) _____ at 6:05 on the
    dot.

4. A: (*you, stay*) _____ home and (*study*) _____ last
    night?

    B: No, _____ . I (*go*) _____ to a new movie,
    The Valley of the Vampires.

    A: (*you, like*) _____ it?

    B: It was okay, I guess, but I don't really like horror movies.

5. A: (*Mary, study*) _____ last night?

    B: No, _____ . She (*watch*) _____ TV.

6. A: (*Mark Twain, write*) _____ *Tom Sawyer*?

    B: Yes, _____ . He also (*write*) _____ *Huckleberry
    Finn.*

7. A: (*the children, go*) _____ to the zoo yesterday?

    B: Yes, _____ . And they (*have*) _____ a wonder-
    ful time.

8. A: (*you, eat*) _____ breakfast this morning?

    B: No, _____ . I (*have, not*) _____ enough time. I
    was late for class because my alarm clock (*ring, not*) _____ .

EXERCISE 7—ORAL: Pair up with a classmate. Practice questions, short answers, and irregular verbs.

STUDENT A: Ask a question beginning with *"Did you . . .?"* Listen carefully to Student B's answers to make sure he or she is using the irregular verbs correctly.* Your book is open.

STUDENT B: In order to practice using irregular verbs, answer *"yes"* to all of Student A's questions. Give full answers. Your book is closed.

> *Example*:   eat breakfast this morning
> *Student A*: Did you eat breakfast this morning?
> *Student B*: Yes, I did. I ate breakfast at 7:30 this morning.

PART I

1. sleep well last night
2. wake up early this morning
3. eat breakfast this morning
4. take the bus to school
5. drive your car to school
6. ride your bicycle to school
7. bring your books to class
8. read the newspaper this morning
9. hear the news about the earthquake
10. say something
11. do your homework last night
12. give your friend a birthday present
13. catch a cold last week
14. feel terrible
15. see a doctor
16. lose your grammar book
17. find your grammar book
18. go to a party last night
19. have a good time
20. think about me

PART II (*Switch roles.*)

21. come to class yesterday
22. buy some books yesterday
23. drink a cup of coffee before class
24. run to class today
25. write your parents a letter
26. send your parents a letter
27. lend your friend some money
28. wear a coat yesterday
29. go to the zoo last week
30. feed the birds at the park
31. make your own dinner last night
32. leave home at eight this morning
33. fly to this city
34. fall down yesterday
35. hurt yourself when you fell down
36. break your arm
37. understand the question
38. speak to John yesterday
39. meet John the first day of class
40. shake hands with John when you met him

---

*Look at Appendix 1 to check the correct form of an irregular verb if necessary.

EXERCISE 8—ORAL (BOOKS CLOSED):   Practice using irregular verbs by answering the questions.

> *Example:*   Where did you sit in class yesterday?
> *Response:*   I sat over there.

1. What time did class begin this morning?
2. What time did the sun rise this morning?
3. What time did you get up this morning?
4. What time did you leave home this morning?
5. What did you have for breakfast?
6. What did you drink this morning?
7. Where did you put your books when you came to class this morning?
8. What did you wear yesterday?
9. What time did you wake up this morning?
10. Where did you grow up?
11. What did you eat for lunch yesterday? How much did it cost?
12. Where did you sit in class yesterday?
13. When did you meet (. . .)?
14. What cities did you fly to on your way to (*name of this city*)?
15. What did you buy last week?
16. Where did you go yesterday?
17. What courses did you take in high school?
18. How long did you sleep last night?

EXERCISE 9—ORAL (BOOKS CLOSED):   Perform the action and then answer the question. Use *just* in your answer.

> *Example*:   Give (. . .) your pen. (*The student performs the action*). What did you just do?
> *Response*:   I just gave (. . .) my pen.

1. Give (. . .) your dictionary.
2. Put your book on your lap.
3. Shut your book.
4. Stand up.
5. Hold up your book.
6. Bend your elbow.
7. Bite your finger.
8. Tear a piece of paper.
9. Shake hands with (. . .).
10. Light a match.
11. Hide your pen.
12. Throw your eraser to (. . .).

13. Draw a picture.
14. Choose a pen, this one or that one.
15. Blow on your finger.
16. Hang your (jacket) on (a hook, your chair).
17. Hit your desk with your hand.
18. Steal (. . .)'s pen.
19. Take (. . .)'s grammar book.
20. Sell your pen to (. . .) for a dime.
21. Stick your pen in your pocket.
22. Speak to (. . .).

2-2 EXPRESSING PAST TIME: THE SIMPLE PAST AND THE PAST PROGRESSIVE

SIMPLE PAST now past — X ———|——— future	(a) Mary **walked** downtown yesterday. (b) I **slept** for eight hours last night.	The simple past is used to talk about activities or situations that *began and ended* at a particular time in the past (e.g., yesterday, last night, two days ago).
PAST PROGRESSIVE now begin — X — end in progress	(c) I sat down at the dinner table at 6:00 p.m. yesterday. My friend came *to my house at 6:10 p.m.* **I was eating dinner** *when my friend came.* (d) I went to bed at 10:00 The phone rang at 11:00. **I was sleeping** *when the phone rang.*	The past progressive expresses an activity that was *in progress* (*was occurring, was happening*) at a particular time in the past.* In (c): eating was in progress at 6:10 when my friend came.
	(e) **When** the phone **rang, I was sleeping**.	In (e): The simple past is used in a "**when** clause" and the past progressive in the main clause.
	(f) **While I was sleeping**, the phone **rang**.	In (f): The past progressive is used in a "**while** clause" and the simple past in the main clause.
		(e) and (f) have the same meaning.

*The past progressive is also called the past continuous or the continuous past.

FORMS OF THE PAST PROGRESSIVE

STATEMENT	I He She It } **was working** when the phone rang.	You We They } **were working** when the phone rang.
NEGATIVE	I He She It } **was not (wasn't) working** when the phone rang.	You We They } **were not (weren't) working** when the phone rang.
QUESTION	**Was** { I he she it } **working** when the phone rang?	**Were** { you we they } **working** when the phone rang?
SHORT ANSWER	Yes, { I he she it } **was.** No, { I he she it } **wasn't.**	Yes, { you we they } **were.** No, { you we they } **weren't.**

EXERCISE 10: Complete the sentences with the words in parentheses. Use *the simple past* or *the past progressive.*

1. At 6:00 p.m. Bob sat down at the table and began to eat. At 6:05 Bob

    (*eat*) _____ dinner.

2. While Bob (*eat*) _____ dinner, Ann (*come*) _____
   through the door.

3. In other words, when Ann (*come*) _____ through the door, Bob

    (*eat*) _____ dinner.

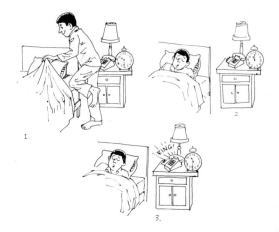

4. Bob went to bed at 10:30. At 11:00 Bob (*sleep*) _____ .

5. While Bob (*sleep*) _____ , the phone (*ring*) _____.

6. In other words, when the phone (*ring*) _____ , Bob (*sleep*)

_____ .

7. Bob left his house at 8:00 a.m. and began to walk to class. While he (*walk*)

_____ to class, he (*see*)_____ Mrs. Smith.

8. When Bob (*see*) _____ Mrs. Smith, she (*sweep*) _____

_____ her front porch.

EXERCISE 11:   Complete the following. Use the words in parentheses. Use *the simple past* or *the past progressive.*

1. Sally (*eat*) _____ dinner last night when someone (*knock*)

_____ on the door.

2. I began to study at seven last night. Fred (*come*) _____ at

    seven-thirty. I (*study*) _____ when Fred (*come*) _____

    _____ .

3. While I (*study*) _____ last night, Fred (*drop by*) _____

    _____ to visit me.

4. My roommate's parents (*call*) _____ him last night while we

    (*watch*) _____ TV.

5. My mother called me around five. My husband came home a little after five.

    When he (*come*) _____ home, I (*talk*) _____ to
    my mother on the phone.

EXERCISE 12:   Complete the sentences with the words in parentheses. Use *the simple past* or *the past progressive.*

1. Yesterday Tom and Janice (*go*) _____ to the zoo around one.

    They (*see*) _____ many kinds of animals. They stayed at the

    zoo for two hours. While they (*walk*) _____ home, it (*begin*)

    _____ to rain, so they (*stop*) _____ at a small

    cafe and (*have*) _____ a cup of coffee.

2. Yesterday afternoon I (*go*) _____ to visit the Parker family.

    When I (*get*) _____ there around two o'clock, Mrs. Parker

    (*be*) _____ in the yard. She (*plant*) _____ flowers

    in her garden. Mr. Parker (*be*) _____ in the garage. He (*work*)

_____ on their car. He (*change*) _____ the oil.

The children (*play*) _____ in the front yard.

3. A: There was a power outage in our part of town last night. (*your lights, go out*) _____ too?

   B: Yes, they did. It (*be*) _____ terrible! I (*take*) _____ _____ a shower when the lights went out. My wife (*find*) _____ a flashlight and rescued me from the bathroom! We couldn't cook dinner, so we (*eat*) _____ sandwiches instead. I (*try*) _____ to study by candlelight, but I couldn't see well enough, so I (*go*) _____ to bed and (*sleep*) _____ _____ .

   A: I (*read*) _____ when the lights (*go out*) _____ . I (*study*) _____ for a history exam. Of course, I couldn't study in the dark, so I (*get up*) _____ very early this morning and finished studying for my test.

2-3 EXPRESSING PAST TIME: USING TIME CLAUSES

time clause	*main clause*	When I was in Chicago = a time clause I visited the art museum = a main clause
(a) **When I was in Chicago,** I visited the art museum.		(a) and (b) have the same meaning. A time clause can:
main clause	*time clause*	(1) come in front of a main clause, as in (a).
(b) I visited the art museum **when I was in Chicago.**		(2) follow a main clause, as in (b).

(c) **After Mary ate dinner**, she went to the library. (d) Mary went to the library **after she ate dinner.** (e) **Before I went to bed,** I finished my homework. (f) I finished my homework **before I went to bed.** (g) **While I was watching TV**, the phone rang. (h) The phone rang **while I was watching TV.**	**When, after, before,** and **while** introduce time clauses. (A *clause* is a structure that has a subject and a verb.) **when** **after** + *subject and verb* = a time clause **before** **while**
	PUNCTUATION: Usually a comma is used at the end of a time clause when the time clause comes first in a sentence (comes in front of the main clause): *time clause* + comma + *main clause* *main clause* + (no comma) + *time clause.*
(i) I was sleeping **when the phone rang.** (j) **While I was sleeping**, the phone rang.	**when** = at that time **while** = during that time (i) and (j) have the same meaning.

EXERCISE 13:   Combine the two sentences into one sentence by using time clauses. Punctuate carefully.

1. *First*:   I got home.
   Then: I ate dinner.

   (a) After _____ I got home, I ate dinner. _____

   (b) _____ I ate dinner _____ after _____ I got home. _____

2. *First*:   I washed the dishes.
   Then: I watched TV.

   (a) After _I washed the dishes_____

   (b) _____ after _____

3. *First*:   I unplugged the coffee pot.
   Then: I left my apartment this morning.

   (a) Before _____

   (b) _____ before _____

4. *First*:   I was eating dinner.
   Then: Jim came.

   (a) While _____

(b) _____ while _____

(c) When _____

(d) _____ when _____

5. *First*: It began to rain.
   Then: I stood under a tree.

   (a) When*_____

   (b) _____ when _____

EXERCISE 14—ORAL: Combine the two sentences into one sentence by using a time clause. Use the word in parentheses to introduce the time clause. Discuss punctuation.

 1. (*before*)   *First*: I did my homework.
                    Then: I went to bed.

 2. (*after*)   *First*: Bob graduated.
                    Then: He got a job.

 3. (*while*)   *First*: I was studying.
                    Then: Mary called me on the phone.

 4. (*when*)   *First*: My alarm clock rang.
                    Then: I woke up.

 5. (*before*)   *First*: I wrote my brother a letter.
                    Then: I watched TV.

 6. (*while*)   *First*: I was falling asleep last night.
                    Then: I heard a strange noise.

 7. (*when*)   *First*: I heard a strange noise.
                    Then: I turned on the light.

 8. (*when*)   *First*: I was eating lunch.
                    Then: Mary came.

 9. (*while*)   *First*: I was eating lunch.
                    Then: Mary came.

10. (*before*)   *First*: I bought some flowers.
                    Then: I went to the hospital to visit my friend.

---

*In a sentence with a time clause introduced by **when**, both the time clause verb and the main verb are often simple past. In this case, usually the action in the "**when** clause" happened first. For example:

When the phone rang, I answered it.   **First***: The phone rang.*
                                             Then*: I answered it.*

The two actions occurred very close in time, but the action in the "**when** clause" happened first.

EXERCISE 15—ORAL/WRITTEN: Pair up with a classmate.

STUDENT A: Tell Student B about your activities yesterday. Think of at least five things you did yesterday to tell Student B about. Also think of two or three things you didn't do yesterday.

STUDENT B: Listen carefully to Student A. Make sure that Student A is using past tenses correctly. Ask Student A questions about his/her activities if you wish. Take notes while Student A is talking. Use your notes to write a composition about Student A's activities yesterday. Use time clauses.
When Student A finishes talking about his/her activities, switch roles.

EXERCISE 16:   Complete the sentences with the correct form of the words in parentheses.

(1)   Last Friday was a holiday. It (*be*) _____ Independence

(2) Day, so I didn't have to go to classes. I (*sleep*) _____ a little

(3) later than usual. Around ten, my friend Larry (*come*) _____

(4) over to my apartment. We (*pack*) _____ a picnic basket and

(5) then (*take*) _____ the bus to Forest Park. We (*spend*) _____

(6) _____ most of the day there.

(7)   When we (*get*) _____ to the park, we (*find*) _____

(8) _____ an empty picnic table near a pond. There were some

(9) ducks on the pond, so we (*feed*) _____ them. We (*throw*)

(10) _____ small pieces of bread on the water, and the ducks (*swim*)

(11) _____ over to get them. One duck was very clever. It (*catch*)

(12) _____ the bread in midair before it (*hit*) _____

(13) the water. Another duck was a thief. It (*steal*) _____ bread

(14) from the mouths of other ducks. While we (*feed*) _____ the

(15) ducks, Larry and I (*meet*) _____ a man who usually (*come*)

(16) _____ to the park every day to feed the ducks. We (*sit*) _____

(17) _____ on a park bench and (*speak*) _____ to him
for fifteen or twenty minutes.

(18)   After we (*eat*) _____ our lunch, I (*take*) _____

(19) a short nap under a tree. While I (*sleep*) _____ , a mosquito

(20) (*bite*) _____ my arm. When I (*wake*) _____ up,

(21) my arm itched, so I scratched it. Suddenly I (*hear*) _____ a

(22) noise in the tree above me. I (*look*) _____ up and (*see*)

(23) _____ an orange and gray bird. After a few moments, it (*fly*)

(24) _____ away.

(25)   During the afternoon, we (*do*) _____ many things. First

(26) we (*take*) _____ a long walk. When we (*get*) _____

(27) back to our picnic table, I (*read*) _____ a book, and Larry,

(28) who (*be*) _____ an artist, (*draw*) _____ pictures.

(29) Later we (*play*) _____ a game of chess. Larry (*win*) _____

(30) _____ the first game, but I (*win*) _____ the second

(31) one. Then he (*teach*) _____ me how to play a new game with

(32) dice. While we (*play*) _____ this new game, one of the dice

(33) (*fall*) _____ from the picnic table onto the ground. We finally

(34) (*find*) _____ it in some tall grass.

(35)   In the evening, we (*join*) _____ a huge crowd to watch

(36) the fireworks display. The fireworks (*be*) _____ beautiful.

(37) Some of the explosions (*be*) _____ very loud, however. They

(38) (*hurt*) _____ my ears. When the display (*be*) _____

(39) _____ over, we (*leave*) _____ . All in all, it (*be*)

(40) _____ a very enjoyable day.

EXERCISE 17—WRITTEN: Write a composition about one of the following:

1. Write about an enjoyable day in your life.
2. Write about an important event in your life.

2-4   EXPRESSING PAST HABIT: *USED TO*

(a)	I **used to live** with my parents. Now I live in my own apartment.	**Used to** expresses a past situation or habit that no longer exists at present.	
(b)	Bob **used to work** for the telephone company, but now he works for the power company.	FORM: *I you he she it we they* } **used to** + *simple form of a verb*	
(c)	Ann **used to be** afraid of dogs, but now she likes dogs.		
(d)	**Did** you **use to live** in Paris?	QUESTION FORM: **did** + *subject* + **use to** . . .	

EXERCISE 18—ORAL: Make sentences with a similar meaning by using **used to.**

1. When I was a child, I was shy. Now I'm not shy.
   (*I used to be shy, but now I'm not.*)
2. When I lived in my hometown, I went to the beach every weekend. Now I don't go to the beach every weekend.
   (*I used to go to the beach every weekend, but now I don't.*)
3. Ann worked in a law office for many years. Now she doesn't have a job.
4. When I was in high school, I wore a uniform to school.
5. When I was a child, I watched cartoons on TV. I don't watch cartoons anymore.
6. I lived with my parents for many years.
7. When I was a child, I drank a lot of milk.
8. When I lived at home, I ate bread and cheese for breakfast.

EXERCISE 19—ORAL AND/OR WRITTEN: Use **used to.**

1. You are an adult now. What did you use to do when you were a child that you don't do now?
2. You are living in a foreign country. What did you use to do in your own country that you don't do now?
3. Think of a particular time in your past (e.g., when you were in high school, when you lived in Paris, when you worked at your uncle's store). Describe a typical day in your life at that time. What did you use to do?

EXERCISE 20—PREPOSITIONS: Complete the sentences with prepositions. (See Appendix 4 for a list of preposition combinations.)

1. Tom paid _____for_____ his airplane ticket in cash.

2. Joan graduated _____ high school two years ago.

3. I waited _____ the bus.

4. Jim is a waiter. He waits _____ customers at a restaurant.

5. I have a different opinion. I don't agree _____ you.

6. I arrived _____ this city last month.

7. I arrived _____ the airport around eight.

8. I listened _____ the news on TV last night.

9. This exercise consists _____ verbs that are followed by certain prepositions.

10. Jack invited me _____ his party.

11. I complained _____ the landlord _____ the leaky faucet in the kitchen.

12. Did you talk _____ Professor Adams _____ your grades?

13. We're hoping _____ good weather tomorrow so we can go on a picnic.

14. Did you hear _____ the earthquake in Turkey?

15. I heard _____ my sister last week. She wrote me a letter.

16. I spoke _____ the Foreign Student Advisor _____ my problem.

chapter 3

Future Time

3-1 EXPRESSING FUTURE TIME: *BE GOING TO* AND *WILL*

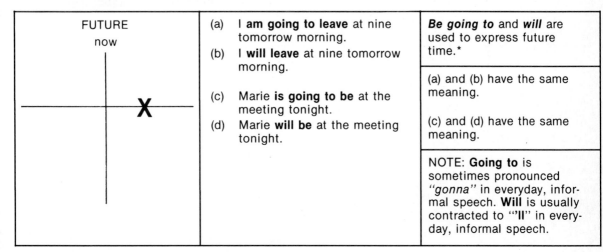

FUTURE now X	(a)	I **am going to leave** at nine tomorrow morning.	**Be going to** and **will** are used to express future time.*
	(b)	I **will leave** at nine tomorrow morning.	
	(c)	Marie **is going to be** at the meeting tonight.	(a) and (b) have the same meaning.
	(d)	Marie **will be** at the meeting tonight.	(c) and (d) have the same meaning.
			NOTE: **Going to** is sometimes pronounced *"gonna"* in everyday, informal speech. **Will** is usually contracted to *"'ll"* in everyday, informal speech.

*__*Shall__ is also used (primarily with *I* and *we*) to express future time.*

    I shall leave at nine tomorrow morning.
    We shall leave at nine tomorrow morning.

The use of **shall** to express future time is infrequent and indicates strong emphasis.

FORMS WITH *WILL*

STATEMENT	I You He She } **will work** tomorrow. It We They	(I'll) (you'll) (he'll) (she'll) (it'll) (we'll) (they'll)	QUESTION	**Will** { I you he she } **work** tomorrow? it we they
NEGATIVE	I You He She } **will not (won't) work** tomorrow. It We They		SHORT ANSWER	Yes, { I you he she } **will.** No, { I you he she } **won't.** it it we we they they

EXERCISE 1—ORAL (BOOKS CLOSED):   Make sentences with ***be going to*** about your future activities.

> *Example:*   tomorrow morning
> *Student A:*   I'm going to go to class tomorrow morning.
> *Student B:*   What is (Student A) going to do tomorrow morning?
> *Student C:*   S/he's going to go to class.

1. tomorrow afternoon
2. tomorrow night
3. tonight
4. next week
5. later today
6. in a couple of hours
7. this weekend
8. the day after tomorrow
9. pretty soon
10. after a while
11. next year
12. sometime

EXERCISE 2—ORAL (BOOKS CLOSED):   Make sentences about your activities. Use present, past, or future verbs.

1. yesterday
2. tomorrow
3. right now
4. every day

5. today*

6. this morning*

7. this afternoon*

8. tonight*

9. the day before yesterday

10. the day after tomorrow

11. last week

12. this week*

13. next week

14. two days ago

15. in a few days (from now)

16. a few minutes ago

EXERCISE 3:   Complete the sentences by using *a pronoun + a form of **be going to**.*

1. I ate lunch with Alan today, and _____I'm going to eat_____ lunch with him tomorrow too.*

2. Ann wasn't in class today, and _____she isn't going to be_____ in class tomorrow either.*

3. Margaret walked to school this morning, and _____She will go_____ to school tomorrow morning too.

4. Harry didn't go to work today, and _____he isn't going_____ to work tomorrow either.

5. My friends came over last night, and _____he will come_____ over this evening too.

6. I didn't eat lunch at the cafeteria this noon, and _____I not going to eat_____ lunch there tomorrow either.

7. We're doing exercises in class today, and _____we will do_____ exercises in class tomorrow too.

8. It isn't raining today, and according to the weather report _____it isn't going_____ _____ tomorrow either.

---

*Time expressions such as *today, this morning, this afternoon, this evening, tonight, this week, this month, this year, this semester* can be used with past, present, or future verbs.

Past: It **rained** this morning.

Present: It **is raining** this morning.

Future: I'm **going to go** downtown this morning.

EXERCISE 4—ORAL: Complete the sentences with *a pronoun + a form of* **be go-ing to.** Use a future time expression. Use **too** (with affirmative sentences) or **either** (with negative sentences).*

> *Example*: I didn't study last night, and . . .
> *Response*: I didn't study last night, and I'm not going to study tonight either.

1. I came to class today, and. . . . *I'm goin to class tomorrow*
2. I did my homework yesterday, and. . . . *I'm going to do my*
3. I wasn't at home last night, and. . . *home*
4. We didn't have a grammar quiz today, and. . *we're not* *aswell*
5. Our teacher is in class today, and. . . *She is going to be in class*
6. Keith studied at the library last night, and. . . *tomorrow Too:*
7. Susan didn't come to class today, and. . . *She isn't come to morrow eider*
8. It's cold today, and. . . *It's going To be cold tomorrow too:*

we won't

EXERCISE 5: Practice using contractions with **will.**

> **NOTE:** **Will** is usually contracted with pronouns (*I, she, etc.*) in both speech and informal writing.
> **Will** is usually contracted with nouns (*Bob, my friend, etc.*) in speech but usually not in writing.

Write the correct contraction for the words in parentheses. Practice pronunciation.

1. (*I will*) _____ I'll _____ be home at eight tonight.

2. (*we will*) ___ We'll ___ see you tomorrow.

3. (*you will*) ___ You'll ___ probably get a letter today.

4. (*she will*) Mary is tired tonight. ___ She'll ___ probably go to bed early.

5. (*he will*) Dennis has a cold. ___ He'll ___ probably stay home in bed today.

6. (*it will*) ___ It'll ___ probably be too cold to go swimming tomorrow.

7. (*they will*) I invited some guests for dinner. ___ They'll ___ probably get here around seven.

---

*See 8–2 for more information about *too* and *either*.

EXERCISE 6:   Read the following sentences aloud. Practice contracting *will* with nouns in speech.

1. Mary will be here at six tomorrow.
2. Dinner will be at seven.
3. Bob will probably call tonight.
4. The weather will probably be a little colder tomorrow.
5. The party will start at eight.
6. John will help us move into our new apartment.
7. My friends will be here soon.
8. The sun will rise at 6:08 tomorrow morning.

EXERCISE 7:   Study the examples.

(a) Ann **will probably go** to the park tomorrow. (b) Bob **probably won't go** to the park tomorrow. (*More formal: Bob will probably not go to the park tomorrow.*)	People often use *probably* with *will*. *Probably* comes between *will* and the main verb, as in (a); or in front of *won't*, as in (b).*

Complete the sentences. Use *a pronoun + will/won't*. Use *probably*.

1. I went to the library last night, and _____I'll probably go_____ there tonight too.

2. Ann didn't come to class today, and _____she probably won't come_____ to-morrow either.

3. I watched TV last night, and _I'll watched Tomorrow_ TV tonight too.   _as well/by probably_

4. I wasn't at home last night, and _I'll probably not be_ , at home tonight either.

5. Bob went to bed early last night, and _He'll probably go_ to bed early tonight too.

6. Jack didn't hand his homework in today, and _____ _____ it in tomorrow either.

7. It's hot today, and _it'll_____ hot tomorrow too.

8. My friends didn't come over last night, and _____ _____ over tonight either.

————————

*See 6–7 for more information about placement of midsentence adverbs such as *probably*.

9. The students had a quiz today, and _____They'll probably have_____ one tomorrow too.

10. Alice didn't ride her bike to school today, and _____She'll probably won't ride her bike_____ it to school tomorrow either.

3-2 EXPRESSING FUTURE TIME IN TIME CLAUSES AND "*IF* CLAUSES"

(a) *Before I **go** to class tomorrow*, I'm going to eat breakfast. (b) I'm going to eat dinner at 6:00 tonight. *After I **eat** dinner*, I'm going to study in my room. (c) I'll give Mary your message *when I **see** her tomorrow.* (d) It's raining right now. *As soon as the rain **stops**,* I'm going to walk downtown.	The simple present is used in a future time clause. ***Be going to*** and ***will*** are not used in a future time clause. **before** **after** + subject and verb = a time **when** clause **as soon as*** In (a): The speaker is talking about two events: going to class and eating breakfast. Both events are in the future. However, the speaker uses the simple present (not *be going to* or *will*) to talk about going to class because the verb occurs in a time clause: *Before I **go** to class tomorrow.* . . .
(e) Maybe it will rain tomorrow. *If it **rains** tomorrow,* I'm going to stay home.	When the meaning is future, the simple present (not *be going to* or *will*) is used in an "*if* clause." *if* + subject and verb = an "*if* clause"†

As soon as means *immediately after.*
†See Chapter 14 for other uses of "*if* clauses."

EXERCISE 8: Combine the ideas of the two sentences into one sentence by using a time clause. Use the word in parentheses to introduce the time clause. Punctuate carefully.*

1. (*after*)   *First*: I'm going to finish my homework.
             Then: I'm going to go to bed.
   After I finish my homework, I'm going to go to bed. OR: I'm going to go to bed after I finish my homework.

———————

*See 2-3 for punctuation of time clauses.

2. (*before*)　　*First*: I'm going to write a letter.
　　　　　　　　Then: I'm going to go to bed.

　　before I go to bed. Then I'm write a letter

3. (*when*)　　*First*: I'm going to go to Chicago next week.
　　　　　　　　Then: I'm going to visit the art museum.

　　When I go to Chicago next week then I visit the art museum

4. (*after*)　　*First*: I'll go to the drug store.
　　　　　　　　Then: I'll go to the post office.

　　First After I'll go to drug store The I'll go to post office

5. (*before*)　　*First*: Ann will finish her homework.
　　　　　　　　Then: She will watch TV tonight.*

　　before ann Finishes her homework, she will watch T.v.

6. (*after*)　　*First*: Jim will get home this evening.
　　　　　　　　Then: He's going to read the newspaper.

　　First Jim get home this evening Then he's going To read newspaper

7. (*when*)　　*First*: I'll call John tomorrow.
　　　　　　　　Then: I'll ask him to my party.

　　First

8. (*as soon as*)　*First*: The rain will stop.
　　　　　　　　Then: The children are going to go outside and play.

　　The children will go ouside and play so

9. (*as soon as*)　*First*: The teacher will get here.
　　　　　　　　Then: Class will begin.

10. (*before*)　　*First*: The Robertsons will get some travelers' checks.
　　　　　　　　Then: They will leave on vacation.

11. (*as soon as*)　*First*: I will get home tonight.
　　　　　　　　Then: I'm going to take a hot bath.

　　as soon as I get home tonight Then I'll take a Hotboth.

---

*A noun usually comes before a pronoun:

　　After **Ann** eats dinner, **she** is going to study.

　　Ann is going to study after **she** eats dinner.

12. (**when**)   *First*: I'm going to go shopping tomorrow.
                   Then: I'm going to buy a new pair of shoes.

___

EXERCISE 9—WRITTEN: Complete the following sentences with your own words.

1. I'm going to eat dinner before I. . . *go to bed*
2. As soon as I get home tonight, I. . . *go stored*
3. I'm going to call my friend after I. . . . *leeft front class*
4. My life will be easy after I. . . *Finish my carria.*
5. Before I go to bed tonight, I. . . *will read a magassing*
6. When I'm in Florida next month, I. . *will go to the Beach*
7. I'll call you as soon as I. . *Can*
8. I'm going to visit my aunt and uncle when. . *I get my Vacation*

EXERCISE 10:   Combine the ideas of the two sentences into one sentence by using an "*if* clause."

1. *Possible condition*: Maybe it will rain tomorrow.
            Result: I'm going to stay home.
   If it rains tomorrow, I'm going to stay home. OR: I'm going to stay home
   if it rains tomorrow.*

2. *Possible condition*: Maybe it will be hot tomorrow.
            Result: I'm going to go swimming.
   IF it is hot tomorrow I'm going to go Swimming

3. *Possible condition*: Maybe it will snow tomorrow.
            Result: Elizabeth isn't going to ride her bike to school.
   IF it is Snow tomorrow Elizabeth isn't going To ride her bike to school

4. *Possible condition*: Maybe I will have enough money.
            Result: I'm going to go to Hawaii for my vacation.
   IfI will have enough money,

5. *Possible condition*: Maybe Tom will have enough time.
            Result: He'll finish his composition tonight.
   IF Tom has enought time He will Finish his com pposition

*Notice the punctuation in the example. A comma is used when the "*if* clause" comes before the main clause. No comma is used when the "*if* clause" follows the main clause.

6. *Possible condition*: Maybe I won't get a letter tomorrow.
           Result: I'll call my parents.

   IF I don't get a letter tomorrow I

7. *Possible condition*: Perhaps the weather will be nice tomorrow.
           Result: We're going to go on a picnic.

   IF the weather

8. *Possible condition*: Maybe Tom won't study for his test.
           Result: He'll get a bad grade.

9. *Possible condition*: Maybe I won't study tonight.
           Result: I probably won't pass the chemistry exam.

10. *Possible condition*: Maybe I will study for the test.
            Result: I'll probably get a good grade.

EXERCISE 11—ORAL (BOOKS CLOSED):   Make sentences from the given possibilities. Use *if*.

    Example: Maybe you'll go downtown tomorrow.
    Response: If I go downtown tomorrow, (I'm going to buy some new clothes/I'm going to go to a department store/I can go to the post office, etc.).

1. Maybe it'll be nice tomorrow.   *IF is nice tomorrow I will go to the Beach,*
2. Maybe it'll be hot/cold tomorrow.   *If is hot and cold tomorrow I will stay home*
3. Maybe it won't be nice/hot/cold tomorrow.   *it won't be nice tomorrow*   *hot and cold I will go to*
4. Maybe it'll rain tomorrow.   *IF is rain tomorrow I won't wash my works*
5. Maybe it won't rain tomorrow.   *IF is not raining tomorrow I will wash my car.*
6. Maybe you'll be tired tonight.   *IF you are tired tonight probably go to bed early*
7. Maybe you won't be tired tonight.   *IF you are not tire tonight— you will go to the tenniss score early*
8. Maybe you'll have enough time tomorrow.   *IF you have time tomorrow you can starting English in the morning.*   *tomorrow*
9. Maybe you won't feel good tomorrow.   *IF you feel bad tomorrow you not will play soccer,*
10. Maybe you'll have some free time tomorrow.   *IF you have*
11. Maybe you'll go downtown tomorrow.
12. Maybe you'll be hungry after class.

EXERCISE 12—ORAL (BOOKS CLOSED)

(To the teacher: Using the entries in Exercise 11, involve both a Student A and a Student B. Student B continues Student A's idea, but uses the third person.)

  Example: Maybe you'll go downtown tomorrow.
  Student A: If I go downtown tomorrow, I'm going to buy some new shoes.
  Student B: If (. . .) buys some new shoes, his/her feet will be warm this winter.

EXERCISE 13: REVIEW OF TIME CLAUSES AND "IF CLAUSES." Complete the sentences by using a form of the words and parentheses. Read carefully for time expressions.

1. (a) Before Tom (*go*) _____goes_____ to bed, he always (*brush*) _____

    _____brushes_____ his teeth.

  (b) Before Tom (*go*) _goes_____ to bed later tonight, he (*write*) *will*

    _____ a letter to his girlfriend.

  (c) Before Tom (*go*) _____ to bed last night, he (*take*)

    _____ a shower.

  (d) While Tom (*take*) _took_____ a shower last night, the phone

    (*ring*) _rang_____ .

  (e) As soon as the phone (*ring*) _rang_____ last night, Tom (*jump*)

    _jumped_____ out of the shower to answer it.

  (f) As soon as Tom (*get*) _gets_____ up tomorrow morning, he

    (*brush*) _will ~~brushes~~ brushes_ his teeth.

  (g) Tom always (*brush*) _____ his teeth as soon as he (*get*)

    _____ up.

2. (a) After I (*get*) _will get_____ home from school every afternoon, I

    usually (*drink*) _____ a cup of tea.

  (b) After I (*get*) _get_____ home from school tomorrow afternoon,

    I (*drink*) _I will drink_ a cup of tea.

(c) After I (*get*) _got_ home from school yesterday, I (*drink*) _drunk_ a cup of tea.

(d) While I (*drink*) _was drinking_ a cup of tea yesterday afternoon, my neighbor (*come*) _came_ over, so I (*offer*) _offered them to_ her a cup of tea, too.

(e) My neighbor (*drop*) _will_ over again tomorrow. When she (*come*) _____ , I (*make*) _____ a cup of tea for her.

3. Jane (*meet*) _will meet_ me at the airport when my plane (*arrive*)_s_ _____ tomorrow.

4. If I (*see*) _If I sees_ Mike tomorrow, I (*tell*) _I will tell him_ him about the party.

5. I go to New York often. When I (*be*) _I'm_ in New York, I usually (*see*) _see_ a Broadway play.

6. When I (*be*) _'m_ in New York next week, I (*stay*) _I will stay_ _____ at the Park Plaza Hotel.

7. Jack (*watch*) _is watching_ a football game on TV right now. As soon as the game (*be*) _is over_ over, he (*mow*) _will mow at_ the grass in the back yard.

8. Cindy and I (go) _will go_ to the beach tomorrow if the weather
   (be) _is_ warm and sunny.

9. As soon as the test (be) _was_ over in class yesterday, the
   students (leave) _left_ the room.

10. As soon as I (get) _get_ home every day, my children always
    (run) _runs_ to the door to meet me.

EXERCISE 14: Study the examples.

(a) Jim **makes** his bed *and* **cleans** up his room every morning.	Often a subject has two verbs which are connected by *and*. This is called parallel structure: V + **and** + V *makes* **and** *cleans* = parallel structure
(b) Ann **is cooking** dinner *and* (is) **talking** on the phone at the same time. (c) I **will stay** home *and* (will) **study** tonight. (d) I **am going to stay** home *and* (am going to) **study** tonight.	It is not necessary to repeat a helping verb (an auxiliary verb) when two verbs are connected by *and*.

Complete the sentences by using a form of the words in parentheses.

1. When I (walk) _walked_ into the living room yesterday evening,
   Grandpa (read) _was reading_ a newspaper and (smoke) _he was_
   his pipe.

2. Helen will graduate next semester. She (move) _will move_ to New
   York City and (look) _look_ for a job after she (graduate)
   graduate from school.

3. Every day my neighbor (call) _calling_ me on the phone and
   (complain) _to complain_ about the weather.

4. Look at Ann! She (cry) _is crying_ and (laugh) _laughtin_
   at the same time. I wonder if she is happy or sad.

5. I'm beat! I can't wait to get home. After I (get) _get_ home, I
   (take) _the_ a hot shower and (go) _I will go_ straight
   to bed.

6. Yesterday my dog (*dig*) _____ a hole in the back yard and

   (*bury*) _____ a bone.

7. I'm tired of this cold weather. As soon as spring (*come*) *come* ,

   I (*play*) *I'll play* tennis and (*jog*) *jog* in the park as

   often as possible.

EXERCISE 15:   Complete the sentences by using a form of the words in parentheses.

1. It's getting late, but before I (*go*) *I go* to bed, I (*finish*)

   I will finish my homework and (*write*) *I will write* a couple

   of letters.

2. While I (*make*) *I made* dinner last night, some grease (*spill*)

   spilled out of the frying pan and (*catch*) *catch cought* on

   fire. When the smoke detector on the ceiling (*start*) *started* to

   buzz, my roommate (*run*) *ran* into the kitchen to find out

   what was wrong. He (*think*) *thought* that the house was on fire!

3. Mark is a nut about video games. He (*play*) *He likes plays* video games

   morning, noon, and night. Sometimes he (*cut*) *he cuts* class

   because he (*prefer*) *prefered* to play the games. Right now he (*do,*

   not) *will donot* very well in school. If he (*study, not*) _____

   Right now harder and (*go*) _____ to class every day,

   he (*flunk*) _____ out of school.

4. Sometimes my daughter Susie has temper tantrums. She (*cry*) __crys__
__Somuch__ and (*stomp*) __stomped__ her feet when she (*get*)
_____got_____ angry. Yesterday when she (*get*) __got__
angry, she (*pick*) __picks__ up a toy car and (*throw*) __thrown__
it at her little brother. Luckily, the car (*hit, not*) __hit not__
him. Afterwards, Susie (*feel*) __felt__ very bad. She (*apologize*)
__apologized__ to her little brother and (*kiss*) __kiss__ him.

5. It's October now. The weather (*begin*) __will begin__ to get colder. It
(*begin*) _____ to get cold every October. I (*like, not*) _____
_____ winter, but I (*think*) _____ autumn is
beautiful. In a couple of weeks, my friend and I (*take*) _____
a weekend trip to the country if the weather (*be*)_____ nice. We
(*drive*) __will drive__ through the river valley and (*enjoy*) __enjoyed__
_____ the colors of fall.

3-3 USING THE PRESENT PROGRESSIVE TO EXPRESS FUTURE TIME

(a) **Don is going to come** to the party tomorrow night. (b) **Don is coming** to the party tomorrow night. (c) **We're going to go** to a movie tonight. (d) **We're going** to a movie tonight. (e) **I'm going to stay** home tonight. (f) **I'm staying** home tonight. (g) **Ann is going to fly** to Chicago next week. (h) **Ann is flying** to Chicago next week. (i) **Bob is going to take** a taxi to the airport tomorrow. (j) **Bob is taking** a taxi to the airport tomorrow.	Sometimes the present progressive is used to express future time. (a) and (b) have the same meaning. The present progressive is used to express future time when the sentence concerns *a definite plan, a definite intention, a definite future activity.**
(k) A: You shouldn't buy that used car. It's in terrible condition. It costs too much. You don't have enough money. You'll have to get insurance and you can't afford the insurance. Buying that used car is a crazy idea. B: **I am buying** that used car tomorrow morning! My mind is made up. Nobody—not you, not my mother, not my father—can stop me. **I'm buying** that car, and that's it! I don't want to talk about it anymore. A: Oh well, it's your money.	Verbs such as **come, go, stay, arrive, leave** are frequently used in the present progressive to express future time. Such verbs express definite plans.
	Verbs expressing planned means of transportation in the future are frequently used in the present progressive: for example, **fly, walk, ride, drive, take,** (a bus, a taxi, etc.)
	Sometimes a speaker will use the present progressive when he or she wants to make *a very strong statement* about a future activity, as in (k).

*A future meaning for the present progressive is indicated either by future time words in the sentence or by the context.

EXERCISE 16: Practice using *the present progressive* to express future time by completing the dialogues. Use the words in the list or your own words. Are there any sentences in this exercise in which the present progressive expresses present, not future, time?

call	make
come	meet
drive	stay
fly	take
go	

1. A: What are you doing tomorrow afternoon?

   B: I __am going__ downtown. I __am going__ shopping. How about you? What __are__ you __doing__ tomorrow afternoon?

   A: I __will go__ to a movie with Tom. After the movie, we __we are going__ out to dinner. Would you like to come with us?

   B: No thanks. I can't. I __will take__ Alice at 6:30 at the new seafood restaurant on Fifth Street.

2. A: I __will going__ on vacation tomorrow.

   B: Where __are__ you __going,__ ?

   A: To San Francisco.

   B: How are you getting there? __are__ you __going to Fly__ or __you drive__ your car?

   A: I __will go by car__. I have to be at the airport by seven tomorrow morning.

   B: Do you need a ride to the airport?

   A: No thanks. I __will take__ a taxi. Are you planning to go someplace over vacation?

   B: No. I __will stay with__ here.

3. A: What courses __are__ you __taking__ this semester?

   B: I __'m taking__ English, biology, math, and psychology.

   A: What courses __are__ you __study__ next semester?

   B: I __'m going__ English literature, chemistry, calculus, and history.

4. A: My sister and her husband __will come__ over to my house for dinner tomorrow night. It's my sister's birthday, so I __will make__

a special birthday dinner for her. I ___cooking___ her favorite
food: roast beef and mashed potatoes.

B: ___Is___ anyone else ___come___ over for the birthday
dinner?

A: Yes. Dick and Ann Walker.

5. A: I think I will call the doctor. You have a fever, chills, and a stomach-
ache.

B: No, don't call the doctor. I'll be okay.

A: I'm worried. I___'m going call___ the doctor! And that's it!

EXERCISE 17—WRITTEN: Write a short paragraph on each of the following topics.

1. Write about an interesting experience you had when you were a child (six to
twelve years old).

2. Write about your plans for the future.

EXERCISE 18—PREPOSITIONS: Complete the sentences with prepositions. (See
Appendix 4 for a list of preposition combinations.)

1. I borrowed this dictionary ___From___ Pedro.

2. Could you please help me ___with___ these heavy suitcases?

3. Sue, I'd like to introduce you ___to___ Ed Jones.

4. You shouldn't stare ___at___ other people. It's not polite.

5. Marco Polo traveled ___to___ China in the thirteenth century.

6. Do you believe ___in___ ghosts?

7. Are you laughing ___about___ my mistake?

8. I admire my father ___for___ his honesty and intelligence.

9. I argued ___with___ Jack ___about___ politics.

10. I discussed my educational plans ___with___ my parents.

11. I applied ___To___ the University of Massachusetts. I applied
___For___ admission to the University of Massachusetts.

12. Jack applied ___for___ a job at the automobile factory.

chapter 4

Modal Auxiliaries

4-1 MODAL AUXILIARIES: INTRODUCTION

AUXILIARY + THE SIMPLE FORM OF A VERB			
can	(a)	I **can speak** English.	***Can, could, may, might, should, had better, must, will,** and **would** are followed by the simple form of a verb.*
could	(b)	He **couldn't come** to class.	
may	(c)	It **may rain** tomorrow.	They are not followed by *to:*
might	(d)	It **might rain** tomorrow.	CORRECT: *I can speak English.*
should	(e)	Mary **should study** harder.	INCORRECT: *I can to speak English.*
had better	(f)	I **had better study** tonight.	
must	(g)	John **must see** a doctor today.	The main verb never has a final **-s.**
will	(h)	I **will be** in class tomorrow.	CORRECT: *Mary can speak English.*
would	(i)	**Would** you please **close** the door?	INCORRECT: *Mary can speaks English.*

AUXILIARY + *TO* + THE SIMPLE FORM OF A VERB			
have to	(j)	I **have to study** tonight.	***Have, have got,** and **ought** are followed by an infinitive (**to** + the simple form of a verb).*
have got to	(k)	I **have got to study** tonight.	
ought to	(l)	Mary **ought to study** harder.	

EXERCISE 1: Add *to* where necessary. If no *to* is necessary, put an **X** in the blank.

1. I have _____to_____ go downtown tomorrow.

2. Tom can _____X_____ play soccer.

3. Could you please _____✗_____ open the window?

4. The students must _____✗_____ learn all of the irregular verbs.

5. Sally has _____to_____ do her homework tonight.

6. I think you should _____✗_____ take better care of your health.

7. I ought _____to_____ go to the post office this afternoon.

8. Would you _____✗_____ speak more slowly, please?

9. We may _____✗_____ go on a picnic tomorrow.

10. Will you please _____✗_____ mail this letter for me?

11. Tom and I might _____✗_____ go to the zoo tomorrow.

12. You had better _____✗_____ see a doctor.

13. We can _____✗_____ go shopping tomorrow.

14. The students have _____to_____ take a test next Friday.

15. I have got _____to_____ go to the post office this afternoon.

4-2 EXPRESSING ABILITY OR POSSIBILITY: *CAN* AND *COULD*

(a) Bob **can play** the piano.* (b) You **can buy** a screwdriver at a hardware store.	**Can** expresses *ability or possibility* in the present or future.
(c) I { **can't** / **cannot** / **can not** } understand that sentence.	The negative form of **can** may be written: **can't, cannot,** or **can not.**
(d) Our son **could talk** when he was two years old.	The past form of **can** is **could.**
(e) They { **couldn't** / **could not** } come to class yesterday.	The negative of **could**: **couldn't** or **could not.**

*Notice: CORRECT: *Bob can play the piano.*
              INCORRECT: *Bob can to play the piano.*
              INCORRECT: *Bob can plays the piano.*

EXERCISE 2:   *Can* is often pronounced /kən/. *Can't* is pronounced /kænt/. Try to determine if your teacher is saying *can* or *can't* in the following sentences.

1. I *can/can't* swim.   3. I *can/can't* sing.
2. We *can/can't* go to the movie.   4. Bob *can/can't* whistle.

5. I *can/can't* hear you.

6. Tom *can/can't* play the guitar.

7. I *can/can't* see Ann.

8. I *can/can't* wait.

9. We *can/can't* go to the party.

10. Mr. Reed *can/can't* help you.

EXERCISE 3—ORAL (BOOKS CLOSED): Use *can.*

A. ABILITY

1. What abilities and talents do you have? Tell the class about some of the things you can do. Can you swim? Whistle? Play the piano?

2. Tell the class about some abilities or talents that you don't have—things that you can't do.

3. Ask a classmate if he or she has a certain ability or talent.

> *Example:*   *Student A*: (. . .), can you play pool?
>   *Student B*:   Yes, I can.* OR: No, I can't.

B. POSSIBILITY

1. (. . .) wants to go to the zoo. Tell him/her what he/she can see at the zoo.

2. (. . .) wants to buy a hammer. Tell him/her where he/she can get a hammer.

3. (. . .) has to go to the airport tomorrow. How can he/she get there?

4. (. . .) is bored on weekends. Tell him/her some things he/she can do on weekends in (*this city*).

5. (. . .) wants to go out to eat tonight. Where can he/she get a good meal?

6. (. . .) is interested in science. What are some courses he/she can take at a university?

7. What are some things you can find in a library?

EXERCISE 4—ORAL (BOOKS CLOSED): Use *could.*

1. What could you do when you were a child that you can't do now?

2. What could you do when you were living in your own country or hometown that you can't do now?

3. What did you want to do yesterday or last week but couldn't do? Why couldn't you do it?

4. Who has missed class recently? When? Why couldn't you come to class?

5. Who has had a cold or the flu recently? What couldn't you do when you were sick?

---

*In a short answer, *can* is always pronounced /kæn/, not /kən/.

EXERCISE 5:   For each of the given situations, write two sentences: (a) using **can,** and (b) using **can't.**

1. Jack's friends are going to the park to play soccer. Jack wants to play too, but he has a broken toe, so he's on crutches.

    (a) _Jack can go to the park and watch the game._

    (b) _He can't play in the game._

2. Bob is going to a dinner party at a fancy restaurant. He doesn't know what to wear.

    (a) _Bob can go to a dinner party at_

    (b) _He can't go to a diner party_

3. Mary is at a department store. She has fifty dollars. She intends to spend all of it. She wants to buy the following things: a dress, a sweater, a pair of shoes, a raincoat, a pair of earrings.

    (a) _____

    (b) _____

4. Barbara has to go to the airport. The airport is ten miles from her house. How is she going to get there?

    (a) _____

    (b) _____

5. Alice lives in this city. She has four days to take a trip somewhere. She is going to drive her car. Where can she go?

    (a) _____

    (b) _____

6. The temperature today is around _____ degrees. Ann and Jerry don't have class today. They don't want to stay at home.

    (a) _____

    (b) _____

4-3 EXPRESSING POSSIBILITY: *MAY* AND *MIGHT*; EXPRESSING PERMISSION: *MAY* AND *CAN*

(a) It **may rain** tomorrow. (b) It **might rain** tomorrow. (c) A: Why isn't John in class? B: I don't know. He {**may** / **might**} be sick today.	**May** and **might** express possibility in the present or future. They have the same meaning. There is no difference in meaning between (a) and (b).
(d) It **may not rain** tomorrow. (e) It **might not rain** tomorrow.	Negative: **may not** and **might not**. (Do not contract **may** and **might** with **not**.)
(f) **Maybe** it will rain tomorrow. (g) **Maybe** John is sick. (h) John **may be** sick.	**Maybe** (spelled as one word) is an adverb meaning *perhaps*. Notice (f) and (g). **May be** (spelled as two words) is a verb form, as in (h).
(i) Yes, children, you **may have** a cookie after dinner.	**May** is also used to give *permission*.
(j) Okay, kids, you **can have** a cookie after dinner.	Often **can** is used to give *permission*, too. (i) and (j) have the same meaning, but **may** is more formal than **can**.

EXERCISE 6—ORAL (BOOKS CLOSED): Answer the questions.

*(To the teacher: Ask the students to begin their responses with "I don't know." It is sometimes helpful to write those words on the board as a reminder. Ask them to include at least three possibilities in their answer to a question, using **may, might,** and **maybe** as in the example.)*

> *Example*: What are you going to do tomorrow?
> *Response*: I don't know. I may go downtown. Or I might go to the laundromat. Maybe I'll study all day. Who knows?

1. What are you going to do tomorrow night?
2. What's the weather going to be like tomorrow?
3. What is (. . .) going to do tonight?
4. I'm taking something out of my briefcase/purse/pocket/wallet. It's small and I'm holding it in my fist. What is it?
5. What does (. . .) have in her purse?
6. What does (. . .) have in his pants pockets?

7. (. . .) isn't in class today. Where is he/she?

8. You have another class after this one. What are you going to do in that class?

9. We have a vacation (*time*). What are you going to do during vacation?

10. What are you going to do this weekend?

11. What is (. . .) going to do after class today?

12. What are you going to do after you graduate?

EXERCISE 7—ORAL: Make sentences with *may, might,* and *maybe* based on the given situations. Notice: Some of the situations are future and some of them are present.

1. You don't have any special plans for this coming weekend.
   (*I may. . . . Or I might . . . . Maybe I'll. . . .*)

2. It's midnight. Your roommate/spouse isn't home. Where is he/she?

3. John wants to buy a sandwich. The sandwich costs 75 cents. John has only 69 cents in his pocket. What is he going to do?

4. Your friends are coming to your home for dinner. What are you going to make for them?

5. You want to go on a picnic tomorrow, but the weather forecaster predicts rain for tomorrow. What are you going to do if you can't go on a picnic?

6. It is late at night. You hear a strange noise. What is it?

7. Look at the picture. What is the man's occupation? What is the woman's occupation?

8. What is your (younger sister/younger brother/daughter/son/niece/nephew) going to be when he or she grows up?

4-4 ASKING FOR PERMISSION: *MAY I, COULD I, CAN I*

	POLITE QUESTION	POSSIBLE ANSWERS	
(a)	**May I** please borrow your pen?	Yes. Yes. Of course. Yes. Certainly. Of course. Certainly. Sure. (*informal*) Okay. (*informal*)	People use **may I, could I,*** and **can I** to ask polite questions. The questions ask for someone's permission. (a), (b), and (c) have basically the same meaning. Note: **can I** is less formal than **may I** and **could I**.
(b)	**Could I** please borrow your pen?		
(c)	**Can I** please borrow your pen?		
		Uh-huh. (*meaning* yes)	**Please** can come at the end of the question: *May I borrow your pen, please?* **Please** can be omitted from the question: *May I borrow your pen?*

*In a polite question, **could** is not the past form of **can**.

EXERCISE 8: Following are some phone conversations. Complete the dialogues. Use **may I, could I,** or **can I** + a verb from the list. Note: The caller is Speaker B.

> *help*
> *leave*
> *speak/talk*
> *take*

1. A: Hello?
   B: Hello. Is Dick there?
   A: Yes, he is.

   B: _____ to him?
   A: Just a minute. I'll get him.

2. A: Hello. Dean Black's office.

   B: _____ to Dean Black?
   A: May I ask who is calling?
   B: Susan Abbott.
   A: Just a moment, Ms. Abbott. I'll connect you.

3. A: Hello?

   B: Hi. This is Bob. _____ to Steve?
   A: Sure. Hang on.

4. A: Good afternoon. Dr. Anderson's office. _____ you?
   B: Yes. I'd like to make an appointment with Dr. Anderson.
   A: Fine. Is Friday morning at ten all right?
   B: Yes. Thank you.
   A: Your name?

5. A: Hello?

   B: Hello. _____ to Mary?

   A: She's not at home right now. _____ a message?
   B: No thanks. I'll call again later.

6. A: Hello?

   B: Hello. _____ to Ann?
   A: She's not here right now.

   B: Oh. _____ a message?
   A: Certainly. Just a minute. I have to get a pen.

7. A: Hello?

   B: Hello. _____ to Jack?
   A: Who?
   B: Jack. Jack Butler.
   A: There's no one here by that name. I'm afraid you have the wrong
      number.
   B: Is this 221-3892?
   A: No, it's not.
   B: Oh. I'm sorry.
   A: That's okay.

EXERCISE 9—ORAL (BOOKS CLOSED): Ask a classmate a polite question. Use *may
I, could I,* or *can I.*

> *Example*:   (. . .) has a book. You want to see it for a minute.
> *Student A*: May/Could/Can I (please) see your book for a
>   minute?
> *Student B*: Of course./Sure./etc.
> *Student A*: Thank you./Thanks.

1. (. . .) has a dictionary. You want to see it for a minute.
2. (. . .) has a pen. You want to use it for a minute.
3. (. . .) has a pencil sharpener. You want to borrow it.
4. (. . .) has a camera. You want to see it for a minute.

5. You want to see something that a classmate has.

6. You want to use something that a classmate has.

7. You want to borrow something that a classmate has.

8. You are at a restaurant. (. . .) is your waiter/waitress. You have finished your meal. You want the check.

9. You are at (. . .)'s house. You want to use the phone.

10. You are speaking to one of your teachers. You want to leave class early today.

11. You smoke, but you left your cigarettes at home today. What are you going to say to your classmate?

12. You're in a store. Your bill is $2.01. You have only $2.00. What are you going to say to your friend?

13. You have a job at (*name of a local store*). A customer walks to your counter. What are you going to say to the customer?

14. You want to talk to your teacher after class.

15. You're making some bread, but you don't have enough flour. You need one more cup. What are you going to say to your neighbor?

4-5 ASKING FOR ASSISTANCE: *WOULD YOU, COULD YOU, WILL YOU, CAN YOU*

POLITE QUESTION	POSSIBLE ANSWERS*	
(a) **Would you** please open the door? (b) **Could you** please open the door? (c) **Will you** please open the door? (d) **Can you** please open the door?	Yes. Yes. Of course. Yes. Certainly. Of course. Certainly. I'd be happy to. I'd be glad to. Of course. I'd be happy/glad to. Certainly. I'd be happy/glad to. Sure. (*informal*) Okay. (*informal*) My pleasure. (*informal*) Uh-huh. (*meaning* yes)	People use **would you, could you, will you,** and **can you** to ask polite questions. The questions ask for someone's help or cooperation. (a), (b), (c), and (d) have basically the same meaning. (The use of **can**, as in (d), is less formal than the others.)
		NOTE: **May** is not used when **you** is the subject of a polite question. INCORRECT: May you please open the door?

*Answers to polite questions are usually affirmative. Examples of possible polite negative responses follow:
I'm sorry, but (I can't / I don't have enough time / my arms are full / etc.)
I'd like to, but (I can't / I don't have enough time / my arms are full / etc.)

EXERCISE 10:   Complete the dialogues. Use a polite question (***would you/could you, will you/can you***) in each. Use the expressions in the list or your own words.

answer the phone for me	*say that again*
get the door for me	*turn it down*
open the window	*turn the volume up*
pick some up	

1. *Teacher:* It's getting hot in here. <u>Would/Could/Will/Can you please open</u>

    <u>the window?</u>

    Student: <u>Of course. I'd be happy to./Sure./etc.</u>

    Teacher: <u>Thank you./Thanks.</u>

    Student: <u>You're welcome.</u>

2. *Friend A:* The phone is ringing, but my hands are full. _____

    _____

    Friend B: _____

    Friend A: _____

    Friend B: No problem.

3. *Roommate A:* I'm trying to study, but the radio is too loud. _____

    _____

    Roommate B: _____

    Roommate A: _____

    Roommate B: That's okay. No problem.

4. *Sister:* I'm trying to listen to the news on television, but I can't hear it.

    _____

    _____

    Brother: _____

    Sister: _____

    Brother: Don't mention it.

5. *Husband:* Honey, I'm out of razor blades. When you go to the store, _____

    _____

Wife: _____

Husband: _____

Wife: Anything else?

6. *Stranger A:* Excuse me. _____

   Stranger B: _____ ~~Prestar Tolend~~

   Stranger A: _____ ~~deber dept~~

   Stranger B: You're welcome.

7. *Acquaintance A:* Hi.

   Acquaintance B: Hi. Walabaxitinpundoozit? ~~sometere~~

   Acquaintance A: Excuse me? ~~Syrup~~ ~~Jarabe~~ ~~dept deber~~

   Acquaintance B: Walabaxitinpundoozit.

   Acquaintance A: Oh. I'm sorry, but I don't understand.

EXERCISE 11—ORAL (BOOKS CLOSED):   Ask a classmate a polite question.

   Example: You want someone to open the door.

   Student A: (. . .), would/could/will/can you please open the door?

   Student B: Certainly./Sure./I'd be happy to./etc.

   Student A: Thank you./Thanks.

You want someone to . . .

1. close the door.
2. lend you his/her eraser.
3. tell you the time.
4. hand you (*something*).
5. lend you a quarter.
6. shut the window.
7. give (*something*) to (. . .).
8. help you.
9. spell (*a particular word*) for you.
10. hold your books for you while you tie your shoe.

11.   (. . .) is at your apartment. The phone is ringing, but your hands are full. You want him/her to answer it for you.

12.   You and (. . .) are on vacation together. You'd like to have a picture of the two of you together. You see a stranger who looks friendly. You want him/her to take a picture of you.

13.   You wrote a letter to a university. You want your teacher to read it and correct the mistakes.

14.   (. . .) is going to the library. You want him/her to return a book for you.

15.   (. . .) and you are at (*name of a nearby restaurant*). You want a sandwich and a Pepsi, but you don't have any money. You want (. . .) to lend you a couple of bucks.

4-6   EXPRESSING ADVICE: *SHOULD, OUGHT TO, HAD BETTER*

(a)	My clothes are dirty. I ⎰ **should** **ought to** ⎱ **wash** them. **had better**	**Should, ought to,** and **had better** have basically the same meaning. They mean: *This is a good idea. This is good advice.*
(b)	You need your sleep. You **shouldn't stay** up late.	Negative: **should** + **not** = **shouldn't.***
(c)	**I'd** better **You'd** better **He'd** better **She'd** better study tonight. **We'd** better **They'd** better	Contraction of **had** = **'d.** NOTE: Usually **had** is the past form of **have.** However, in the expression **had better,** had is used as part of an idiom and the meaning is not past. The meaning is present or future.

***Ought to** is usually not used in the negative.

The negative of **had better** is *had better not*, and it often carries a warning of bad consequences.

  You had better not be late!   If you are late, you will get into a lot of trouble.

EXERCISE 12:   Complete the dialogues. Use **should, ought to,** or **had better.** Choose from the expressions in the list or use your own words.

borrow some money	*hold your breath*
call the landlord and complain	*marry somebody who is rich*
call the police	*put cotton in your ears*
drink a glass of water	*see a dentist*
find a new apartment	*send her a dozen roses*
find a new girlfriend	*soak it in cold water*
get a job	*speak English outside of class every day*
go back to the restaurant and ask if someone found them	*take it back to the store*
use a dictionary when he writes	*watch TV a lot*

deber To owe ought

1. A: I have a toothache. This tooth hurts. What should I do?*

   B: You should/ought to/had better see a dentist. _____
      debe

2. A: I have the hiccups. What should I do?

   B: _____

3. A: Ali wants to improve his English. What should he do?

   B: _____

4. A: I don't have any money. I'm broke. I can't pay my rent. I don't have
      enough money to pay my bills. What should I do?

   B: _____

5. A: Someone stole my bicycle. What should I do?

   B: _____

6. A: I cut my finger. I got blood on my sweater. My finger is okay, but I'm
      worried about my sweater. What should I do?

   B: _____

7. A: Tom's spelling isn't very good. He makes a lot of mistakes when he
      writes compositions. What should he do?

   B: _____

8. A: Ann bought a new tape recorder. After two days, it stopped working.
      What should she do?

   B: _____

9. A: The refrigerator in my apartment doesn't work. The stove doesn't
      work. The air conditioner doesn't work. And there are cockroaches in
      the kitchen. What should I do?

   B: _____

10. A: I asked Mary to marry me. She said no. What should I do?

    B: _____

11. A: I left my sunglasses at a restaurant yesterday. What should I do?

    B: _____

12. A: My husband/wife snores. I can't get to sleep at night. What should I
       do?

    B: _____ *roncar* _____

Should, not *ought to* or *had better*, is usually used in a question. The answer, however, can contain
should, ought to, or *had better*.

EXERCISE 13:   Complete the sentences. Use ***shouldn't*** + the expressions in the list or your own words.

> *be cruel to animals*   *give too much homework*
> *be late for an appointment*   *miss any classes*
> ✔*drive a long distance*   *smoke*
> *exceed the speed limit*   *throw trash out of your car window*

1. If you are tired, you _____ shouldn't drive a long distance. _____

2. Cigarette smoking is dangerous to your health. You _____

3. A good driver _____

4. A teacher _____

5. A student _____

6. Littering is against the law. You _____

7. It is important to be punctual. You _____

8. Animals have feelings, too. You _____

EXERCISE 14—ORAL: Discuss problems and give advice.

(To the teacher: This exercise can be done in pairs, in small groups, or as a class.)

STUDENT A: Think of a problem. It can be your problem or perhaps a friend's problem. Tell your classmates about the problem and then ask for advice.
STUDENT B: Give Student A some advice. Use ***should/ought to/had better***.

> *Example:*   *A:* I can't study at night because the dorm is too noisy.
>   What should I do?
>   *B:* You ought to study at the library. You shouldn't stay in
>   your dorm room in the evening.

4-7   EXPRESSING NECESSITY: *HAVE TO, HAVE GOT TO, MUST*

(a) I have a very important test tomorrow. I have to I have got to study tonight. must	*Have to, have got to,* and *must* have basically the same meaning. They express the idea that something is necessary.
	Have to is used much more frequently than *must* in everyday speech and writing.* *Have got to* is generally used only in informal speech and writing.
(b) I **have to** ("hafta") go downtown today. (c) Mary **has to** ("hasta") go to the bank. (d) I've **got to** ("gotta") study tonight.	Usual pronunciation: *have to* = "hafta" *has to* = "hasta" *(have) got to* = "gotta"
(e) I **had to study** last night.	The past form of *have to, have got to,* and *must* (meaning necessity) is *had to.*

Must means that something is *very* necessary; there is no other choice. *Must* is used much less frequently than *have to* in everyday speech and writing. *Must* is a "strong" word.

EXERCISE 15:   Complete the sentences. Use *have to, has to,* or *had to* in each.

1. I went downtown yesterday because <u>I had to go to City Hall.</u>

2. I can't go to the movie tonight because _____

3. I couldn't go to Pete's party last Saturday because _____

4. John can't go downtown with us this afternoon because _____

5. When I was in high school, _____

6. If you want to travel abroad, _____

7. I'm sorry I was absent from class yesterday, but _____

8. Alice can't come to class tomorrow because _____

9. I need a car because _____

10. When I worked in my uncle's restaurant, _____

11. If you want to enter the university, _____

12. We wanted to go on a picnic yesterday, but we couldn't because _____

    _____

13. I wanted to _____ yesterday, but _____

    _____ instead.

EXERCISE 16—ORAL (BOOKS CLOSED):   Practice using *have to, have got to, must,* and *should.*

(To the teacher: Elicit several responses from different students for each item. Involve a Student B in order to provide practice with third person singular. Encourage usual pronunciation: "hafta," "hasta," and "gotta.")

> *Example*:   Tell me something you have to do this evening.
> *Student A*:   I have to go to a meeting.
> *Teacher*:   What does (Student A) have to do this evening?
> *Student B*:   He/She has to go to a meeting.
> *Teacher*:   How about you, (. . .)? Tell me something you have to do this evening.

A. Use *have to*.
   1. Tell me something you have to do today or tomorrow.
   2. Tell me something you have to do every day.
   3. Tell me something you had to do yesterday or last week.
B. Use *have got to*.
   4. Tell me something you have got to do today or tomorrow.
   5. Tell me something you've got to do tonight.
   6. Tell me something you've got to do after class today.
C. Use *must* or *should*.
   7. Tell me something very important that you must do today or tomorrow.
   8. Tell me something that you should do today or tomorrow (but which you may or may not do).
   9. Tell me something a driver must do according to the law.
   10. Tell me something a good driver should always do.
   11. Tell me something a person should do in order to stay healthy.
   12. Tell me something a person must do to stay alive. (If a person doesn't do this, he or she will die.)
   13. I don't have a driver's license for this state/province, but I want to get one. Tell me something I must do to get a driver's license.

4-8   EXPRESSING LACK OF NECESSITY: *DO NOT HAVE TO;* EXPRESSING PROHIBITION: *MUST NOT*

(a) I finished all of my homework this afternoon. I **don't have to study** tonight.	***Don't/doesn't have to*** expresses the idea that something is *not necessary.*
(b) Tomorrow is a holiday. Mary **doesn't have to go** to class.	

(c) Children, you **must not play** with matches! (d) We **must not use** that door. The sign says: PRIVATE. DO NOT ENTER.	*Must not* expresses *prohibition*. (DO NOT DO THIS!)
(e) You **mustn't** play with matches.	*Must* + *not* = *mustn't*. (Note: The first *t* is not pronounced.)

EXERCISE 17: Complete the sentences with *don't/doesn't have to* or *must not*.

1. Liz finally got a car, so now she usually drives to work. She _____ _____ take the bus.

2. Tommy, you _____ say that word. That's not a nice word.

3. Mr. Moneybags is very rich. He _____ work for a living.

4. If you are in a canoe, you _____ stand up and walk around. If you do, the canoe will probably tip over.

5. A: You _____ tell Jim about the surprise birthday party. Do you promise?
   B: I promise.

6. A: Did Professor Adams make an assignment?
   B: Yes, she assigned Chapters 4 and 6, but we_____ read Chapter 5.

7. A: I _____ forget to set my alarm for 5:30.
   B: Why do you have to get up at 5:30?
   A: I'm going to meet Ron at 6:00. We're going fishing.

8. A: Listen to me carefully, Annie. If a stranger offers you a ride, you _____ get in the car. Never get in a car with a stranger. Do you understand?
   B: Yes, Mom.

9. A: Do you have a stamp?

   B: Uh-huh. Here.

   A: Thanks. Now I _____ go to the post office.

10. A: Children, your mother and I are going to go out this evening. I want you to be good and follow these rules: You must do everything the baby-sitter tells you to do. You _____ go outside after dark. It's Saturday night, so you _____ go to bed at eight. You can stay up until eight-thirty. And remember: you _____ _____ pull the cat's tail. Okay?

    B: Okay, Dad.

4-9 GIVING INSTRUCTIONS: IMPERATIVE SENTENCES

COMMAND (a) *General:* *Soldier:*	**Open the door!** Yes, sir!	Imperative sentences are used to give commands, make polite requests, and give directions.
REQUEST (b) *Teacher:* *Student:*	**Open the door, please.** Okay. I'd be happy to.	The difference between a command and a request lies in the speaker's tone of voice and the use of *please.*
DIRECTIONS (c) *Barbara:* *Stranger:*	Could you tell me how to get to the post office? Certainly. **Walk two blocks down this street. Turn left and walk three more blocks.** It's on the right hand side of the street.	*Please* can come at the beginning or end of a request: *Open the door, please.* *Please open the door.*
(d) **Close** the window. (e) Please **sit** down. (f) **Be** quiet! (g) **Don't walk** on the grass. (h) Please **don't wait** for me. (i) **Don't be** late.		The simple form of a verb is used in imperative sentences. The understood subject of the sentence is *you* (meaning the person the speaker is talking to): *(You) close the window.* Negative form: *Don't + the simple form of a verb.*

EXERCISE 18: Complete the dialogues with imperative sentences. Try to figure out something the first speaker might say in the given situation.

1. *The teacher:* Read this sentence, please./Look at page 33./etc.

   The student: Okay.

2. *The doctor:* _____
   The patient: All right.

3. *The mother:* _____
   The son: I will. Don't worry.

4. *Mrs. Jones:* _____
   The children: Yes, ma'am.

5. *The general:* _____
   The soldier: Yes, sir! Right away, sir!

6. *The father:* _____
   The daughter: Okay, Dad.

7. *A friend:*   _____
   A friend: Why not?

8. *The wife:*   _____
   The husband: Okay.

9. *The husband:* _____
   The wife: Why?

10. *The boss:*   _____
    The employee: I'll do it immediately.

11. *The father:* _____
    The son: Okay. I won't.

EXERCISE 19—ORAL:

1. Give a classmate explicit directions on how to get to another place in this building. (*Walk out the door and turn left/right. Go to the end of the hall and. . . . etc.*)
2. Give a classmate explicit directions on how to get to a place that is near the classroom building. (*Go out the main door. Turn left and. . . . etc.*)

EXERCISE 20—WRITTEN: Write about one of the following.

1. Give general advice to people who want to (*choose one*):
   (a) improve their health, or
   (b) get good grades, or
   (c) lose weight, or
   (d) improve their English.

Tell your readers: Do this. Don't do that. You should do this. You shouldn't do that. You ought to do this. You have to do this. You don't have to do that. You must do this. You must not do that. You can do this. You had better do that, etc.

Begin your composition with: *If you want to. . . , there are several things you should do. First. . . .*

2. Explain how to prepare one of your favorite recipes. Try to write without looking at a cookbook. Be sure to give the directions in chronological order (in order of time: *first, second, next, then, etc.*).

Begin your composition with: *One of my favorite recipes is for. . . . I would like to tell you how to make it/them.*

3. One of your friends wants to come to this city. S/he wants to go to school here or get a job here. Write your friend a letter. Give your friend advice about coming to this city to study or work.

4-10 MAKING SUGGESTIONS: USING *LET'S* AND *WHY DON'T*

(a) A: It's hot today. **Let's go** to the beach. B: Okay. Good idea. (b) A: It's hot today. **Why don't we go** to the beach? B: Okay. Good idea.	**Let's** (*do something*) and **why don't we** (*do something*) have the same meaning. They are used to make suggestions about activities for you and me. **Let's** = *let us.*
(c) A: I'm tired. B: **Why don't you take** a nap. A: That's a good idea. I think I will.	People use **why don't you** (*do something*) to make a friendly suggestion, to give friendly advice.

EXERCISE 21: Complete the dialogues. Use *let's* or *why don't we.*

1. A: The weather's beautiful today. _____
   B: Good idea.

2. A: I'm bored.
   B: Me too. _____
   A: Great idea!

3. A: Are you hungry?
   B: Yes. Are you?

   A: Yes. _____
   B: Okay.

4. A: What are you going to do over spring break?
   B: I don't know. What are you going to do?

A: I haven't made any plans.

B: _____

A: That sounds like a terrific idea, but I can't afford it.

5. A: I need to go shopping.
    B: So do I.
    A: _____

    B: I can't go then. _____
    A: Okay. That's fine with me.

6. A: Do you have any plans for this weekend?
    B: Not really.
    A: I don't either. _____
    B: Okay. Good idea.

7. A: What time should we leave for the airport?

    B: _____
    A: Okay.

8. A: What should we do tonight?

    B: _____
    A: Sounds okay to me.

9. A: _____

    B: Let's not. _____ instead.
    A: Okay.

EXERCISE 22—ORAL: Give suggestions. Use *"Why don't you*. . .?

1. I'm thirsty.
2. I'm sleepy.
3. I have a headache.
4. I have a toothache.
5. It's too hot in this room.
6. Brrr. I'm cold.
7. I'm broke.
8. I'm hungry.
9. I have to take a science course next semester. What should I take?
10. Tomorrow is my sister's birthday. What should I give her?
11. I'd like to go to (. . .)'s party tonight, but I probably should stay home and study. What do you think I should do?
12. I'm going to take a vacation this summer. Where should I go?

EXERCISE 23: Make sentences by combining one of the ideas in Column A with one of the ideas in Column B. Use *if* with the ideas in Column A.*

Example: If you need some help when you move into your new apartment, please call me.

COLUMN A (*condition*)

    ✔ 1. You may need some help when you move into your new apartment.
    2. The weather may be nice tomorrow.
    3. You may have a problem with your visa.
    4. I may not be at the airport when your plane gets in.
    5. John may want to lose some weight.
    6. You may be tired.
    7. Mary may not get better soon.
    8. You may not know the answer to a question on the test.
    9. Alice may call while I'm out.
   10. You may be hungry.

COLUMN B (*suggestion*)

    1. Guess.
    2. You should see the International Student Advisor.
    3. Why don't you take a nap?
    4. Wait for me by the United Airlines counter.
    5. Please take a message.
    6. I'd be happy to make a sandwich for you.
    7. He should stop eating candy.
  ✔ 8. Please call me.
    9. She should see a doctor.
   10. Let's go to the zoo.

4-11 STATING PREFERENCES: *PREFER, LIKE . . . BETTER, WOULD RATHER*

(a) I **prefer** apples **to** oranges. (b) I **like** apples **better than** oranges. (c) I **would rather have** an apple **than** an orange.	Pattern: **prefer** X **to** Y. Pattern: **like** X **better than** Y. Pattern: **would rather** + *verb* + X **than** Y.
(d) **I would rather have** an apple. **He would rather have** an orange. **They would rather have** some bananas.	**Would rather** is used to state preferences. NOTICE: The verb following **would rather** is always in the simple form. INCORRECT: *He would rather has an orange.*

---

*Use the simple present in the "*if* clause." (See 3-2.) Do not use *may* in the "*if* clause."

(e)	**I'd** **You'd** **He'd** **She'd** **We'd** **They'd** } rather have an apple.	Contraction of **would** = **'d.** *
(f)	**I would rather watch** TV this evening **than go** to the library.	Sometimes a verb follows **than.** This verb is in the simple form.
(g)	**I would rather have** an apple **than (have)** an orange.	A verb following **than** is always possible, but it is usually omitted if it is the same as the verb
(h)	**I would rather visit** Chicago **than (visit)** Miami.	which immediately follows **would rather.**

*The contraction of **had** is also **'d**.

 I'd better study: **'d** = **had**.
 I'd rather study: **'d** = **would**.

See 6-9, Forms of the Past Perfect, for more information about **had** as an auxiliary verb.

EXERCISE 24—ORAL (BOOKS CLOSED): Answer the questions in complete sentences.

Example: Which do you prefer, apples or oranges?
Response: I prefer (oranges) to (apples).
Example: Which do you like better, bananas or strawberries?
Response: I like (bananas) better than (strawberries).
Example: Which would you rather have right now, an apple or a banana?
Response: I'd rather have (a banana).

 1. Which do you like better, rice or potatoes?
 2. Which do you prefer, rice or potatoes?
 3. Which would you rather have for dinner tonight, rice or potatoes?
 4. Which do you prefer, fish or beef?
 5. Which do you like better, fish or beef?
 6. Which would you rather have for dinner tonight, fish or beef?
 7. Which do you like better, Chinese food or Mexican food?
 8. Which do you prefer, tea or coffee?
 9. Would you rather have a cup of tea after class or a cup of coffee?
10. Which do you like better, hot weather or cold weather?
11. Which do you prefer, rock music or classical music?
12. What kind of music would you rather listen to, rock or classical music?

13. Name two vegetables. Which do you prefer?
14. Name two kinds of fruit. Which do you like better?
15. Name two sports. Which do you like better?
16. Name two sports that you play. Which sport would you rather play this afternoon?
17. Name two TV programs. Which do you like better?
18. Name two movies. Which one would you rather see?

EXERCISE 25—ORAL (BOOKS CLOSED): Answer the questions in complete sentences. Use *would rather . . . than. . . .*

Would you rather . . .
1. have a cup of coffee or (have) a cup of tea right now?
2. be a doctor or (be) a dentist?
3. be married or (be) single?
4. live in an apartment or (live) in a house?*
5. go to Paris or (go) to London for your vacation?
6. visit Niagara Falls or (visit) the Grand Canyon?
7. take a nap or go downtown this afternoon?
8. watch TV or read a good book?
9. study chemistry or (study) accounting?
10. be a plumber or (be) a carpenter?
11. go to a football game or (go) to a soccer game?
12. study tonight or go to a movie?
13. after dinner, wash the dishes or dry the dishes?
14. go to (*name of a place in this city*) or (go) to (*name of a place in this city*)?
15. have straight hair or (have) curly hair?
16. be a student or (be) a teacher?
17. have six children or (have) two children?
18. take your vacation in Greece or (take your vacation) in Brazil?
19. be at home right now or (be) in class?

---

*It is possible but not necessary to repeat a preposition after *than*.

CORRECT: *I'd rather live in an apartment than in a house.*
CORRECT: *I'd rather live in an apartment than a house.*

20. have a car or (have) an airplane?
21. be a bird or (be) a fish?
22. take a long walk this afternoon or go swimming?

EXERCISE 26:   Complete the dialogues with your own words.

1. A: Do you feel like going to a show tonight?

   B: Not really. I'd rather _____

2. A: Which do you like better, _____ or _____

   B: I like _____ better _____

3. A: What are you going to do this weekend?

   B: I may _____ , but I'd rather _____

4. A: What kind of music do you like?

   B: All kinds. But I prefer _____ to _____

5. A: What are you going to do tonight?

   B: I should _____ , but I'd rather _____

6. A: Let's go on a picnic next Saturday.

   B: That sounds good, but I'd rather _____

7. A: I like _____ better _____
   B: Oh? Why?

   A: _____

8. A: Are you going to _____ tonight?

   B: I'd like to, but I can't. I have to _____

      _____ , but I'd much rather _____

chapter 5

Asking Questions

5-1 YES/NO QUESTIONS AND SHORT ANSWERS

	YES/NO QUESTIONS	SHORT ANSWER (+ LONG ANSWER)	
(a)	**Do you know** Jim Smith?	**Yes, I do.** (I know Jim Smith.) **No, I don't.** (I don't know Jim Smith.)	A *yes/no question* is a question that can be answered by **yes** or **no.**
(b)	**Did it rain** last night?	**Yes, it did.** (It rained last night.) **No, it didn't.** (It didn't rain last night.)	
(c)	**Are you studying** English?	**Yes, I am.** (I'm studying English.) **No, I'm not.** (I'm not studying English.)	NOTE: In an affirmative answer (*yes*), a helping verb is not contracted with the subject. In (c): CORRECT: *Yes, I am.* INCORRECT: *Yes, I'm.*
(d)	**Was Ann** in class?	**Yes, she was.** (Ann was in class.) **No, she wasn't.** (Ann wasn't in class.)	In (e): CORRECT: *Yes, he will.* INCORRECT: *Yes, he'll.*
(e)	**Will Bob be** here soon?	**Yes, he will.** (Bob will be here soon.) **No, he won't.** (Bob won't be here soon.)	
(f)	**Can you swim?**	**Yes, I can.** (I can swim.) **No, I can't.** (I can't swim.)	

EXERCISE 1: In the following dialogues, the long answer is given in parentheses. Look at the long answer, and then make the appropriate *yes/no question* and *short answer* to complete each dialogue. Do not use a negative verb in the question.

1. A: _____ Do you know my brother? _____
    B: No, _____I don't._____ (I don't know your brother.)

2. A: ___Does Jane eats lunch at the cafeteria everyday___
    B: Yes, _She does_ (Jane eats lunch at the cafeteria every day.)

3. A: ___Does the pen belong to you?___
    B: No, _it doesn't_ (That pen doesn't belong to me.)

4. A: ___Does the students in this class speak Englishwell___
    B: Yes: _they does_ (The students in this class speak English well.)

5. A: ___Do you slept well last night?___
    B: Yes, _I Did_ (I slept well last night.)

6. A: ___Did Ann and Jim didn't come to class yesterday?___
    B: No, _they didn't_ (Ann and Jim didn't come to class yesterday.)

7. A: _____
    B: Yes, _____ (I'm studying my grammar book.)

8. A: _____
    B: No, _____ (The children aren't watching TV.)

9. A: _____
    B: Yes, _he is_ (Tim Wilson is in my class.)

10. A: _____
    B: No, _____ (It wasn't foggy yesterday.)

11. A: ___will you be in class to morrow___
    B: No, _I Won't_ (I won't be in class tomorrow.)

12. A: _____
    B: No, _____ (Larry isn't going to be in class tomorrow.)

13. A: ___Does Karen wi___
    B: Yes, _____ (Karen will finish her work before she goes to bed.)

14. A: _____
    B: No, _____ (I can't play the piano.)

15. A: _____
    B: Yes, _can._____ (Some birds can swim under water.)

16. A: _Should I_____
    B: Yes, _you should_ (You should make an appointment to see the
    doctor.)

17. A: _do I need_____
    B: Yes, _you do___ (You need to make an appointment to see the
    doctor.)

18. A: _____
    B: Yes, _____ (I have a bicycle.)*

19. A: _Does_____
    B: No, _She doesn't_ (Al doesn't have a roommate.)

20. A: _Do I have to study tonight_____
    B: Yes, _you Do'__ (I have to study tonight.)

EXERCISE 2—ORAL (BOOKS CLOSED): Answer the questions. Use short answers.

Example: Do you know how to swim?
Response: Yes, I do. OR: No, I don't.
Example: Is (. . .) wearing blue jeans today?
Response: Yes, s/he is. OR: No, s/he isn't.

1. Is (. . .) in class today?
2. Does (he) have a mustache?
3. Is (he) wearing a sweater today?
4. Was (the teacher) in class yesterday?

5. Did (I) come to class yesterday?
6. Is (. . .) from (*name of a country*)?

_____

*In American English, a form of *do* is usually used when *have* is the main verb:

   Do you have a car?

In British English, a form of *do* with main verb *have* is not necessary:

   Have you a car?

7. Does (. . .) speak (*name of a language*)?
8. Are you going downtown tomorrow?
9. Will you be in class tomorrow? *No I'm not*
10. Can you play the piano? *Yes I can*
11. Do you know how to play the violin?
12. Are we going to have a test tomorrow?
13. Can turtles swim?
14. Should people smoke cigarettes?
15. Did you watch TV last night?

16. Do you have a bicycle?
17. Will class begin at (*time*) tomorrow?
18. Does class begin at (*time*) every day?
19. Do giraffes eat meat?
20. Were all of the students in class yesterday?
21. Should I speak more slowly?
22. Is English grammar easy?
23. Are you going to study tonight?
24. Was this exercise difficult?

EXERCISE 3—ORAL (BOOKS CLOSED): Make questions and give short answers.

> *Example:*   (. . .) is wearing jeans today.
> *Student A:* Is (. . .) wearing jeans today?
> *Student B:* Yes, s/he is.
>
> *Example:*   (. . .) isn't wearing jeans today.
> *Student A:* Is (. . .) wearing jeans today?
> *Student B:* No, s/he isn't.

1. (. . .) has curly hair.
2. (. . .) doesn't have a mustache. *Does The Doctor*
3. (. . .) is going to be in class tomorrow.
4. (. . .) won't be in class tomorrow.
5. (. . .) studied at the library last night.
6. (. . .) can't play the piano.
7. (. . .) has to study tonight.
8. (. . .) went to a party last night.
9. (. . .) is wearing earrings.
10. (. . .) has dark eyes.
11. (. . .)'s grammar book isn't open.
12. (. . .) should close his/her grammar book.

13. That book belongs to (. . .). *Did Mary was in class yesterday*
14. (. . .) and (. . .) came to class yesterday. *Did*
15. (. . .) wasn't in class yesterday.
16. This book has an index.
17. Most books have indexes.
18. This exercise is easy.
19. (. . .) will be at home tonight.
20. An ostrich can't fly.

5-2 YES/NO QUESTIONS AND INFORMATION QUESTIONS

A *yes/no question* = a question that may be answered by **yes** or **no.**

A: Does Ann live in Montreal?
B: Yes, she does. OR: **No, she doesn't.**

An *information question* = a question that asks for information by using a question word: **where, when, why, who, whom, what, which, whose, how.**

A: Where does Ann live?
B: In Montreal.

(QUESTION WORD) +	HELPING VERB +	SUBJECT +	MAIN VERB		
(a)	**Does**	**Ann**	**live**	in Montreal?	The same subject-verb word order is used in both yes/no and information questions:
(b) **Where**	**does**	**Ann**	**live?**		
(c)	**Is**	**Mary**	**studying**	at the library?	
(d) **Where**	**is**	**Mary**	**studying?**		
(e)	**Will**	**you**	**graduate**	next year?	**HELPING VERB + SUBJECT + MAIN VERB**
(f) **When**	**will**	**you**	**graduate?**		
(g)	**Did**	**you**	**see**	Jack at the party?	
(h) **Who(m)***	**did**	**you**	**see**	at the party?	
(i)		**Who**	**came**	to the party?	When the question word (e.g., **who** or **what**) is the subject of the question, usual question word order is not used. No form of **do** is used. Notice examples (i) and (j).
(j)		**What**	**happened**	yesterday?	

*See 5-3 for a discussion of **who(m)**.

EXERCISE 4—ORAL: Make questions from the following sentences. Make *(a)* a *yes/no question* and *(b)* an *information question* with **where**.

Example: I live there.
Response: (a) Do you live there?
(b) Where do you live?

Reminder:
(QUESTION WORD) + HELPING VERB + SUBJECT + MAIN VERB

Does She lived there

1. She lives there.
Do the student
2. The students live there.

3. Bob lived there.
are you
4. I'm living there.

5. Mary is living there.

6. I was living there.

7. He was living there.

8. They are going to live there.

9. John will live there.

10. The students can live there.

11. Alice should live there.

12. Tom has to live there.*

EXERCISE 5: Make information questions. Use **where, why, when**, or **what time**.

1. A: _____ When/What time† did you get up this morning? _____
   B: At 7:30. (I got up at 7:30 this morning.)

2. A: _whar do you ate lunch today_ ?
   B: At the cafeteria. (I ate lunch at the cafeteria today.)

3. A: _when wa't time did you ate lunch today_
   B: At 12:15. (I ate lunch at 12:15.)

4. A: _why DO you eat lunch at the Cafeteria_
   B: Because the food is good. (I eat lunch at the cafeteria because the food is good.)

5. A: _Where DO your aunt and uncle live_
   B: In Chicago. (My aunt and uncle live in Chicago.)

6. A: _when are you going to visit your aun, and_
   B: Next week. (I'm going to visit my aunt and uncle next week.) _next week'anche,_

7. A: _at what time you will get home to night._
   B: Around six. (I'll get home around six tonight.)

8. A: _where is George is goin_
   B: At the library. (George is going to study at the library tonight.)

9. A: _____
   B: Because it's quiet. (George studies at the library because it's quiet.)

10. A: _____
    B: At that corner. (You can catch a bus at that corner.)

---

*In a question, a form of **do** is used with **have to.**

    Do you have to go there? Where do you have to go?

    Does she have to go there? Where does she have to go?

†A question with **what time** usually asks about time on a clock. The answer can be *7:30, a quarter past ten, around five o'clock,* etc.

A question with **when** can be answered by any time expression: *7:30, around five o'clock, last night, next week, in a few days, yesterday,* etc.

11. A: _what time do yo have to leve_

     B: Ten o'clock. (I have to leave at ten o'clock.)

12. A: _where was you liven_

     B: In Japan. (I was living in Japan in 1980.)

13. A: _why are the students are_

     B: Because they're working on an exercise. (The students are writing in their books because they're working on an exercise.)

14. A: _what time should I Call you,_

     B: Around seven. (You should call me around seven.)

EXERCISE 6: Make information questions. Use *where, why, when*, or *what time*.

1. A: _when are you goin to morror_

     B: Tomorrow. (I'm going to go downtown tomorrow.)

2. A: _____

     B: Because I didn't feel good. (I stayed home yesterday because I didn't feel good.)

3. A: _where do you go thursday_

     B: To a movie. (I went to a movie last night.)

4. A: _Where Can I buy a hammer_

     B: At a hardware store. (You can buy a hammer at a hardware store.)

5. A: _____

     B: At 1:10. (Class begins at 1:10.)

6. A: _____

     B: Because I need to buy some stamps. (I have to go to the post office because I need to buy some stamps.)

7. A: _where will your dau_

     B: Next June. (My daughter will graduate from college next June.)

8. A: _where do your childrens go to school_

     B: At Lincoln Elementary School. (My children go to school at Lincoln Elementary School.)

9. A: _____

     B: Four years ago. (I met the Smiths four years ago.)

10. A: _Why are you study English_

   B: Because I need to know it in order to study in the United States. (I'm
   studying English because I need to know it in order to study in the
   United States.)

EXERCISE 7—ORAL: Pair up with a classmate. Practice asking questions with *why*.

STUDENT A's book is open. STUDENT B's book is closed.

STUDENT A: Say the sentence in the book. (Then listen carefully to B's question
with *why* and make sure it is correct.)
STUDENT B: Ask a question using *why*.*
STUDENT A: Make up an answer to the question.

   Example: A: I'm tired today.
   B: Why are you tired today?
   A: Because I stayed up late last night.

1. A: I was absent from class yesterday.
2. A: I'm going to go to the bank after class.
3. A: I went downtown yesterday.
4. A: I took a taxi to school today.
5. A: I need to go to the drugstore.
6. A: I'm going to buy a new dictionary.

   Example: A: I didn't study last night.
   B: Why didn't you study last night?
   (*Notice: Use a negative verb in the question
   with why.*)
   A: Because I was tired.

 7. A: I didn't do my homework last night.
 8. A: I'm not coming to class tomorrow.
 9. A: I can't come to your party this weekend.
10. A: I didn't eat breakfast this morning.
11. A: I won't be in class tomorrow.
12: A: I don't like the weather in this city.

---

*In normal daily conversation, the second speaker (Student B) would usually ask only "Why?" or "Why
not?" However, to practice question word order, Student B should ask the full question in this exercise.

5-3   USING *WHO, WHO(M)*, **AND** *WHAT*

QUESTION	ANSWER	
(a) **S** **Who** came?	**S** **Someone** came.	In (a): **Who** is used as the subject (**S**) of a question.

(b) **O**   **S**
Who(m) did you see?
	S **O**
	I saw **someone**.
		In (b): **Who(m)** is used as the object (**O**) in a question.
		Whom is used in formal English. In everyday spoken English, **who** is usually used instead of **whom:**
		    FORMAL: *Whom did you see?*
		    INFORMAL: *Who did you see?*

(c) **S** **What** happened?	**S** **Something** happened.	**What** can be used as either the subject or the object in a question.

(d) **O**   **S**
What did you see?
	S **O**
	I saw **something**.
		Notice in (a) and (c): When **who** or **what** is used as the subject of a question, usual question word order is not used; no form of **do** is used.
		    CORRECT: *Who came?*
		    INCORRECT: *Who did come?*

EXERCISE 8:   Make questions. Use *what, who,* or *who(m)*.

1. A: <u>What did you see?</u>
    B: An accident. (I saw an accident.)

2. A: <u>What Did Mary See?</u>
    B: An accident. (Mary saw an accident.)

3. A: <u>Who Saw an accident?</u>
    B: Mary. (Mary saw an accident.)

4. A: <u>Whom did Mary see?</u>
    B: John. (Mary saw John.)

5. A: <u>Whom saw john?</u>
    B: Mary. (Mary saw John.)

6. A: <u>what happened?</u>
    B: An accident. (An accident happened.)

General Education
GE Development

7. A: _what did Alice buy?_
   B: A new coat. (Alice bought a new coat.)

8. A: _Whom did bay a knew Coat?_
   B: Alice. (Alice bought a new coat.)

9. A: _what are you looking? at_
   B: A map of the world. (I'm looking at a map of the world.)*

10. A: _Whom did you looking?_
    B: Jane. (I'm looking at Jane.)

11. A: _Whom did you talked?_
    B: The secretary. (I talked to the secretary.)

12. A: _what Did Tom talk about?_
    B: His problems. (Tom talked about his problems.)

13. A: _what Did the teacher look?_
    B: The board. (The teacher looked at the board.)

14. A: _Whom Did look at the board_
    B: The teacher. (The teacher looked at the board.)

15. A: _whom Did The Teacher look?_
    B: The students. (The teacher looked at the students.)

EXERCISE 9—ORAL: In spoken English, *is, are, did,* and *will* are often contracted with question words. Listen to your teacher say the following questions and practice saying them yourself.

1. Where is my book?†
2. What is in that drawer?†
3. Why is Mary absent?
4. Who is that man?†
5. Who are those men?
6. Where are you going?
7. What are you doing?
8. Where did Bob go last night?

---

*A preposition may come at the beginning of a question in very formal English:

>   *At what are you looking?*
>   *At whom* (not *who*) *are you looking?*

In everyday English, a preposition usually does not come at the beginning of a question.

†Often *is* is contracted with *where, what,* and *who* in informal writing as well as in spoken English.

>   *Where's my pen?*
>   *What's that?*
>   *Who's he?*

9. What did you say?
10. Why did you say that?
11. Who did you see at the party?
12. Where will you be?

13. When will you arrive?
14. Who will meet you at the airport?

EXERCISE 10:   Make any appropriate question for the given answer.

1. A: *Whom did you see at the party?*
   B: Yesterday.

2. A: *What did you see?*
   B: A new pair of shoes.

3. A: *Who will meet you at the airport?*
   B: Mary.

4. A: *at what time you will arrive?*
   B: Six-thirty.

5. A: *where will you be on Sunday?*
   B: To the zoo.

6. A: *why are you rest?*
   B: Because I was tired.

7. A: *what are you eaten?*
   B: A sandwich.

8. A: *where is the Zoo?*
   B: I don't know.

9. A: *when will you arrive?*
   B: Tomorrow.

10. A: *Whom is going to work tomorrow*
    B: My brother.

5-4   USING *WHAT* + A FORM OF *DO*

	QUESTION	ANSWER	
(a)	**What does** Bob **do** every morning?	He goes to class.	***What*** + *a form of* ***do*** *is used to ask questions about activities.*
(b)	**What did** you **do** yesterday?	I went downtown.	
(c)	**What is** your roommate **doing**?	She's studying.	
(d)	**What are** you **going to do** tomorrow?	I'm going to go to the beach.	

(e)	**What do** you **want to do** tonight?	I want to go to a movie.
(f)	**What would** you **like to do** tomorrow?	I would like to visit Jim.
(g)	**What will** you **do** tomorrow?	I'll go downtown.
(h)	**What should** I **do** about my headache?	You should take an aspirin.

EXERCISE 11: Make questions. Use **what** + *a form of* **do**.

1. A: <u>What are you doing</u> right now?
    B: I'm studying.

2. A: _____ last night?
    B: I studied.

3. A: _____ tomorrow?
    B: I'm going to visit my relatives.

4. A: <u>what do you want to do</u> tomorrow?
    B: I want to go to the beach.

5. A: <u>what do you need to do</u> tomorrow?
    B: I need to go to the library.

6. A: _____ tomorrow?
    B: I would like to go to a movie.

7. A: _____ tomorrow?
    B: I'm planning to stay home and relax most of the day.

8. A: <u>what do you study</u> in class every day?
    B: I study English.

9. A: _____ (for a living)?*
    B: I'm a teacher. (I teach.)

10. A: <u>what will you do</u> if it snows tomorrow and you
    can't get to the airport?
    B: I'll cancel my reservation and book a flight for the next day.

11. A: <u>what should I do</u> to improve my English?
    B: You should speak English as much as possible.

12. A: _____ after class yesterday?
    B: He (Bob) went to the post office.

_____

*__What do you do?__ has a special meaning. It means: *What is your occupation, your job?* Another way
of asking the same question: **What do you do for a living?**

13. A: _____ after class yesterday?
    B: She (Jane) went swimming.

14. A: _____ when he stopped you for
    speeding?
    B: He (the police officer) gave me a ticket.

15. A: _____ ?
    B: She (Yoko) is writing in her book.

16. A: _____ in the winter?
    B: It (a bear) hibernates.

17. A: I have the hiccups. _____ ?
    B: You should drink a glass of water.

18. A: Mike is in trouble with the law. _____ ?
    B: He should see a lawyer.

19. A: _____ ?
    B: He (my husband) is a businessman. He works for General Electric.

20. A: _____ ?
    B: She (my wife) is a computer programmer. She works for the telephone
    company.

EXERCISE 12—ORAL (BOOKS CLOSED): Ask a classmate a question. Use
what + do.

> *Example:*   tomorrow
> *Student A:*   What are you going to do tomorrow?/What do
>   you want to do tomorrow?/What would you like
>   to do tommorow?/etc.
> *Student B:*   (answer the question)

1. last night   4. this afternoon
2. right now   5. tonight
3. next Saturday   6. yesterday

7. every day

8. yesterday afternoon

9. this morning

10. last weekend

11. on weekends

12. tomorrow afternoon

13. after class yesterday

14. after class today

15. every morning

5-5 USING *WHAT KIND OF*

QUESTION	ANSWER	

(a) **What kind of shoes** did you buy?	Boots.
	Sandals.
	Tennis shoes.
	Loafers.
	Running shoes.
	High heels.
	(etc.)
		What kind of asks for information about a specific type (a specific kind) in a general category.
		In (a):
		  general category = shoes
		  specific kinds = boots,
		                      sandals,
		                      tennis shoes,
		                      etc.

(b) **What kind of fruit** do you like best?	Apples. Bananas. Oranges. Grapefruit. Grapes. Strawberries. (etc.)	

NOTE: **What kind of** can be followed by a singular count noun, a plural count noun, or a noncount noun. (See Chapter 11 for a discussion of nouns.)

    singular count noun: What kind of **tree** is that?

    plural count noun: What kind of **shoes** are those?

    noncount noun: What kind of **fruit** is that?

EXERCISE 13: Name the general category. Complete the question, using **what kind of**. Answer the question.

    Example: *lamb, beef, pork, chicken, (other):* <u>turkey, duck, ham.</u>

    GENERAL CATEGORY: <u>meat</u>

           QUESTION: <u>What kind of meat</u> do you eat

                    most often?

SPECIFIC ANSWER: <u>Beef. OR: Chicken. OR:</u>
                   <u>I'm a vegetarian.</u>

1. *rock music, classical music, popular music, folk music, Venezuelan music,*
   (other): _music,_____

   GENERAL CATEGORY: _Romantic_____ *music*
              QUESTION: _What kind of____ do you like best?
   SPECIFIC ANSWER: _let it be_____

2. *a Volkswagen, a Mercedes-Benz, a Fiat, a Toyota, a Ford, (other):* _____
   _____ *I would like To have a care*_____

   GENERAL CATEGORY: _Mercedez____
              QUESTION: _what kind_ *of car,* would you like to have?
   SPECIFIC ANSWER: _mercedez___

3. *vegetables, fruit, meat, sweet food, hot food,* junk food, French food,*
   (other): _____

   GENERAL CATEGORY: _____
              QUESTION: _____ do you like best?
   SPECIFIC ANSWER: _____

4. *fiction, nonfiction, biographies, science books, science fiction, love stories,*
   history books, historical fiction, (other): _____

   GENERAL CATEGORY: _____
              QUESTION: _____ do you like to read?
   SPECIFIC ANSWER: _____

EXERCISE 14—ORAL (BOOKS CLOSED):   Answer the questions.

1. What kind of music do you like best?
2. What kind of shoes are you wearing?
3. What kind of food do you like best?
4. What kind of books do you like to read?

   _Poems Books._____

Hot food can mean *spicy food.*

5. Who has a car? What kind of car do you have?*

6. I'm going to buy a car. What kind of car should I buy?

7. Who is wearing a watch? What kind of watch do you have?

8. Who has a camera? What kind of camera do you have?

9. Who smokes cigarettes? What kind of cigarettes do you smoke?

10. Who had a sandwich yesterday/for lunch today? What kind of sandwich did you have?

11. Who had soup yesterday/for lunch today? What kind of soup did you have?

12. Look out the window.
Do you see a tree? What kind of tree is it?
Do you see a bird? What kind of bird is it?
Do you see a car? What kind of car is it?

13. What kind of government does your country have?

14. What kind of job would you like to have?

15. What kind of person would you like to marry?

5-6   USING WHICH

(a)	Tom: May I borrow a pen from you? Ann: Sure. I have two pens. This pen has black ink. That pen has red ink. **Which (pen/one) do you want?** Tom: That one. Thanks.	In (a): Ann uses **which** (not *what*) because she wants Tom to choose. **Which** is used when the speaker wants someone to make a choice, when the speaker is offering alternatives: *this one or that one/these or those.*
(b)	**Which pen** do you want?	
(c)	**Which one** do you want?	(b), (c), and (d) have the same meaning.
(d)	**Which** do you want?	
(e)	Sue: I like these earrings and I like those earrings. Bob: **Which (earrings/ones) are you going to buy?** Sue: I think I'll get these.	**Which** can be used with either singular or plural nouns. (f), (g), and (h) have the same meaning.
(f)	**Which earrings** are you going to buy?	
(g)	**Which ones** are you going to buy?	
(h)	**Which** are you going to buy?	

---

*When a question with *what kind of* involves manufactured products, the answer may either name a particular brand or describe the product's particular attributes (qualities).

A: *What kind of car do you have?*   A: *What kind of car do you have?*
B: *A Ford.*   B: *A four-door station wagon.*

EXERCISE 15:   Make questions. Use *which* or *what*.

1. A: I have two books.   ___Which book/Which one/Which do you want?___
    B: That one. (I want that book.)

2. A: _____What did you buy when you went shopping?_____
    B: A book. (I bought a book when I went shopping.)

3. A: Could I borrow your pen for a minute?

    B: Sure. I have two. _____
    A: That one. (I would like that one.)

4. A: _____
    B: A pen. (Chris borrowed a pen from me.)

5. A: Do you like this tie?
    B: Yes.
    A: Do you like that tie?
    B: It's okay.

    A: _____
    B: This one. (I'm going to buy this one.)

6. A: _____
    B: A tie. (Tony got a tie when he went shopping.)

7. A: These shoes are comfortable, but so are those shoes. _____

    _____ I can't decide.
    B: These. (You should buy these shoes.)

8. A: There are flights to Atlanta at 7:30 a.m. and 8:40 a.m. _____

    _____
    B: The 7:30 flight. (I'm going to take the 7:30 flight.)

9. A: _____
    B: *Very big.* (*Huge* means *very big.*)

10. A: _____
    B: *Fast.* (The meaning of *rapid* is *fast.*)

11. A: Would you please hand me a sharp knife?

    B: I'd be happy to. _____
    A: That one. (I'd like that one.)

12. A: Are you a student in the English program?
    B: Yes, I am.
    A: _____

B: The beginning class. (I'm in the beginning class.)*

13. A: Did you enjoy your trip to Europe?
    B: Yes, I did. Very much.

    A: _____

    B: I visited France, Spain, Portugal, and Italy.*

    A: _____

    B: Spain. (I enjoyed visiting Spain the most.)

5-7 USING *WHOSE*

	QUESTION	ANSWER	
(a) (b) (c)	**Whose (book)** is this? **Whose (books)** are those? **Whose car** did you borrow?	It's John's (book). They're mine (OR: my books). I borrowed Karen's car.	**Whose** asks about possession. Notice in (a): The speaker of the question may omit the noun (*book*) if the meaning is clear to the listener.
(d) (e)	COMPARE: **Who's** that? **Whose** is that?	Mary Smith. Mary's.	**Who's** and **whose** have the same pronunciation. **Who's** = a contraction of **who is**. **Whose** = asks about possession.

EXERCISE 16: Make questions with *whose* or *who*.

1. A: ___Whose pen is_____ this?
   B: Mary's. (It's Mary's pen.)

2. A: ___Whose pens are_____ these?
   B: Jack's. (They're Jack's pens.)

3. A: _____ that?
   B: Bob's. (It's Bob's notebook.)

4. A: _____ those?
   B: Ann's. (They're Ann's papers.)

5. A: _____ this?
   B: Pedro's. (It's Pedro's coat.)

_____

*The differences between *what class* and *which class* and between *what country* and *which country* are often very small.

6. A: _____ these?
   B: Yoko's. (They're Yoko's gloves.)

7. A: _____
   B: Tom's. (I borrowed Tom's umbrella.)

8. A: _____
   B: Linda's. (I used Linda's book.)

9. A: _____
   B: Fred's. (Fred's book is on the table.)

10. A: _____
    B: Fred. (Fred is on the phone.)

11. A: _____
    B: Pat's. (That's Pat's house.)

12. A: _____
    B: Pat. (Pat is living in that house.)

13. A: _____
    B: Sue Smith. (That's Sue Smith.) She's a student in my class.

14. A: _____
    B: Sue's. (That's Sue's.) This one is mine.

EXERCISE 17—ORAL: Ask questions with *whose*.

STUDENT A: Pick up, touch, or point to an object in the classroom. Ask a question with *whose*.
STUDENT B: Answer the question.

   Example: (*Student A picks up a book.*)
   Student A: Whose (book) is this?
   Student B: It's Maria's (book).

   Example: (*Student A points to some books.*)
   Student A: Whose (books) are those?
   Student B: They're Kim's (books).

EXERCISE 18—ORAL: Ask and answer questions about possession. Follow the pattern in the examples. Talk about things in the classroom.

Example: pen
Student A: Is this your pen?/Is this (pen) yours?
Student B: No, it isn't.
Student A: Whose is it?
Student B: It's Ali's.

Example: pens
Student A: Are these Yoko's (pens)?/Are these (pens) Yoko's?
Student B: No, they aren't.
Student A: Whose are they?
Student B: They're mine.

1. dictionary
2. books
3. notebook
4. papers

5. bookbag
6. briefcase
7. glasses
8. eraser

9. purse
10. pencil sharpener
11. things
12. stuff*

EXERCISE 19—WRITTEN: Make questions for the given answers. Use any appropriate question word. Write both the question (A:) and the answer (B:). Use your own paper.

Example: A: . . . ? B: I'm reading.
Written dialogue: A: What are you doing?
B: I'm reading.

1. A: . . . ? B: They're mine.
2. A: . . . ? B: I'm going to study.
3. A: . . . ? B: A Toyota.
4. A: . . . ? B: This one, not that one.
5. A: . . . ? B: It's Bob's.
6. A: . . . ? B: It means *small*.
7. A: . . . ? B: Classical music.

8. A: . . . ? B: Because I didn't feel good.
9. A: . . . ? B: Mr. Smith.
10. A: . . . ? B: You should buy that shirt.
11. A: . . . ? B: A couple of days ago.
12. A: . . . ? B: I would like to go to the zoo.

---

*Stuff is used in informal spoken English to mean miscellaneous things. For example, when a speaker says, "This is my stuff," the speaker may be referring to pens, pencils, books, papers, notebooks, clothes, etc. (Note: *stuff* is a noncount noun; it never has a final *-s*.)

5-8   USING *HOW*

	QUESTION	ANSWER	
(a)	**How** did you get here?	I drove./By car. I took a taxi./By taxi. I took a bus./By bus. I flew./By plane. I took a train./By train. I walked./On foot.	**How** has many uses. One use of **how** is to ask about means (ways) of transportation.
(b) (c) (d) (e) (f) (g) (h) (i)	**How old** are you? **How tall** is he? **How big** is your apartment? **How sleepy** are you? **How hungry** are you? **How soon** will you be ready to leave? **How well** does she speak English? **How quickly** can you get here?	Twenty-one. About six feet. It has three rooms. Very sleepy. I'm starving. In five minutes. Very well. I can get there in 30 minutes.	**How** is often used with adjectives (e.g., *old, big*) and adverbs (e.g., *well, quickly*).

EXERCISE 20:   Make questions with **how.**

1. A: _____ How old is your daughter? _____
   B: Ten. (My daughter is ten years old.)

2. A: _____ how important is your Education _____
   B: Very important. (Education is very important.)

3. A: _____
   B: By bus. (I get to school by bus.)

4. A: _____
   B: Very deep. (The ocean is very deep.)

5. A: _____
   B: Very heavy. (My suitcase is very heavy.) I can hardly lift it.

6. A: _____
   B: By plane. (I'm going to get to Denver by plane.)

7. A: _____ how well Robert speaks English _____
   B: Very well. (Roberto speaks English very well.)

8. A: _____
   B: It's 29,028 feet high. (Mt. Everest is 29,028 feet high.)

9. A: _____ ho am I starving _____
   B: I'm starving! When's dinner? (I'm very hungry.)

10. A: _____
    B: I walked. (I walked to school today.)

11. A: _how should I send the letter by airmail_
    B: By airmail. (You should send that letter by airmail.)

12. A: _____
    B: It's not very safe at all. (That neighborhood isn't very safe at night.)

13. A: _____
    B: Not very. (The test wasn't very difficult.)

14. A: _how tall Mary is about_
    B: About 5½ feet. (Mary is about 5½ feet tall.)

15. A: _____
    B: Not very fast. Usually about 55 miles per hour. (I don't drive very fast.)

5-9 USING *HOW OFTEN*

	QUESTION	ANSWER	
(a)	**How often** do you go shopping?	Every day. Once a week. About twice a week. Every other day or so.* Three times a month.	***How often** asks about frequency.*
(b)	**How many times a day** do you eat?	Three or four.	Other ways of asking ***how often:***
	How many times a week do you go shopping?	Two.	*how many times* ⎰ *a day* ⎱ *a week* *a month* *a year*
	How many times a month do you go to the bank?	Once.	
	How many times a year do you take a vacation?	Once or twice.	

*Every other day means Monday yes, Tuesday no, Wednesday yes, Thursday no, etc. Or so means *approximately.*

EXERCISE 21—ORAL: Ask and answer questions about frequency.

STUDENT A: Ask a question with ***how often*** or ***how many times a day/week/ month/year.***

STUDENT B: Answer the question. (Possible answers are suggested in the list
of frequency expressions.)

FREQUENCY EXPRESSIONS		
every every other once a twice a three times a ten times a } + **day/week/month/year**		**a lot** **occasionally*** **once in a while** **not very often** **hardly ever** **almost never** **never**

*Notice: *Occasionally* is spelled with *two c's* but only *one s.*

Example: eat lunch at the cafeteria
Student A: How often do you eat lunch at the cafeteria?
Student B: About twice a week.

how often do you

1. go to a movie
2. watch TV
3. go out to eat
4. cook your own dinner
5. play cards
6. read a newspaper
7. go to the post office

8. write a letter to your parents
9. see a doctor
10. see a dentist
11. cash a check
12. go to a laundromat
13. go swimming
14. be late for class

5-10 USING *HOW FAR*

(a)	**It is** 289 miles **from** St. Louis **to** Chicago.†		The most common way of expressing distance: **It is** + *distance* + **from/to** + **to/from.**
(b)	**It is** 289 miles	**from** St. Louis **to** Chicago. **from** Chicago **to** St. Louis. **to** Chicago **from** St. Louis. **to** St. Louis **from** Chicago.	In (b): All four expressions with **from** and **to** have the same meaning.
(c)	A: **How far is it** from St. Louis to Chicago? B: 289 miles.		**How far** is used to ask questions about distance.

†1 mile = 1.609 kilometers.
1 kilometer = 0.614 mile.

(d) A: **How far do you** live from school? B: Four blocks.	
(e) **How many miles** is it from St. Louis to Chicago? (f) **How many kilometers** is it to Montreal from here? (g) **How many blocks** is it to the post office?	Other ways to ask **how far:** *how many miles* *how many kilometers* *how many blocks*

EXERCISE 22: Make questions.

1. A: _how many miles are From Washington DC._
   B: 237 miles. (It's 237 miles from New York City to Washington, D.C.)

2. A: _how many kilometers are From montreal to qucbec_
   B: 257 kilometers. (It's 257 kilometers from Montreal to Quebec.)

3. A: _how many miles are From Chicago to New Orleans_
   B: 919 miles. (It's 919 miles to Chicago from New Orleans).

4. A: _how many blocks are to the post office_
   B: Six blocks. (It's six blocks to the post office.)

5. A: _how many blocks are here to the bookstore_
   B: Two and a half blocks. (It's two and a half blocks to the bookstore
   from here.)

6. A: _how many miles do you living From the school._
   B: About three miles. (I live about three miles from school.)

7. A: Karen is really into physical fitness these days. She jogs every day.

   B: Oh? _how many miles does she jogs everyday_
   A: Five miles. (She jogs five miles every day.)
   B: That's great. I usually don't even walk five miles a day.

8. A: I had a terrible day yesterday.
   B: What happened?
   A: I ran out of gas while I was driving to work.

   B: _____ before you ran out of gas?
   A: To the junction of I–90 and 480. (I got to the junction of I–90 and 480.)
   Luckily, there was a gas station about half a mile down the road.

EXERCISE 23—ORAL (BOOKS CLOSED): Ask and answer questions with *how far.*

*(To the teacher: Bring to class some road maps of your area. The maps should have mileage charts. Divide the class into small groups and have them ask each other questions with **how far.** The student who is asking the question should find on the map the places s/he is asking about and point to them. The other students should use the mileage chart to find the answer or, if necessary, add up the miles on the map itself.)*

5-11 USING *HOW LONG*

QUESTION	ANSWER	
(a) **How long does it take** to drive to Chicago from here?	Two days.	*How long* asks for information about length of time.
(b) **How long did you study** last night?	Four hours.	
(c) **How long will you be** in Florida?	Ten days.	
(d) **How many days will you be** in Florida?	Ten.	Other ways of asking *how long:*
		how many + { minutes, hours, days, weeks, months, years }

EXERCISE 24: Study the examples.

	IT +	*TAKE* +	(SOMEONE) +	TIME EXPRESSION +	INFINITIVE	
(a)	**It**	**takes**		**six hours**	**to drive**	to Chicago from here.
(b)	**It**	**took**	Janet	**a long time**	**to finish**	her composition.

Make sentences using *it* + *take* to express length of time.

1. I drove to Los Angeles. (*Length of time: three days*)

> It took me three days to drive to Los Angeles.

2. I walk to class. (*Length of time: twenty minutes*)

_____ *it take him* _____

3. George finished the test. (*Length of time: an hour and a half*)

_____

4. We will drive to the airport. (*Length of time: forty-five minutes*)

_____

5. Ann made a dress. (*Length of time: six hours*)

_____

6. Alan hitchhiked to Alaska. (*Length of time: two weeks*)

_____ *it take her Five minutes* _____

7. Mary puts on her makeup. (*Length of time: five minutes*)

_____ *it takes me tow hours* _____

8. I wash my clothes at the laundromat. (*Length of time: two hours*)

I wash my clothes at the laundromat. it take me tow hours.
to wash my laundromat

EXERCISE 25:   Make questions using *how long*.

1. A: _____How long did it take you to drive to New York?_____
    B: Five days. (It took me five days to drive to New York.)

2. A: _____
    B: Twenty minutes. (It takes me twenty minutes to walk to class.)

3. A: *howlong did it tak bob To Finish his Composition*
    B: Two hours. (It took Bob two hours to finish his composition.)

4. A: *howlong will it take to Drive to the stadium*
    B: Thirty minutes. (It will take us thirty minutes to drive to the stadium.)

5. A: _____
    B: For a week. (Mr. McNally is going to be in the hospital for a week.)

6. A: _____
    B: Four years. (I'll be at the University of Maryland for four years.)

7. A: *howlong did it takes to bake acake*
    B: About an hour. (It takes about an hour to bake a cake.)

A: How about cookies? *how long did tate to bake Cookies.*
B: Oh, it depends. Maybe forty minutes. (It takes maybe forty minutes to bake cookies.)

8. A: *how long were you take out of town,*
B: Five days. (I was out of town for five days.)

A: How about Mary? _____
B: A week. (She was out of town for a week.)

9. A: *howlong does it take you to change a flattire.*
B: About fifteen minutes. (It takes me about fifteen minutes to change a flat tire.)

A: How about a spark plug? *how long it take you to change*
B: Not long at all. Maybe three minutes. (It takes me maybe three minutes to change a spark plug.)

10. A: _____
B: A long time. (It takes a long time to learn a second language.)

A: How about a computer language? _____
B: That takes a long time, too. (It takes a long time to learn a computer language.)

EXERCISE 26:   Make questions. Use any appropriate question words.

1. A: What are you going to do this weekend?
B: I'm going to go to a baseball game. (I'm going to go to a baseball game this weekend.)

2. A: There are two games this weekend, one on Saturday and one on Sunday. *witch one are you going to do da*
B: The one on Sunday. (I'm going to go to the one on Sunday.)

3. A: _did you get to the game yesterday._

   B: No, I didn't. (I didn't go to the game yesterday.)

4. A: _who went to the game yesterday_

   B: Sara and Jim. (Sara and Jim went to the game yesterday.)

5. A: _how often do you go to the_

   B: About once a month. (I go to a baseball game about once a month.)

6. A: _____

   B: Bob. (I'm going to go to the game with Bob on Sunday.)

7. A: _____

   B: At the corner of Fifth and Grand. (The stadium is at the corner of Fifth and Grand.)

8. A: _____

   B: Six miles. (It's six miles to the stadium from here.)

9. A: _____

   B: Twenty minutes. (It takes twenty minutes to get there.)

10. A: _what time does the game starts?_

    B: One o'clock. (The game starts at one o'clock.)

11. A: _____

    B: Because I have fun. (I like to go to baseball games because I have fun.)

12. A: _____

    B: I yell, enjoy the sunshine, eat peanuts, and drink beer. (I yell, enjoy the sunshine, eat peanuts, and drink beer when I go to a baseball game.)

EXERCISE 27—ORAL (BOOKS CLOSED):   Make questions. Use question words.

Example: I'm studying English grammer.
Response: What are you doing? OR: What are you studying?

1. I studied last night.
2. I studied at the library.
3. I studied for two hours at the library last night.
4. I'm going to study tonight.
5. I'm going to study at home.
6. I'm going to study with (. . .).
7. We're going to study together because we have a test tomorrow.
8. I saw (. . .) yesterday.
9. (. . .) called me last night.
10. I talked to (. . .) last night.

11. I go to the library twice a week.
12. The library is two blocks from here.
13. I live in (*name of this city*).
14. I was born in (*name of town*).
15. I grew up in (*name of town*).
16. I stayed home yesterday because I didn't feel good.
17. I'm looking at the board.
18. I'm looking at (. . .).
19. That is (. . .)'s pen.
20. I want this pen, not that one.
21. (. . .) is wearing (*kind of shoes*).
22. I'm going to wear jeans tomorrow.
23. I'm going to write a letter to (. . .).
24. (. . .) wrote me a letter.
25. It's (*distance*) to (*name of city*) from here.
26. My plane will arrive at 6:30.
27. I have a (*kind of car*).
28. It takes (*length of time*) to drive to (*name of city*) from here.
29. I drive to (*name of city*) once or twice a year.
30. *Glad* means *happy.*

5-12   MORE QUESTIONS WITH *HOW*

	QUESTION	ANSWER	
(a)	**How do you spell** "coming"?	C-O-M-I-N-G.	To answer (a): Spell the word.
(b)	**How do you say** "yes" in Japanese?	*Hai.*	To answer (b): Say the word.
(c)	**How do you say/pronounce** this word?	— — — —	To answer (c): Pronounce the word.
(d)	**How are you getting along?**	Great.	In (d), (e), and (f): How is your life? Is your life okay? Do you have any problems?
(e)	**How are you doing?**	Fine.	NOTE: (f) is often used in greetings: *Hi, Bob. How's it going?*
(f)	**How's it going?**	Okay.	
		So-so.	
(g)	**How do you feel?** **How are you feeling?**	Terrific!	The questions in (g) ask about health or about general emotional state.
		Wonderful!	
		Great!	
		Fine.	
		Okay.	
		So-so.	
		A bit under the weather.	
		Not so good.	
		Terrible!	
		Awful!	

(h) **How do you do?**	**How do you do?**	**How do you do?** is used by both speakers when they are introduced to each other in a somewhat formal situation: A: *Dr. Erickson, I'd like to introduce you to a friend of mine, Dick Brown. Dick, this is my biology professor, Dr. Erickson.* B: **How do you do,** *Mr. Brown?* C: **How do you do,** *Dr. Erickson? I'm pleased to meet you.*

EXERCISE 28—ORAL (BOOKS CLOSED):

(To the teacher: Divide the class into two teams for a spelling bee. Say a word in the list. Have a student on Team A ask someone on Team B how to spell the word. Student A then has to decide if Student B spelled the word correctly. Award points to the teams if you wish.)

> *Example:*   country
> *Student A:*   How do you spell "country"?
> *Student B:*   C-O-N-T-R-Y
> *Student A:*   Yes, that's right. OR: No, that isn't right. The correct spelling is C-O-U-N-T-R-Y.

1. together
2. purple
3. daughter
4. planned
5. rained
6. neighbor

7. different
8. foreign
9. studying
10. bought
11. people
12. beautiful

13. beginning
14. intelligent
15. writing
16. assignment
17. family
18. Mississippi

EXERCISE 29—ORAL: Ask your classmates how to say these words in their native languages:

> *Example:*   yes
> *Student A:*   How do you say "yes" in Japanese?
> *Student B:*   Hai.

1. Yes.
2. No.

3. Thank you.
4. I love you.

EXERCISE 30—ORAL: Ask your classmates how to pronounce these words.

> *Example:*   *Student A:* How do you pronounce number 9?
> *Student B:* (*Student B pronounces the word.*)
> *Student A:* Good. OR: No, I don't think that's right.

Group A:	(1) beat	(2) bit	(3) bet	(4) bite	(5) bait	(6) bat	(7) but	(8) boot	(9) boat	(10) bought

Group B:	(1) zoos	(2) Sue's	(3) shoes	(4) chews	(5) choose	(6) chose	(7) those	(8) toes	(9) doze	(10) dose

EXERCISE 31—WRITTEN: Make questions for the given answers. Write both the question (A:) and the answer (B:). Use your own paper.

> *Example:*   A: . . . ? B: I'm reading.
> *Written dialogue:*   A: What are you doing?
>   B: I'm reading.

1. A: . . . ? B: It means *big*.
2. A: . . . ? B: Three days ago.
3. A: . . . ? B: Once a week.
4. A: . . . ? B: This one, not that one.
5. A: . . . ? B: By bus.
6. A: . . . ? B: Mine.
7. A: . . . ? B: 100 miles.
8. A: . . . ? B: B-E-A-U-T-I-F-U-L.
9. A: . . . ? B: The park.
10. A: . . . ? B: Because I. . . .
11. A: . . . ? B: Fine.
12. A: . . . ? B: Nonfiction.
13. A: . . . ? B: I'm going to study.
14. A: . . . ? B: A bit under the weather.
15. A: . . . ? B: How do you do?
16. A: . . . ? B: Two hours.
17. A: . . . ? B: Six o'clock.
18. A: . . . ? B: Mary.

EXERCISE 32—PREPOSITIONS: Complete the sentences with prepositions. (See Appendix 4 for a list of preposition combinations.)

1. What's the matter _____*with*_____ you? What's wrong?
2. We can go out for dinner, or we can eat at home. It doesn't matter _____*to*_____ me.

3. To make this recipe, you have to separate the egg whites ___From___ the yolks.

4. I don't know anything ___about___ astrology.

5. I'm looking forward ___To___ my vacation next month.

6. Dennis dreamed ___about___ his girlfriend last night.

7. Right now I'm doing an exercise. I'm looking ___in___ my book.

8. Jim can't find his book. He's looking ___For___ it.

9. Jim is searching ___For___ his book.

10. I asked the waitress ___For___ another cup of coffee.

11. I asked Mary ___to___ her trip to Japan.

12. Does this pen belong ___to___ you?

13. We had mice in the house, so we set some traps to get rid ___For___ them.

14. What happened ___to___ your finger? Did you cut it?

chapter 6

The Present Perfect and the Past Perfect

6-1 THE PAST PARTICIPLE

	SIMPLE FORM	SIMPLE PAST	PAST PARTICIPLE	PRESENT PARTICIPLE	
REGULAR VERBS	finish arrive	finished arrived	**finished** **arrived**	finishing arriving	English verbs have four principal forms: (1) the simple form (2) the simple past (3) the past participle (4) the present participle
IRREGULAR VERBS	see eat make sing go	saw ate made sang went	**seen** **eaten** **made** **sung** **gone**	seeing eating making singing going	The past participle is used in the present perfect tense and the past perfect tense.* The past participle of regular verbs is the same as the simple past form: both end in *-ed*. See Appendix 1 for a list of irregular verbs.

*The past participle is also used in the passive. See Chapter 9.

EXERCISE 1:   Write the past participle.

SIMPLE FORM	SIMPLE PAST	PAST PARTICIPLE	SIMPLE FORM	SIMPLE PAST	PAST PARTICIPLE
1. finish	finished	finished	11. eat	ate	eaten
2. see	saw	seen	12. study	studied	studied
3. go	went	gone	13. stay	stayed	stayed
4. have	had	had	14. come	came	come
5. meet	met	met	15. ride	rode	ridden
6. call	called	called	16. write	wrote	wroten
7. be	was, were	been	17. rain	rained	rained
8. do	did	done	18. read	read	read
9. know	knew	known	19. start	started	started
10. fly	flew	flown	20. begin	began	begun

6-2   FORMS OF THE PRESENT PERFECT

STATEMENT		
	(a) I **have** **finished** my work. (b) Jim **has** **eaten** lunch. ***HAVE/HAS*** + PAST PARTICIPLE	The basic form of the present perfect: *have/has* + *past participle*
	(c) **I've** finished my work. (d) **He's** eaten lunch.	Contractions with ***have*** and ***has***: 　**I've** eaten 　**you've** eaten 　**we've** eaten **they've** eaten 　**he's** eaten 　**she's** eaten 　**it's** eaten
NEGATIVE	(e) I **have not (haven't) finished** my work. (f) Jim **has not (hasn't) eaten** lunch.	***have*** + ***not*** = ***haven't*** ***has*** + ***not*** = ***hasn't***

QUESTION		(QUESTION WORD)	+	HELPING VERB	+ SUBJECT +	MAIN VERB		In a question, the helping verb (*have* or *has*) precedes the subject.
	(g)			**Have**	you	**finished**	your work?	
	(h)			**Has**	Jim	**eaten**	lunch?	
	(i)	How long		**have**	you	**lived**	here?	
	(j)	A: Have you seen that movie? B: **Yes, I have** OR: **No, I haven't.**						The helping verb (**have** or **has**) is used in the short answer to a yes/no question.
	(k)	A: Has Jim eaten lunch? B: **Yes, he has.** OR: **No, he hasn't.**						

6-3 USING THE PRESENT PERFECT

"before now" (no exact time) now **X** ──── **X**	(a) (b) (c) (d)	Jim **has** already **eaten** lunch. Ann **hasn't eaten** lunch yet. **Have** you ever **eaten** at that restaurant? I **have** never **eaten** at that restaurant.	The present perfect expresses activities or situations that occurred (or did not occur) *"before now,"* at *some unspecified time in the past.* *
	(e) (f) (g)	I **have eaten** at that restaurant many times. I **have flown** in an airplane many times. It **has rained** three times so far this week.	The present perfect often expresses activities that were *repeated several or many times in the past.* The exact times are unspecified.
now **X** ──── **X** │ └───► length of time	(h) (i) (j)	Alice **has lived** in this city *since 1980.* I **have known** Bob *for ten years.* We **have been** in class *since ten o'clock this morning.*	When the present perfect is used with **since** or **for**, it expresses a situation that *began in the past and continues to the present.*

*If the exact time is specified, the simple past tense is used.

   SPECIFIED TIME: Jim **ate** lunch at 12:00/two hours ago/yesterday. (*simple past tense*)
UNSPECIFIED TIME: Jim **has** already **eaten** lunch. (*present perfect tense*)

EXERCISE 2:   Complete the sentences. Use the words in parentheses. Use *the present perfect*. Discuss the meaning of the present perfect.

1. (*I, meet*)   _____I've (I have) met_____ Ann's husband. I met him at a party last week.

2. (*I, finish*)   _____I finished_____ my work. I finished it two hours ago.

3. (*she, fly*)   Ms. Parker travels to Washington, D.C., frequently. _____She have been Flying Flownmanytime_____ there many times.

4. (*they, know*)   Bob and Jane are old friends. _____known_____ each other for a long time. *it has been*

5. (*it, be*)   I don't like this weather. _____it willbe_____ cold and cloudy for the last three days.

6. (*you, learn*)   Your English is getting better. _____You are learned_____ a lot of English since you came here.

7. (*we, be*)   My wife and I came here two months ago. _____we have been_____ in this city for two months.

8. (*he, finish*)   Tom can go to bed now. _____he already finish_____ his *he has Finish* homework.

EXERCISE 3:   When speakers use the present perfect, they often contract **have** and **has** with nouns in everyday speech. Listen to your teacher say these sentences in normal contracted speech and practice saying them yourself.

1. Bob has been in Chicago since last Tuesday. ("Bob's been . . . . ")
2. Jane has been out of town for two days.
3. The weather has been terrible lately.
4. My parents have been married for forty years.
5. Dick has already eaten breakfast.
6. My friends have moved into a new apartment.
7. My roommate has been in bed with a cold for the last couple of days.
8. My aunt and uncle have lived in the same house for 25 years.

EXERCISE 4:   Complete the sentences. Use the words in parentheses. Use *the present perfect*. Discuss the meaning of the present perfect.

1. (*I, write, not*)   _____I haven't written_____ my sister a letter in a long time. I should write her soon.

2. (*I, write, never**) I've never written _____ a letter to the President of the United States.

3. (*he, finish, not*) Greg is working on his composition, but _____ _____ it yet. He'll probably finish it in a couple of hours.

4. (*I, meet, never*) _____ Nancy's parents. I hope I get the chance to meet them soon.

5. (*Ron, never, be*) _____ in Hong Kong, but he would like to go there someday.

6. (*Linda, be, not*) _____ in class for the last couple of days. I hope she's okay.

7. (*they, come, not*) The children are late. _____ home from school yet. I hope nothing's wrong.

8. (*we, finish, not*) _____ this exercise yet.

9. (*Alice, go, never*) _____ to the Museum of Science and Industry in Chicago, but she would like to.

10. (*I, call, not*) _____ Irene yet. I'll call her tomorrow.

EXERCISE 5—ORAL: Ask and answer questions using the present perfect.

STUDENT A: Use *ever* in the question. *Ever* comes between the subject (*you*) and the main verb.†

STUDENT B: Give a short answer first and then a complete sentence answer.

Use
{
many times
several times
a couple of times
once in my lifetime
never
}
in the complete sentence.

---

*Never has the same usual position as frequency adverbs. (See 6–7.) With the present perfect, *never* comes between the helping verb (*have* or *has*) and the main verb.

†In these questions, *ever* means *in your lifetime, at any time(s) in your life before now.*

Example: be in Florida*
Student A: Have you ever been in Florida?
Student B: Yes, I have. I've been in Florida many times.
              OR: No, I haven't. I've never been in Florida.

1. be in Europe
2. be in Africa
3. be in the Middle East
4. be in Asia

5. eat Chinese food
6. eat Mexican food
7. eat ??? food
8. eat at (*name of a restaurant*)

9. play soccer
10. play baseball
11. play pool
12. play a video game
13. ride a horse

14. ride a motorcycle
15. ride an elephant
16. ride in a taxi

17. be in (*name of a city*)
18. be in (*name of a state/province*)
19. be in (*name of a country*)
20. be in love

21. walk downtown (*or to a place in this city*)
22. stay up all night
23. go to (*a place in this city*)
24. use a computer

EXERCISE 6:   Study the examples.

(a) PRESENT PERFECT		In (a): The present perfect expresses an activity that occurred *at an unspecified time (or times) in the past.*
I **have been** in Europe	many times. several times. a couple of times. once. (*no mention of time*).	In (a): The present perfect expresses an activity that occurred *at an unspecified time (or times) in the past.*
(b) SIMPLE PAST		In (b): The simple past expresses an activity that occurred *at a specific time (or times) in the past.*
I **was** in Europe	last year. three years ago. in 1984. in 1979 and 1984. when I was ten years old.	In (b): The simple past expresses an activity that occurred *at a specific time (or times) in the past.*

---

*When using the present perfect, a speaker might also use the idiom *be to (a place): Have you ever been to Florida?*

Complete the sentences with the words in parentheses.　Use *the present perfect* or *the simple past.*

1. A: Have you ever been in Europe?

   B: Yes, I _____ . I (*be*) _____ in Europe several

   times. In fact, I (*be*) _____ in Europe last year.

2. A: Have you ever eaten at Al's Steak House?

   B: Yes, I _____ . I (*eat*) _____ there many

   times. In fact, my wife and I (*eat*) _____ there last night.

3. A: Have you ever talked to Professor Alston about your grades?

   B: Yes, I _____ . I (*talk*) _____ to him about

   my grades a couple of times. In fact, I (*talk*) _____ to him

   after class yesterday about the F I got on the last test.

4. A: What European countries (*you, visit*) _____ ?

   B: I (*visit*) _____ France, Germany, and Switzerland.

   I (*visit*) _____ France in 1983. I (*be*) _____

   in Germany and Switzerland in 1984.

5. A: (*Bob, have, ever*) _____ a job?

   B: Yes, he _____ . He (*have*) _____ lots of part-

   time jobs. Last summer he (*have*) _____ a job at his

   uncle's bakery.

EXERCISE 7:　Study the examples.

(a) PRESENT PERFECT 　　I **have** already* **finished** my work.	In (a): I finished my work at an unspecified time in the past.
(b) SIMPLE PAST 　　I **finished** my work two hours ago.	In (b): I finished my work at a specific time in the past.

*****Already** has the same usual placement in a sentence as frequency adverbs. (See 6–7.) **Already** means "before."

Complete the sentences with the words in parentheses. Use *the present perfect* or *the simple past*. Use *the present perfect* with **already**.*

1. A: Are you going to finish your work before you go to bed?

   B: I (*finish, already*) _____ it. I (*finish*)

   _____ my work two hours ago.

2. A: Is Jim going to eat lunch with us today?

   B: No. He (*eat, already*) _____ . He (*eat*)

   _____ lunch an hour ago.

3. A: Do you and Virginia want to go to the movie at the Bijou with us tonight?

   B: No thanks. We (*see, already*) _____ it. We (*see*)

   _____ it last week.

4. A: When are you going to write your paper for Dr. Roth?

   B: I (*write, already*) _____ it. I (*write*)

   _____ it two days ago.

5: A: When is Jane going to call her parents and tell them about her engagement?

   B: She (*call, already*) _____ them. She (*call*)

   _____ them last night.

6. A: This is a good book. Would you like to read it when I'm finished?

   B: Thanks, but I (*read, already*) _____ it. I (*read*)

   _____ it a couple of months ago.

---

*In informal spoken English, the simple past is often used with **already**. However, practice using the present perfect with **already** in this exercise.

6-4 USING *SINCE* AND *FOR*

SINCE			
	(a) I **have been** here	since eight o'clock. since Tuesday. since May. since 1982. since January 3, 1983. since the beginning of the semester. since yesterday. since last month.	*Since* is followed by the mention of *a specific point in time:* an hour, a day, a month, a year, etc. *Since* expresses the idea that an activity began at a specific time in the past and continues to the present. The present perfect also expresses the idea that an activity began in the past and continues to the present. The present perfect is used in sentences with *since*.

			INCORRECT: *I am living here since May.* INCORRECT: *I live here since May.* INCORRECT: *I lived here since May.* CORRECT: *I have lived here since May.**

	MAIN CLAUSE (*present perfect*)	*SINCE* CLAUSE (*simple past*)	
(b)	I **have lived** here	**since** I **was** a child.	**Since** may also introduce a time clause (i.e., a subject and verb may follow **since**.) Notice in the examples: The present perfect is used in the main clause; the simple past is used in the "**since** clause."
(c)	Al **has met** many people	**since** he **came** here.	

FOR				
(d)	I have been here	for ten minutes. for two hours. for five days. for about three weeks. for almost six months. for many years. for a long time.		**For** is followed by the mention of *a length of time*: two minutes, three hours, four days, five weeks, etc.
(e)	I **have lived** here **for two years**. I moved here two years ago, and I still live here.			In (e): The use of the present perfect in a sentence with **for** + *a length of time* means that the action began in the past and continues to the present.
(f)	I **lived** in Chicago **for two years**. I don't live in Chicago now.			In (f): The use of the simple past means that the action began and ended in the past.

*ALSO CORRECT: *I have been living here since May.* See 6-6 for a discussion of the present perfect progressive.

EXERCISE 8:   Complete the sentence "I have been here . . . ." Use **since** or **for** with the given expressions.

I have been here . . .

1.   for   two months.

2.   since   September.

3. _____ 1983.

4. _____ last year.

5. _____ two years.

6. _____ fifteen minutes.

7. _____ 9:30.

8. _____ about five weeks.

9. _____ the first of January.

10. _____ almost four months.

11. _____ the beginning of the semester.

12. _____ the semester started.

13. _____ a couple of hours.

14. _____ last Friday.

15. _____ a long time.

16. _____ yesterday.*

EXERCISE 9: Complete the sentences.

Example:

I've been in class
{
since   nine o'clock this morning. _____

for   27 minutes. _____
}

1. We've been in class
{
since _____

for _____
}

2. I've been in this city,
{
since _____

for _____
}

3. I've had a driver's license
{
since _____

for _____
}

4. I've had this book
{
since _____

for _____
}

EXERCISE 10—ORAL (BOOKS CLOSED): Answer the questions.

*(To the teacher: Ask Student A to use **since** in his/her answer. Ask Student B to use **for**.)*

    Example: How long have you had this book?

    Student A: I've had this book since (the beginning of the term).

---

*Note: Past time expressions such as *yesterday, the day before yesterday, last night, last Wednesday, last month, last year* can follow *since*, but expressions with *ago* do not usually follow *since*.

    CORRECT: *I've been here since last Friday.*
        RARE: *I've been here since three days ago.*
    CORRECT: *I've been here for three days.*

Teacher: How long has (. . .) had this book?

Student B: S/he has had this book for (five weeks).

1. How long have you been in (*this country*)?
2. How long have you been at (*this school*)?
3. How long have you been up today?
4. How long have you known (. . .)?
5. Where do you live? How long have you lived there?
6. How long have you had your wristwatch?
7. Who has a car/bicycle? How long have you had it?
8. How long have you been in this room today?
9. Who is wearing new clothes? What? How long have you had it/them?
10. Who is married? How long have you been married?

EXERCISE 11:   Complete the sentences with the words in parentheses. Use *the present perfect* or *the simple past.*

1. Carol and I are old friends. I (*know*) _____ her since I (*be*)

    _____ a freshman in high school.

2. Maria (*have*) _____ a lot of problems since she (*come*)

    _____ to this country.

3. I (*have, not*) _____ any problems since I (*come*)

    _____ here.

4. Since the semester (*begin*) _____ , we (*have*) _____

    _____ four tests.

5. Mike (*be*) _____ in school since he (*be*) _____
   six years old.

6. My mother (*be, not*) _____ in school since she (*graduate*)

    _____ from college in 1958.

7. Since we (*start*) _____ doing this exercise, we (*complete*)

    _____ six sentences.

8. My name is Surasuk Jutukanyaprateep. I'm from Thailand. Right now I'm

    studying English at this school. I (*be*) _____ at this school since

    the beginning of January. I (*arrive*) _____ here January 2, and my classes (*begin*) _____ January 6. Since I (*come*)

_____ here, I (*do*) _____ many things, and I

(*meet*) _____ many people. I (*go*) _____

to several parties. Last Saturday I (*go*) _____ to a party at my

friend's house. I (*meet*) _____ some of the other students from

Thailand at the party. Of course, we (*speak*) _____ Thai, so I

(*practice, not*) _____ my English that night. There (*be*)

_____ only people from Thailand at the party. However, since

I (*come*) _____ here, I (*meet*) _____ a lot of

other people. I (*meet*) _____ students from Latin America,

Africa, the Middle East, and Asia. I enjoy meeting people from other
countries.

EXERCISE 12—ORAL (BOOKS CLOSED):   Answer the questions.

(*To the teacher: Ask a question that prompts the use of the present perfect, and then
immediately follow up with a related question that prompts the use of the simple past.*)

> *Example:*   What countries have you been in?
> *Response:*   Well, I've been in England, and I've been in France.
> *Teacher:*   Oh? When were you in England?
> *Response:*   I was in England three years ago.
> *Teacher:*   How about you, (. . .)? What countries have you been in?
> *etc.*

1. What countries have you been in?
2. What cities (*in the United States, in Florida, etc.*) have you been in?
3. What are some of the things you have done since you came to (*this city*)?
4. Who are some of the people you have met since you came to (*this city*)?
5. What have we studied in this class since (*the beginning of the term*)?
6. What have we done in class today since (*nine o'clock*)?

EXERCISE 13:   Write the simple past and the past participles of these irregular verbs.

1. see   ___saw___   ___seen___   3. give   _____   _____

2. eat   _____   _____   4. fall   _____   _____

5. take _____ _____   9. write _____ _____

6. shake _____ _____   10. bite _____ _____

7. drive _____ _____   11. hide _____ _____

8. ride _____ _____

EXERCISE 14—ORAL: Ask and answer questions using the present perfect in order to practice using past participles of irregular verbs.

STUDENT A: Ask a question beginning with "Have you ever . . .?"
STUDENT B: Answer the question.

Example: eat at the student cafeteria
Student A: Have you ever eaten at the student cafeteria?
Student B: Yes, I have. I've eaten there many times. In fact, I
              ate breakfast there this morning. OR: No, I haven't.
              I usually eat all my meals at home.

1. ride a horse
2. take a course in chemistry
3. write a poem
4. give the teacher an apple
5. shake hands with (. . .)
6. bite into an apple that had a
   worm inside

7. drive a semi (a very large truck)
8. eat raw fish
9. hide money under your mattress
10. fall down stairs
11. see the skeleton of a dinosaur

EXERCISE 15:   Write the simple past and the past participles.

1. break _____ _____   5. wear _____ _____

2. speak _____ _____   6. draw _____ _____

3. steal _____ _____   7. grow _____ _____

4. get _____ _____   8. throw _____ _____

9. blow _____ _____

10. fly _____ _____

11. drink _____ _____

12. sing _____ _____

13. swim _____ _____

14. go _____ _____

EXERCISE 16—ORAL: Ask questions beginning with "Have you ever . . . ?" and give answers.

1. fly in a private plane
2. break your arm
3. draw a picture of a mountain
4. swim in the ocean
5. speak to (. . .) on the phone
6. go to a costume party
7. wear a costume to a party
8. get a package in the mail
9. steal anything
10. grow tomatoes
11. sing "You Are My Sunshine"
12. drink carrot juice
13. throw a football
14. blow a whistle

EXERCISE 17: Write the simple past and the past participles.

1. have _____ _____

2. make _____ _____

3. build _____ _____

4. lend _____ _____

5. send _____ _____

6. spend _____ _____

7. leave _____ _____

8. lose _____ _____

9. sleep _____ _____

10. feel _____ _____

11. meet _____ _____

12. sit _____ _____

13. win _____ _____

14. hang* _____ _____

*_Hang_ is a regular verb (_hang, hanged, hanged_) when it means to kill a person by putting a rope around his/her neck.

EXERCISE 18—ORAL: Ask questions beginning with "Have you ever . . .?" and give answers.

1. lose the key to your house

2. meet (. . .)

3. have the flu

4. feel terrible about something

5. send a telegram

6. sit on a cactus

9. lend (. . .) any money

10. sleep in a tent

11. make a birthday cake

12. build sand castles

7. leave your sunglasses at a restaurant

8. spend one whole day doing nothing

13. win any money at a racetrack

14. hang a picture on the wall

EXERCISE 19:   Write the simple past and the past participles.

1. sell _____ _____

2. tell _____ _____

3. hear _____ _____

4. hold _____ _____

5. feed _____ _____

6. read _____ _____

7. find _____ _____

8. buy _____

9. think _____ _____

10. teach _____ _____

11. catch _____ _____

12. cut _____ _____

13. hit _____ _____

14. quit _____ _____

15. put _____ _____

EXERCISE 20—ORAL: Ask questions beginning with "Have you ever. . . ?" and give answers.

1. teach a child to count to ten
2. hold a newborn baby
3. find any money on the sidewalk
4. cut your own hair
5. think about the meaning of life
6. hear strange noises at night
7. read *Tom Sawyer* by Mark Twain
8. feed pigeons in the park

9. tell a little white lie
10. quit smoking
11. buy a refrigerator
12. sell a car
13. hit another person with your fist
14. put off doing your homework
15. catch a fish

6-5 FORMS OF THE PRESENT PERFECT PROGRESSIVE

	HAVE/HAS + *BEEN* + *-ING*				Form of the present perfect progressive:
(a)	I **have**	**been**	**living**	here since January.	***have/has*** + ***been*** + ***-ing***
(b)	Bob **has**	**been**	**studying**	for two hours.	
(c)	How long **have you been living** here?				Question form:
(d)	How long **has Bob been studying?**				***have/has*** + *subject* + ***been*** + ***-ing***

6-6 USING THE PRESENT PERFECT PROGRESSIVE

Compare the present progressive (a) and the present perfect progressive (b).	
PRESENT PROGRESSIVE (a) **I am sitting** in class **right now.**	The present progressive expresses an activity that is in progress (is happening) right now.

PRESENT PERFECT PROGRESSIVE	The present perfect progressive expresses the duration (the length of time) of an activity that is in progress.
(b) I **have been sitting** in class { **since 9 o'clock.** **for 45 minutes.**	Time expressions with ***since*** or ***for*** are usually used with the present perfect progressive.

EXERCISE 21:   Complete the sentences. Use *the present progressive* or *the present perfect progressive.*

1. Mark isn't studying right now. He (*watch*) _____ TV. He
    (*watch*) _____ TV since seven o'clock.

2. Carol is standing at the corner. She (*wait*) _____ for the bus.
    She (*wait*) _____ for the bus for twenty minutes.

3. Right now we're in class. We (*do*) _____ an exercise. We (*do*)
    _____ this exercise for a couple of minutes.

4. John and Mary (*talk*) _____ on the phone right now. They
    (*talk*) _____ on the phone for over an hour.

5. I (*sit*) _____ in class right now. I (*sit*) _____
    since ten minutes after one.

EXERCISE 22—ORAL (BOOKS CLOSED):   Answer the questions. Use ***since*** or ***for***
in your answer.

1. How long have you been sitting in class?
2. How long have you been studying English?
3. How long have you been living in (*this city*)?
4. I began to teach English in (*year*). How long have I been teaching English?
5. Who lives in an apartment/a dormitory? How long have you been living there?
6. I am standing up/sitting down. How long have I been standing up/sitting down?
7. I began to work at this school in (*month or year*). How long have I been working here?
8. We're doing an exercise. How long have we been doing this exercise?
9. Who drives? How long have you been driving?

10. Who drinks coffee? How old were you when you started to drink coffee? How long have you been drinking coffee?

11. Who smokes? When did you start? How long have you been smoking?

12. How long have you been wearing glasses?

EXERCISE 23: Study the examples.

(a) Ann **has talked** to John on the phone *many times.* (b) Ann **has been talking** to John on the phone *for twenty minutes.*	In (a): The present perfect is used to express repeated actions in the past. In (b): The present perfect progressive is used to express the duration of an activity that is in progress.
(c) I **have lived** here *for two years.* (d) I **have been living** here *for two years.*	With some verbs (e.g., *live, work, teach*), duration can be expressed by either the present perfect or the present perfect progressive. (c) and (d) have essentially the same meaning.

Complete the sentences. Use *the present perfect* or *the present perfect progressive*. In some sentences, either form is possible.

1. The zoo isn't far from here. I (*walk*) _____ there many times.

2. I'm tired. We (*walk*) _____ for over an hour. Let's stop and rest for a while.

3. Mr. Curtis (*work*) _____ at the power company for fifteen years. He likes his job.

4. I (*read*) _____ this chapter in my chemistry text three times, and I still don't understand it!

5. My eyes are getting tired. I (*read*) _____ for two hours. I think I'll take a break.

6. Mrs. Jackson (*teach*) _____ kindergarten for twenty years. She's one of the best teachers at the elementary school.

7. Marge is writing a letter to her boyfriend. She (*write*) _____ it since she got home from class. It's going to be a long letter!

8. I (*write*) _____ my folks at least a dozen letters since I left home and came here.

EXERCISE 24:   Following is a general review of verb tenses. Complete the sentences by using the proper forms of the words in parentheses.

1. A: (*you, have*) _____Do you have____ any plans for vacation?

    B: Yes, I do. I (*plan*) _____am planning____ to go to New Orleans.

    A: (*you, be, ever*) __Have you ever been__ there before?

    B: Yes, I have. I (*be*) _____was_____ in New Orleans two months ago.

    My brother (*live*) ___lives/is living___ there, so I (*go*) _____

    _____go_____ there often.

2. A: Where's Margaret?

    B: She (*study*) _____ at the library.

    A: When (*she, get*) _____ back home?
    B: In an hour or so. Probably around five o'clock.

    A: How long (*she, study*) _____ at the library?
    B: Since two o'clock this afternoon.

    A: (*she, study*) _____ at the library every day?
    B: Not every day, but often.

3. A: Shhh. Irene (*talk*) _____ on the phone long-distance.

    B: Who (*she, talk*) _____ to?

    A: Her brother. They (*talk*) _____ for almost an hour.
    I think her brother is in some kind of trouble.
    B: That's too bad. I hope it's nothing serious.

4. A: (*you, know*) _____ Don's new address?

    B: Not off the top of my head. But I (*have*) _____ it at

    home in my address book. When I (*get*) _____ home

    this evening, I'll call and (*give*) _____ you his address.
    A: Thanks. I'd appreciate it.

5. A: Where's Juan? He (*be*) _____ absent from class for the

    last three days. (*anyone, see*)_____ him lately?

    B: I have. I (*see*)_____ him yesterday. He has a bad cold,

    so he (*be*) _____ home in bed since the weekend. He (*be,*

    probably) _____ back in class tomorrow.

6. A: How long (*you, have to*) _____ wear glasses?

    B: Since I (*be*) _____ ten years old.

    A: (*you, be*) _____ nearsighted or farsighted?
    B: Nearsighted.

7. A: Let's go to a restaurant tonight.
    B: Okay. Where should we go?

    A: (*you, like*) _____ Thai food?

    B: I don't know. I (*eat, never*) _____ any. What's it like?
    A: It's delicious, but it can be pretty hot!

    B: That's okay. I (*love*) _____ really hot food.

    A: There (*be*) _____ a Thai restaurant on Second Avenue.

    I (*go*) _____ there a couple of times. The food is
    excellent.

    B: Sounds good. I (*be, never*) _____ to a Thai

    restaurant, so it (*be*) _____ a new experience for me.

    After we (*get*) _____ there, can you explain the menu to
    me?
    A: Sure. And if I can't, our waiter or waitress can.

8. A: (*you, smoke*) _____ ?
    B: Yes, I do.

    A: How long (*you, smoke*) _____ ?
    B: Well, let me see. I (*smoke*) _____ since I (*be*)

    _____ seventeen. So I (*smoke*) _____
    for almost four years.

    A: Why (*you, start*) _____ ?

    B: Because I (*be*) _____ a dumb, stupid kid.

    A: (*you, want*) _____ to quit?

    B: Yes. I (*plan*) _____ to quit very soon. In fact, I (*decide*)

    _____ to quit on my next birthday. My twenty-first
    birthday is two weeks from now. On that day, I (*smoke*)

    _____ my last cigarette.

    A: That's terrific! You (*feel*) _____ much better after you

    (*stop*) _____ smoking.

B: (*you, smoke, ever*) _____ ?

A: No, I haven't. I (*have, never*) _____ a cigarette in my

life. When I (*be*) _____ ten years old, I (*smoke*)

_____ one of my uncle's cigars. My sister and I (*sneak*)

_____ a couple of his cigars out of the house and (*go*)

_____ behind the garage to smoke them. Both of us (*get*)

_____ sick. I (*have, not*) _____ anything to

smoke since then.

B. That's smart.

6-7 MIDSENTENCE ADVERBS

<table>
<tr><td colspan="2" align="center">COMMON MIDSENTENCE ADVERBS</td><td rowspan="2">The adverbs in the list frequently occur in the middle of a sentence.

When these adverbs occur in the middle of a sentence, they have special positions. See below.</td></tr>
<tr><td>FREQUENCY ADVERBS</td><td>OTHER MIDSENTENCE ADVERBS</td></tr>
<tr><td>positive
ever
always
almost always
usually*
often*
frequently*
generally*
sometimes*
occasionally*</td><td>already
finally*
just
probably*</td><td></td></tr>
<tr><td>negative
seldom
rarely
hardly ever
almost never
never
not ever</td><td></td><td></td></tr>
</table>

*The adverbs with an asterisk (*) sometimes also occur at the beginning or end of a sentence:

  middle: I **sometimes** get up at 6:30.
beginning: **Sometimes** I get up at 6:30.
      end: I get up at 6:30 **sometimes.**

The other adverbs in the list (the ones without an asterisk) rarely occur at the beginning or end of a sentence; their usual position is in the middle of a sentence.

STATEMENT	(a)	He **always comes** She **finally finished**	to class. her work.	Midsentence adverbs come in front of simple present and simple past verbs (except be).
	(b)	They **are always** He **was probably**	on time for class. at home last night.	Midsentence adverbs follow **be** (simple present and simple past).
	(c)	I **will always remember** She **is probably sleeping** They **have finally finished**	her. right now. their work.	Midsentence adverbs come between a helping verb and a main verb.
QUESTION	(d)	**Do you always eat** **Did Tom finally finish** **Is she usually**	breakfast? his work? on time for class?	In a question, the adverb comes directly after the subject.
NEGATIVE	(e) (f)	She **usually doesn't eat** I **probably won't go** She **doesn't always eat** He **isn't ever**	breakfast. to the party. breakfast. on time for class.	In a negative sentence, most adverbs come in front of the negative verb (except **always** and **ever**). **Always** and **ever** follow a negative helping verb or negative **be**.
	(g)	CORRECT: She never eats breakfast. INCORRECT: She doesn't never eat breakfast.		Negative adverbs (**seldom, rarely, hardly ever, never**) are not used with a negative verb.

EXERCISE 25:   Add the word in parentheses to the sentence. Put the word in its usual midsentence position.

1. (*always*)   Tom studies at home in the evening.
2. (*always*)   Tom is at home in the evening.
3. (*always*)   You can find Tom at home in the evening.
4. (*usually*)   The mail comes at noon.
5. (*usually*)   The mail is here by noon.
6. (*probably*)   The mail will be here soon.
7. (*often*)   Ann stays home at night.

8. (*often*)   Ann is at home at night.

9. (*probably*)   Ann will stay home tonight.

10. (*finally*)   Jack wrote me a letter.

11. (*finally*)   The semester is over.

12. (*finally*)   I have finished my composition.

13. (*always*)   Does Tom study at home in the evening?

14. (*always*)   Is Tom at home in the evening?

15. (*always*)   Can you find Tom at home in the evening?

16. (*usually*)   Do you study at the library?

17. (*ever*)   Is the teacher absent?

18. (*just*)   What did you say?

19. (*usually*)   When do you go to bed?

20. (*generally*)   What time do you eat lunch?

21. (*occasionally*)   My son stays overnight with a friend.

22. (*frequently*)   We have company for dinner.

23. (*sometimes*)   Do you feel homesick?

24. (*already*)   I have read that book.

25. (*already*)   The mail is here.

EXERCISE 26:   Add the given words to the sentence. Put the adverbs in their usual midsentence position. Make any necessary changes in the sentence.

1. Jack doesn't shave in the morning.
   - (a). usually
     (*Jack usually doesn't shave in the morning.*)
   - (b). often
     (*Jack often doesn't shave in the morning.*)
   - (c). frequently
   - (d). generally
   - (e). sometimes
   - (f). occasionally
   - (g). always
   - (h). ever
   - (i). never
   - (j). hardly ever
   - (k). rarely
   - (l). seldom

2. I don't eat breakfast.
   - (a). generally
   - (b). always
   - (c). seldom
   - (d). usually
   - (e). never
   - (f). ever
   - (g). occasionally
   - (h). rarely
   - (i). hardly ever

3. Jane doesn't come to class on time.
   - (a). never
   - (b). usually
   - (c). seldom
   - (d). occasionally
   - (e). always
   - (f). hardly ever
   - (g). ever

4. My roommate isn't at home in the morning.
   - (a). usually
   - (b). generally
   - (c). always
   - (d). ever
   - (e). never
   - (f). seldom
   - (g). frequently
   - (h). hardly ever

EXERCISE 27:   Add the word in parentheses to the sentence. Put the word in its usual midsentence position. Make any necessary changes.

1. (*probably*) Tom knows the answer.
2. (*usually*) Is Pat at home in the evening?
3. (*finally*) They have finished their work.
4. (*seldom*) Jack doesn't write letters.
5. (*generally, generally*) I don't stay up late. I go to bed early.
6. (*probably, probably*) Susan won't come to the party. She will stay home.
7. (*never*) You shouldn't allow children to play with matches.
8. (*hardly ever*) Jerry isn't in a bad mood.
9. (*frequently*) My chemistry lecturer came to class late last semester.
10. (*seldom*) The temperature doesn't drop below freezing in Miami.
11. (*always*) Mary rides the bus to school.
12. (*always*) I don't ride the bus to school.
13. (*usually*) Tom doesn't ride the bus to school.
14. (*never*) Jim doesn't ride his bike to his office.
15. (*often*) Our classroom is too hot.

EXERCISE 28—ORAL   (BOOKS CLOSED):   Respond in complete sentences.

Example: What is something that you always do in the morning?

Response: I always drink a cup of coffee.

What is something that. . .

1. you seldom do?
2. you will probably do tomorrow?
3. you probably won't do tomorrow?
4. you are probably going to do next week?
5. you hardly ever do?
6. you almost always do before you go to bed?
7. you have never done?
8. your roommate/spouse occasionally does?
9. a lazy person seldom does?
10. is always or usually expensive?
11. a polite person usually does?
12. a polite person never does?
13. drivers generally do?
14. your classmates sometimes do?
15. you have already done?
16. you just did?
17. I frequently do in class?
18. I usually don't do in class?
19. you rarely eat?
20. people in your country always or usually do to celebrate the New Year?
21. you usually do, but don't always do?
22. you usually don't do?

6-8   USING *ALREADY, YET, STILL,* **AND** *ANYMORE*

ALREADY	(a)	The mail came an hour ago. **The mail is *already* here.**	Idea of *already:* Something happened before now, before this time. *Position: midsentence.**
YET	(b)	I expected the mail an hour ago, but **it hasn't come *yet*.**	Idea of *yet:* Something did not happen before now (up to this time), but it may happen in the future. *Position: end of sentence.*
STILL	(c)	It was cold yesterday.**It is *still* cold today.**	Idea of *still:* A situation continues to exist from past to present without change. *Position: midsentence.**
	(d)	I could play the piano when I was a child. **I can *still* play the piano.**	
	(e)	The mail didn't come an hour ago. **The mail *still* hasn't come.**	
ANYMORE	(f)	I lived in Chicago two years ago, but then I moved to another city. **I don't live in Chicago *anymore*.**	Idea of *anymore:* A past situation does not continue to exist at present; a past situation has changed. *Position: end of sentence.*

*See 6-7 for the usual positions of midsentence adverbs.

> NOTE: **Already** is used in *affirmative* sentences.
> **Yet** and **anymore** are used in *negative* sentences.
> **Still** is used in either *affirmative* or *negative* sentences.

EXERCISE 29:   Complete the sentences with **already, yet, still,** or **anymore.**

1. It's 1:00 p.m. I'm hungry. I haven't eaten lunch _____yet_____ .

2. It's 1:00 p.m. I'm not hungry. I've _____ eaten lunch.

3. Bob was hungry, so he ate a candy bar a few minutes ago. But he's

   _____ hungry, so he's going to have another candy bar.

4. I used to eat lunch at the cafeteria every day, but now I bring my lunch to school in a paper bag instead. I don't eat at the cafeteria

   _____ .

5. It started raining an hour ago. We can't go for a walk because it's

   _____ raining. I hope it stops soon.

6. Look! The rain has stopped. It isn't raining _____ . Let's go for a walk.

7. I didn't understand this chapter in my biology book when I read it

   yesterday. Since then, I've read it three times, but I _____ don't understand it!

8. I don't have to study tonight. I've _____ finished all of my homework.

9. I started a letter to my parents yesterday, but I haven't finished it

   _____ . I'll finish it later today and put it in the mail.

10. I started a letter to my parents yesterday. I thought about finishing it last

    night before I went to bed, and I didn't. I _____ haven't finished it.*

---

*In negative sentences, *still* and *yet* express similar meanings. The meanings of *I haven't finished it yet* and *I still haven't finished it* are similar.

EXERCISE 30:   *Yet* and *still* are frequently used in questions. Complete the following dialogues by using *yet* or *still.*

1. A: Is Mary home _____ ?
   B: No, but I'm expecting her soon.

2. A: Is Mary _____ in class?
   B: Yes, she is. Her class doesn't end until 11:30.

3. A: Has Dennis graduated _____ ?
   B: No. He's still in school.

4. A: Did you eat _____ ?
   B: No. Did you?

5. A: Do you _____ live on Fifth Street?
   B: Not anymore. I moved.

6. A: Has Karen found a new apartment _____ ?
   B: Not that I know of. She's still living on Elm Street.

7. A: Do you _____ love me?
   B: Of course I do! I love you very much.

8. A: Is the baby _____ sleeping?
   B: Yes. Shh. We don't want to wake him up.

9. A: Is the baby asleep _____ ?
   B: I think so. I don't hear anything from the nursery. I put him down for his nap fifteen minutes ago, so I'm pretty sure he's asleep by now.

EXERCISE 31:   Complete the dialogues by using *already, yet, still,* or *anymore.*

1. A: Has Bob found a new job _____ ?

   B: No. He _____ works at the bookstore.

2. A: When is your sister going to come to visit you?

   B: She's _____ here. She got here yesterday.

3. A: Do you _____ live on Pine Avenue?

   B: No, I don't live there _____ . I moved to another apartment closer to school.

4. A: Is Ann home _____ ?

B: No, she isn't. I'm getting worried. She was supposed to be home at

eight. It's almost nine and she _____ isn't here.

A: Don't worry. She'll probably be here any minute.

5. A: I'm going to have another sandwich.

B: What? You just ate three sandwiches!

A: I know, but I'm not full _____ . I'm _____
hungry.

6. A: Would you like to see today's newspaper?

B: Thanks, but I've _____ read it.

7. A: Did you try to call Peter again?

B: Yes, but the line was _____ busy. I'll try again in a few
minutes.

8. A: How does Dick like his job at the hardware store?

B: He doesn't work there _____ . He found a new job.

9. A: Is your younger sister a college student?

B: No. She's _____ in high school.

10. A: When are you going to make Tommy's birthday cake?

B: I've _____ made it.

11. A: How did you do on your calculus exam?

B: I haven't taken it _____ . The exam is tomorrow.

I'm _____ studying for it.

EXERCISE 32:   Using the given information, rewrite the sentences in parentheses.
Add *already, yet, still,* or *anymore* to the sentences.

1. I finished my work two hours ago. (*I have finished my work.*)

  ___ I have already finished my work. _____

2. Ann didn't finish her work yesterday. She's doing her work now. (*She
hasn't finished it*).

  ___ She hasn't finished it yet./She still hasn't finished it.* ____

3. I expected Mike to come home an hour ago, but he didn't come. (*He isn't
home.*)

  _____

_____

*Reminder: In negative sentences, *yet* and *still* often express a similar meaning.

4. I was hungry an hour ago, but I didn't eat anything. (*I'm hungry.*)

   _____

5. Margaret used to work at the drugstore, but she quit her job. (*She doesn't work there.*)

   _____

6. Susan has been working at the bookstore for a year. She has tried to find a different job, but she hasn't found one yet. (*She is working at the bookstore.*)

   _____

7. The movie started half an hour ago. We're late. (*The movie has started.*)

   _____

8. Bob started smoking four years ago. (*He smokes. He hasn't quit.*)

   _____

9. We studied Chapter 5 last week. (*We've studied Chapter 5. We haven't studied Chapter 7.*)

   _____

10. When I was a child, I used to read comic books. But they are for kids. (*I don't read comic books.*)

    _____

11. We started this exercise ten minutes ago. (*We haven't finished it. We are doing this exercise.*)

    _____

12. When we were little, my sister and I could speak a little French. (*I can't speak French, but my sister can speak French.*)

    _____

    _____

    _____

EXERCISE 33—WRITTEN: Write about one (or both) of the following topics.

1. Think of two or three important events that have occurred in your life in the past year or two. In a paragraph for each, briefly tell your reader about these events and give your opinions and/or predictions.
2. Think of two or three important events that have occurred in the world in the past year or two. In a paragraph for each, briefly tell your reader about these events and give your opinions and/or predictions.

6-9 FORMS OF THE PAST PERFECT

AFFIRMATIVE	CONTRACTIONS	NEGATIVE	
I You He She } **had eaten.** It We They	I + had = **I'd** you + had = **you'd** he + had = **he'd** she + had = **she'd** it + had = **it'd** we + had = **we'd** they + had = **they'd**	had + **not** = **hadn't** I **hadn't eaten.**	Form of the past perfect: *had* + *past participle*

6-10 USING THE PAST PERFECT

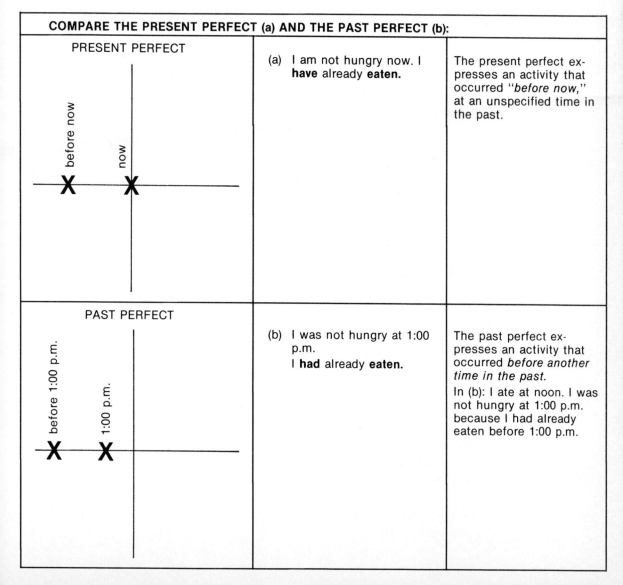

COMPARE THE PRESENT PERFECT (a) AND THE PAST PERFECT (b):		
PRESENT PERFECT	(a) I am not hungry now. I **have** already **eaten.**	The present perfect expresses an activity that occurred "*before now*," at an unspecified time in the past.
PAST PERFECT	(b) I was not hungry at 1:00 p.m. I **had** already **eaten.**	The past perfect expresses an activity that occurred *before another time in the past.* In (b): I ate at noon. I was not hungry at 1:00 p.m. because I had already eaten before 1:00 p.m.

COMPARE THE PAST PROGRESSIVE (c) AND THE PAST PERFECT (d):

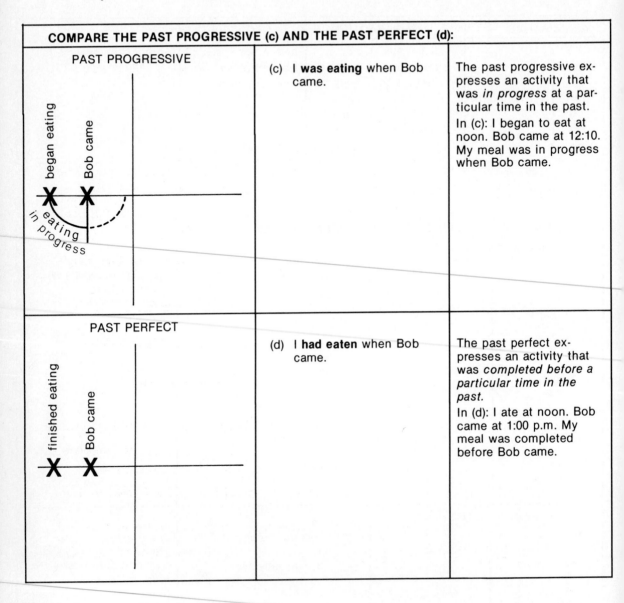

PAST PROGRESSIVE

began eating / Bob came / eating in progress

(c) I **was eating** when Bob came.

The past progressive expresses an activity that was *in progress* at a particular time in the past.

In (c): I began to eat at noon. Bob came at 12:10. My meal was in progress when Bob came.

PAST PERFECT

finished eating / Bob came

(d) I **had eaten** when Bob came.

The past perfect expresses an activity that was *completed before a particular time in the past.*

In (d): I ate at noon. Bob came at 1:00 p.m. My meal was completed before Bob came.

EXERCISE 34:   Complete the sentences with the words in parentheses. Use *the present perfect* or *the past perfect.*

1. I am not hungry. I (*eat, already*) ___I have already eaten___ .

2. I was not hungry. I (*eat, already*) ___I had already eaten___ .

3. It's ten o'clock. I (*finish, already*) _____ my homework, so I'm going to go to bed.

4. Last night I went to bed at ten o'clock. I (*finish, already*)_____
    _____ my homework.

5. By the time* I went to bed last night, I (*finish, already*) _____
    _____ my homework.

6. I was late. The party (*start, already*) _____ by
    the time I got there.

7. We're late. The party (*start, already*) _____ .

8. Carol missed her plane yesterday because of a traffic jam on her way to the
    airport. By the time she got to the airport, her plane (*leave, already*)

    _____ .

EXERCISE 35: Complete the sentences with the words in parentheses. Use *the past progressive* or *the past perfect.*

1. When I left for school this morning, it (*rain*) _____was raining_____ , so I used
    my umbrella.

2. By the time class was over this morning, the rain (*stop*) __had stopped__ ,
    so I didn't need my umbrella anymore.

3. Last night I started to study at 7:30. Dick came at 7:35. I (*study*)

    _____ when Dick came.

4. Last night I started to study at 7:30. I finished studying at 9:00. Dick came

    at 9:30. By the time Dick came, I (*finish*)_____ my homework.

5. When I walked into the kitchen after dinner last night, my wife (*wash*)

    _____ the dishes, so I picked up a dish towel to help
    her.

6. By the time I walked into the kitchen after dinner tonight, my husband

    (*wash, already*) _____ the dishes and _____
    (*put*) them away.

EXERCISE 36: Complete the sentences with the words in parentheses.

1. A: (*you, enjoy*) ___Did you enjoy___ the concert last night?

    B: Very much. I (*go, not*) ___hadn't gone___ to a concert in a long time.

_____

by the time = before

2. A: (*you, see*) _____ John yesterday?

   B: Yes, I did. It (*be*) _____ good to see him again. I (*see, not*) _____ him in a long time.

3. A: Hi, Jim! It's good to see you again. I (*see, not*) _____ you in weeks.

   B: Hi, Sue! It (*be*) _____ good to see you again, too. I (*see, not*) _____ you since the end of last semester. How's everything going?

4. A: (*you, get*) _____ to class on time yesterday morning?

   B: No. By the time I (*get*) _____ there, it (*begin, already*) _____ .

5. A: (*you, go*) _____ out to eat last night?

   B: No. By the time I (*get*) _____ home, my husband (*make, already*) _____ dinner for us.

   A: How (*be*) _____ it?

   B: Terrific. We (*have*) _____ chicken, rice, and a salad. While we (*eat*) _____ , George Drake (*stop*) _____ by to visit us, so we (*invite*) _____ him to join us for dinner. But he (*eat, already*) _____ his dinner, so he (*be, not*) _____ hungry.

   A: What (*you, do*) _____ after dinner?

   B: I wanted to go a movie—*Galaxy Invaders*. But George and my husband (*see, already*) _____ it, so we (*go*) _____ to *Ghost Ship* instead. It (*be*) _____ pretty good.

chapter 7

Gerunds and Infinitives

7-1 GERUNDS AND INFINITIVES: INTRODUCTION

(a) I enjoy *noun* — music.	**S V O** I enjoy *something.* (*something* = the object of the verb.	
(b) I enjoy *gerund* — **listening** — to music.	The object of a verb is usually a noun or pronoun, as in (a).	
(c) I enjoy *gerund phrase* — **listening** to music.	The object of a verb can also be a gerund. A gerund is *the -ing form of a verb.** It is used as a noun. In (b): **listening** is a gerund. It is the object of the verb **enjoy.**	
(d) I want *noun* — a sandwich.	**S V O** I want *something.* (*something* = the object of the verb.) In (d): The object of the verb is a noun (*a sandwich*).	
(e) I want *infinitive* — **to eat** — a sandwich.	The object of a verb can also be an infinitive. An infinitive is **to** + *the simple form of a verb.*	
(f) I want *infinitive phrase* — **to eat** a sandwich.	In (e): **to eat** is an infinitive. It is the object of the verb **want.**	

*The *-ing* form of a verb can be used as a present participle:

I **am listening** to the teacher right now. (**listening** = a present participle, used in the present progressive)
The *-ing* form of a verb can be used as a gerund:

I **enjoy listening** to music. (**listening** = a gerund, used as the object of the verb **enjoy**)

(g) I **enjoy going** to the beach.	Some verbs (*e.g.*, *enjoy*) are followed by gerunds. (See 7–2.)
(h) Bob **wants to go** to the beach.	Some verbs (*e.g.*, *want*) are followed by infinitives. (See 7–4.)
(i) It **began raining.** It **began to rain.**	Some verbs (*e.g.*, *begin*) are followed by either gerunds or infinitives. (See 7–5.)

7-2   VERB + GERUND

COMMON VERBS FOLLOWED BY GERUNDS		
enjoy	(a) I **enjoy working** in my garden	Gerunds are used as the objects of the verbs in the list.
finish	(b) Bob **finished studying** at midnight.	
stop	(c) It **stopped raining** a few minutes ago.	
quit	(d) David **quit smoking.**	The list also contains two-word verbs (see Appendix 4) that are followed by gerunds.
postpone	(e) I **postponed doing** my homework.	
put off	(f) I **put off doing** my homework.	
keep	(g) **Keep working.** Don't stop.	(e) and (f) ⎫
keep on	(h) **Keep on working.** Don't stop.	(g) and (h) ⎬ have the
consider	(i) I'm **considering going** to Hawaii for my vacation.	(i) and (j) ⎭ same meaning
think about	(j) I'm **thinking about going** to Hawaii for my vacation.	(k) and (l)
discuss	(k) They **discussed getting** a new car.	
talk about	(l) They **talked about getting** a new car.	

EXERCISE 1:   Complete the sentences by using *gerunds.* Add a preposition after the gerund if necessary.

1. It was cold and rainy yesterday, so we postponed __going to/visiting__ the zoo.

2. The Porter's house is too small. They're considering _____ __buying/moving into/renting__ a bigger house.

3. We discussed _____ Colorado for our vacation.

4. When Martha finished _____ the floor, she dusted the furniture.

5. Sometimes students put off _____ their homework.

6. We had a blizzard yesterday, but it finally stopped _____ around ten p.m.

7. I quit _____ comic books when I was twelve years old.

8. I'm thinking about _____ a biology course next semester.

9. Beth doesn't like her job. She's talking about _____ a different job.

10. I enjoy _____ sports.

11. I'm considering_____ New York City.

12. A: Are you listening to me?

    B: Yes. Keep _____ . I'm listening.

13. A: Do you want to take a break?

    B: No. I'm not tired yet. Let's keep on _____ for another hour or so.

EXERCISE 2:   Complete the sentences in the dialogues. Use the expressions in the list or your own words. Be sure to use a gerund in each sentence.

buy a new car	*rain*
do my homework	*read a good book*
do things	*smoke*
get a Toyota	*tap your fingernails on the table*
go to the zoo on Saturday	*try*
help him	

1. A: Would you like to go for a walk?

    B: Has it stopped ___raining?_____

    A: Yes.

    B: Let's go.

2. A: I've been having a lot of trouble with my old Volkswagen the last couple of months. It's slowly falling apart. I'm thinking about

    _____

    B: Do you think you'll get another Volkswagen?

    A: No. I'm considering _____

3. A: What do you usually do in your free time in the evening?

    B: I enjoy _____

4. A: Good news! I feel great. I don't cough any more, and I don't run out of breath when I walk up a hill.

   B: Oh?

   A: I quit _____

   B: That's wonderful!

5. A: I've been working on this math problem for the last half hour, and I still don't understand it.

   B: Well, don't give up. Keep _____ If at first you don't succeed, try, try again.

6. A: Are you a procrastinator?

   B: A what?

   A: A procrastinator. That's someone who always postpones

   _____

   B: Oh. Well, sometimes I put off _____

7. A: What are you doing?

   B: I'm helping Teddy with his homework.

   A: When you finish _____ , could you help me in the kitchen?

   B: Sure.

8. A: Could you please stop doing that?

   B: Doing what?

   A: Stop _____ It's driving me crazy.

9. A: Do you have any plans for this weekend?

   B: Henry and I talked about _____

7-3   GO + -ING

(a) **Did** you **go shopping** yesterday?
(b) I **went swimming** last week.
(c) Bob **hasn't gone fishing** in years.
	Go is followed by a gerund in certain idiomatic expressions about activities.
	Notice: There is no *to* between *go* and the gerund.
	    INCORRECT: *Did you go to shopping?*
	    CORRECT: *Did you go shopping?*

COMMON EXPRESSIONS WITH *GO* + *-ING*		
go boating	*go hiking*	*go shopping*
go bowling	*go jogging*	*go skating*
go camping	*go running*	*go skiing*
go dancing	*go sailing*	*go swimming*
go fishing		

EXERCISE 3:   Answer the questions. Use the expressions with **go** + **-ing** in Chart 7–3.*

1. Ann often goes to the beach. She spends hours in the water. What does she like to do?

    (*She likes to go swimming.*)

2. Nancy and Frank like to spend the whole day on a lake with poles in their hands. What do they like to do?

3. Last summer Tom went to a national park. He slept in a tent and cooked his food over a fire. What did Tom do last summer?

4. Bob likes to go to stores and buy things. What does he like to do?

5. Laura takes good care of her health. She runs a couple of miles every day. What does Laura do every day? (*Note: There are two possible responses.*)

6. On weekends in the winter, Fred and Jean sometimes drive to a resort in the mountains. They like to race down the side of a mountain in the snow. What do they like to do?

7. Joe is a nature lover. He likes to take long walks in the woods. What does Joe like to do?

8. Mary prefers indoor sports. She goes to a place where she rolls a thirteen-pound ball at some wooden pins. What does Mary often do?

9. Liz and Greg know all the latest dances. What do they probably do a lot?

10. The Taylors are going to go to a little lake near their house tomorrow. The lake is completely frozen now that it's winter. The ice is smooth. What are the Taylors going to do tomorrow?

11. Barbara and Alex live near the ocean. When there's a strong wind, they like to spend the whole day in their sailboat. What do they like to do? (*Note: There are two possible responses.*)

12. What do you like to do for exercise and fun?

---

*To the teacher: If you wish, do the exercise with books closed and use the names of class members.

7-4 VERB + INFINITIVE

(a) Tom **offered to lend** me some money. (b) I have **decided to buy** a new car.	Some verbs are followed by an infinitive: *an infinitive = **to** + the simple form of a verb.*

COMMON VERBS FOLLOWED BY AN INFINITIVE				
want to *need to* *would like to*	*hope to* *expect to* *plan to* *intend to** *promise to* *decide to*	*offer to* *agree to* *refuse to*	*seem to* *appear to* *pretend to*	*can/can't afford to* *try to***

*Sometimes *intend* is followed by a gerund:

> *I **intend to go** to Florida over vacation.*
> *I **intend going** to Florida over vacation.*

The use of an infinitive after *intend* is more common.

**Usually *try* is followed by an infinitive and gives the idea of making an effort:

> *I'm **trying to learn** English.*
> *Joe **tried to finish** his work before 5:00 p.m.*

Sometimes *try* is followed by a gerund and gives the idea of experimenting with a new approach:

> *It was hot in the room. I **tried opening** the windows, but that didn't help. Then I **tried turning** on the fan, but that didn't help either. Finally I **tried turning** on the air conditioner. That helped.*

EXERCISE 4: Complete the sentences by using infinitives. Add a preposition after the infinitive if necessary.

1. I'm planning <u>to go to/to visit/to fly to/to drive to/etc.</u> Chicago next week.

2. Jack promised _____ my party.

3. I've decided _____ a new apartment.

4. I forgot _____ some milk when I went to the grocery store.

5. Did you remember _____ the door?

6. I would like _____ the Grand Canyon.

7. I need _____ my homework tonight.

8. What time do you expect _____ Chicago?

9. I want _____ a ball game on TV after dinner tonight.

10. You seem _____ in a good mood today.

11. Susie appeared _____ asleep, but she wasn't. She was only pretending.

12. Susie pretended _____ asleep.

13. The Millers can't afford _____ a house.

14. George is only seven, but he intends _____ a doctor when he grows up.

15. My friend offered _____ me five bucks.

16. Tommy doesn't like green vegetables. He refuses _____ them.

17. My wife and I wanted to do different things this weekend. Finally, I agreed

    _____ a movie with her Saturday, and she agreed _____

    _____ the zoo with me tomorrow.

18. I hope _____ all of my courses this term. So far my grades have been pretty good.

19. I try _____ class on time every day.

7-5 VERB + GERUND OR INFINITIVE

COMMON VERBS FOLLOWED BY EITHER A GERUND OR AN INFINITIVE		
begin	(a) It **began to rain.**	Some verbs are followed by either an infinitive or a gerund. Usually there is no difference in meaning.
	(b) It **began raining.**	
start	(c) It **started to snow.**	(a) and (b)
	(d) It **started snowing.**	(c) and (d)
continue	(e) Bob **continued to work.**	(e) and (f)
	(f) Bob **continued working.**	(g) and (h) have the same meaning.
like*	(g) I **like to go** to the zoo.	(i) and (j)
	(h) I **like going** to the zoo.	(k) and (l)
hate	(i) Kathy **hates to go** to the dentist.	
	(j) Kathy **hates going** to the dentist.	
can't stand	(k) I **can't stand to wait** in lines.	
	(l) I **can't stand waiting** in lines.	

*__Like__ can be followed by either an infinitive or a gerund.
__Would like__ is followed by an infinitive, not a gerund.

   I like to go to movies. OR: I like going to movies.
   I would like to go to a movie tonight.

EXERCISE 5:   Complete the sentences with the *infinitive* or *gerund* form of the words in parentheses.

1. I need (*study*) ___to study___ tonight.

2. I enjoy (*cook*) ___cooking___ fancy meals.

3. Ellen started (*talk*) ___to talk/talking___ about her problem.

4. Bud and Sally have decided (*get*) _____ married.

5. We finished (*eat*) _____ around seven.

6. Are you planning (*take*) _____ a vacation this year?

7. I like (*meet*) _____ new people.

8. The Wilsons went (*camp*) _____ in Yellowstone National Park last summer.

9. My roommate offered (*help*) _____ me with my English.

10. It began (*snow*) _____ yesterday in the middle of the afternoon.

11. Please stop (*crack*) _____ your knuckles!

12. Did you remember (*feed*) _____ the cat this morning?

13. I won't be late. I promise (*be*) _____ on time.

14. I'm considering (*move*) _____ to a new apartment.

15. What time do you expect (*arrive*) _____ in Denver?

16. Some children hate (*go*) _____ to school.

17. I forgot (*lock*) _____ the door when I left my apartment this morning.

18. Our teacher seems (*be*) _____ in a bad mood today.

19. Don't put off (*write*) _____ your composition until the last minute.

20. Let's go (*ski*) _____ this weekend.

21. I want (*go*) _____ (*shop*)_____ this afternoon.

22. Fred had to quit (*jog*) _____ because he hurt his knee.

EXERCISE 6:   Complete the sentences with the *infinitive* or *gerund* form of the words in parentheses.

1. Cindy intends (*go*) _____ to graduate school next year.

2. Pierre can't afford (*buy*) _____ a new car.

3. Janice is thinking about (*look*) _____ for a new job.

4. My boss refused (*give*) _____ me a raise, so I quit.

5. Mr. Carter continued (*read*) _____ his book even though the children were making a lot of noise.

6. Shhh. My roommate is trying (*take*) _____ a nap.

7. Dick appears (*have*) _____ a lot of money.

8. John agreed (*meet*) _____ us at the restaurant at seven.

9. Have you discussed (*change*) _____ your major with your academic advisor?

10. I haven't heard from Mary in a long time. I keep (*hope*) _____ that I'll get a letter from her soon.

11. My wife can't stand (*sleep*) _____ in a room with all of the windows closed.

12. Sam's tomato crop always failed. Finally he quit (*try*) _____ (*grow*) _____ tomatoes in his garden.

13. Would you like (*go*) _____ (*dance*) _____ tonight?

14. The Knickerbockers talked about (*build*) _____ a new house.

15. Children like (*play*) _____ make-believe games. Yesterday Tommy pretended (*be*) _____ a doctor, and Bobby pretended (*be*) _____ a patient.

16. My cousin offered (*take*) _____ me to the airport.

17. I'm planning (*go*) _____ (*shop*) _____ tomorrow.

18. Sally enjoys (*go*) _____ to her grandmother's house.

19. Tim expects (*go*) _____ (*fish*) _____ this weekend.

20. When Tommy broke his toy, he started (*cry*) _____ .

21. Jerry likes (*go*) _____ to parties.

22. Would you like (*go*) _____ to Sharon's house next Saturday?

23. I expect (*be*) _____ in class tomorrow.

24. I enjoy (*teach*) _____ .

25. I enjoy (*be*) _____ a teacher.

EXERCISE 7—ORAL (BOOKS CLOSED):   Complete the sentences with either ***to go there*** or ***going there.***

*(To the teacher: It is helpful to write **to go there** and **going there** on the board. Go through the exercise with only those two possible responses first. Then go through the exercise again, but have the students name specific places [e.g., to class, to Hawaii, to Mack's Bar and Grill]. Encourage the students to expand upon these responses [e.g., Why do you put off going to the dentist? When did you stop going to Mack's Bar and Grill?]).*

> *Example:*   I expect. . .
> *Response:*   . . . to go there.
>
> *Example:*   I like. . .
> *Response:*   . . . to go there. OR: . . . going there.

1. I want. . .
2. I need. . .
3. I like. . .
4. I would like. . .
5. I enjoy. . .
6. I intend. . .
7. I am thinking about. . .
8. I'm considering. . .
9. I'm going to try. . .
10. I hope. . .
11. I expect. . .
12. I've decided. . .
13. I enjoy. . .
14. I don't like. . .
15. I hate. . .
16. I can't stand. . .
17. I refuse. . .
18. I started. . .
19. I stopped. . .
20. I began. . .
21. I quit. . .
22. I can't afford. . .
23. Yesterday I remembered. . .
24. Yesterday I forgot. . .
25. My friend and I discussed. . .
26. My friend and I agreed. . .
27. I promised. . .
28. Sometimes I put off. . .
29. My friend and I postponed. . .
30. I've always wanted. . .

EXERCISE 8: Complete the sentences with a form of the words in parentheses.

1. I enjoy (*get*) _____ up early in the morning.

2. I enjoy (*watch*) _____ the sunrise.

3. I enjoy (*get*) _____ up early in the morning and (*watch*)

   _____ the sunrise.

4. I enjoy (*get*) _____ up early in the morning, (*watch*)

   _____ the sunrise, and (*listen*) _____ to the

   birds.

5. I want (*stay*) _____ home tonight.

6. I want (*relax*) _____ tonight.

7. I want (*stay*) _____ home and (*relax*)* _____

   tonight.

8. I want (*stay*) _____ home, (*relax*) _____ , and

   (*go*) _____ to bed early tonight.

9. Mr. and Mrs. Brown are thinking about (*sell*) _____ their old

   house and (*buy*) _____ a new one.

10. Kathy plans (*move*) _____ to New York City, (*find*)

    _____ a job, and (*start*) _____ a new life.

EXERCISE 9: Complete the sentences with a form of the words in parentheses.

1. Have you finished (*paint*) _____ your apartment yet?

2. Steve needs (*go*) _____ to the shopping mall tomorrow and

   (*buy*) _____ some winter clothes.

3. Don't forget (*call*) _____ the dentist's office this afternoon.

---

*When infinitives are connected by *and*, it is not necessary to repeat *to:*
*I need **to stay** home **and** (to) **study** tonight.*

4. Do you enjoy (*go*) _____ to an expensive restaurant and (*have*) _____ a fancy dinner?

5. Most nonsmokers can't stand (*be*) _____ in a smoke-filled room.

6. Let's postpone (*go*) _____ to the zoo until the weather is better.

7. The children promised (*stop*) _____ (*make*) _____ so much noise.

8. How do you expect (*pass*) _____ your courses if you don't study?

9. Tom is thinking about (*quit*) _____ his job and (*go*) _____ back to school.

10. Linda plans (*leave*) _____ for Chicago on Tuesday and (*return*) _____ on Friday.

11. I often put off (*wash*) _____ the dinner dishes until the next morning.

12. Shhh. I'm trying (*concentrate*) _____ . I'm doing a problem for my accounting class, and I can't afford (*make*) _____ any mistakes.

13. I'm sleepy. I'd like (*go*) _____ home and (*take*) _____ a nap.

14. When are you going to start (*do*) _____ the research for your term paper?

15. Why did Marcia refuse (*help*) _____ us?

16. I remembered (*unplug*) _____ the coffee pot, (*turn off*) _____ all the lights, and (*lock*) _____ the door before I left for work this morning.

17. Sometimes when I'm listening to someone who is speaking English very fast, I nod my head and pretend (*understand*) _____ .

18. After Isabel got a speeding ticket and had to pay a fine of $75, she decided

(*stop*) _____ (*drive*) _____ 70 miles an hour on interstate highways.

19. Khalid tries (*learn*) _____ at least 25 new words every day.

20. I considered (*drive*) _____ to Minneapolis. Finally I decided

(*fly*) _____ .

21. Our teacher agreed (*postpone*) _____ the test until Friday.

22. I've been trying (*reach*) _____ Carol on the phone for the

last three days, but she's never at home. I intend (*keep*) _____

(*try*) _____ until I finally get her.

EXERCISE 10—ORAL (BOOKS CLOSED):   Make sentences from the given words. Use *I.* Use any tense.

Example: *want* and *go*
Response: I want to go (to New York City next week).

Example: *remember* and *pay*
Response: I remembered to pay (my phone bill yesterday).

1. *plan* and *go*
2. *consider* and *go*
3. *offer* and *lend*
4. *like* and *visit*
5. *enjoy* and *read*
6. *intend* and *get up*
7. *decide* and *get*
8. *seem* and *be*
9. *put off* and *write*
10. *forget* and *go*
11. *can't afford* and *buy*
12. *try* and *learn*
13. *need* and *learn*
14. *would like* and *take*
15. *would like* and *go* and *swim*
16. *promise* and *come*
17. *finish* and *study*
18. *remember* and *buy*
19. *hope* and *go*
20. *think about* and *go*
21. *quit* and *drink*
22. *expect* and *stay*
23. *stop* and *eat*
24. *refuse* and *lend*
25. *agree* and *lend*
26. *postpone* and *go*
27. *begin* and *study*
28. *continue* and *walk*
29. *talk about* and *go*
30. *keep* and *try* and *improve*

7-6   USING GERUNDS AS SUBJECTS; USING *IT* + INFINITIVE

(a) **Riding horses** is fun. (b) It is fun **to ride** horses.	(a) and (b) have the same meaning. In (a): A gerund phrase (*riding horses*) is used as the subject of the sentence.* Notice: The verb (*is*) is singular.
(c) **Coming to class on time** is important. (d) **It** is important **to come to class on time.**	In (b): The word *it* is used as the subject of the sentence. The word *it* has the same meaning as the infinitive phrase at the end of the sentence: *it* means *to ride horses.*

*It is also correct (but less common) to use an infinitive as the subject of a sentence: *To ride horses is fun.*

EXERCISE 11:   Make sentences with the same meaning by using *it* + *infinitive.*

1. Having good friends is important. (*It is important to have good friends.*)
2. Playing tennis is fun.
3. Riding the bus to school every day is expensive.
4. Learning how to cook is easy.
5. Walking alone at night in that part of the city is dangerous.
6. Is learning a second language difficult?
7. Being polite to other people is important.
8. Learning about other cultures is interesting.
9. Eating nutritious food is important.
10. Is riding a motorcycle easy?
11. Having a cold isn't much fun.
12. Looking up words in a dictionary takes a lot of time.
13. Learning a second language takes a long time.
14. Cooking a soft-boiled egg takes three minutes.

EXERCISE 12:   Make sentences with the same meaning by using a gerund phrase as the subject:

1. It is important to get daily exercise. (*Getting daily exercise is important.*)
2. It is fun to meet new people.
3. It is easy to cook rice.
4. It is boring to spend the whole weekend in the dorm.
5. It is relaxing to take a long walk.
6. Is it difficult to learn a second language?
7. It isn't hard to make friends.

8. It is wrong to cheat during a test.
9. Is it dangerous to smoke cigarettes?
10. Is it expensive to live in an apartment?
11. It isn't easy to live in a foreign country.
12. It takes time to make new friends.
13. It takes time and effort to lose weight.

EXERCISE 13—ORAL: Use infinitive phrases and gerund phrases.

STUDENT A: Complete the sentence with *an infinitive phrase.*
STUDENT B: Make a sentence with the same meaning by using *a gerund phrase*
   as the subject.

1. It's relaxing. . . .
   A: It's relaxing to watch TV.
   B: Watching TV is relaxing.
2. It's important. . . .
3. It's fun. . . .
4. It's easy. . . .
5. It's difficult. . . .

6. It's dangerous. . .
7. It's interesting. . . .
8. Is it hard. . .?
9. Is it fun. . .?
10. It isn't hard. . . .
11. It's against the law. . . .
12. It takes a lot of time. . . .

EXERCISE 14—ORAL: Answer the questions.

STUDENT A: Use *it + infinitives.*
STUDENT B: Use *gerunds.*

1. Which is easier: to make money or to spend money?
   A: It is easier to spend money than (it is) to make money.
   B: Spending money is easier than making money.
2. Which is more fun: to study at the library or to go to the zoo?
3. Which is more difficult: to write English or to read English?
4. Which is easier: to write English or to speak English?
5. Which is more expensive: to go to a movie or to go to a concert?
6. Which is more interesting: to talk to people or to watch people?
7. Which is more comfortable: to wear shoes or to go barefoot?
8. Which is more satisfying: to give gifts or to receive them?
9. Which is more dangerous: to ride in a car or to ride in an airplane?
10. Which is more important: to come to class on time or to get an extra hour of sleep in the morning?
11. Which is better: to light one candle or to curse the darkness?

7-7 *IT* + **INFINITIVE: USING** *FOR (SOMEONE)*

(a) You should study hard. (b) It is important **for you** to study hard. (c) Mary should study hard. (d) It is important **for Mary** to study hard. (e) We don't have to go to the meeting. (f) It isn't necessary **for us** to go to the meeting. (g) A dog can't talk. (h) It is impossible **for a dog** to talk.	(a) and (b) have a similar meaning. Notice the pattern in (b): *it is* + *adjective* + *for (some-one)* + *infinitive phrase*

EXERCISE 15: Use the given information to complete each sentence. Use *for (some-one) and an infinitive phrase* in each completion.

1. *(Students should do their homework.)*

   It's important ___for students to do their homework.___

2. *(Teachers should speak clearly.)*

   It's important _____

3. *(We don't have to hurry.)*
   There's plenty of time. It isn't necessary _____

4. *(A fish can't live out of water for more than a few minutes.)*

   It's impossible _____

5. *(Students have to budget their time carefully.)*

   It's necessary _____

6. *(A child usually can't sit still for a long time.)*

   It's difficult _____

7. *(Americans usually eat turkey on Thanksgiving Day.)*

   It's traditional _____

8. *(People can take trips to the moon.)*

   Will it be possible _____ in the next century?

9. *(Chemistry students should do lab experiments.)*

It's important _____

10. *(The bride usually feeds the groom the first piece of wedding cake.)*

It's traditional _____

11. *(The guests usually wait until the hostess begins to eat.)*

At a formal dinner party, it's customary _____

_____ After she takes the first bite, the guests also start to eat.

12. *(I usually can't understand Mr. Allen.)*

It's hard _____ He talks too fast.

13. *(I can understand our teacher.)*

It's easy _____

7-8 INFINITIVE OF PURPOSE: USING *IN ORDER TO*

Why did you go to the post office?	*In order to* expresses purpose.
(a) I went to the post office because I wanted to mail a letter. (b) I went to the post office **in order to mail** a letter. (c) I went to the post office **to mail** a letter.	*In order to* answers the question "Why?"
	In (c): *in order* is frequently omitted. (a), (b) and (c) have the same meaning.

EXERCISE 16: Add *in order* to the sentences whenever possible.

1. I went to the bank to cash a check.
   I went to the bank in order to cash a check.

2. I'd like to see that movie.
   (No change. The infinitive does not express purpose.)

3. Sam went to the hospital to visit a friend.
4. I need to go to the bank today.
5. I need to go to the bank today to deposit my pay check.
6. On my way home from school, I stopped at the drug store to buy some shampoo.
7. Carmen looked in her dictionary to find the correct spelling of a word.
8. Masako went to the cafeteria to eat lunch.
9. Jack and Linda have decided to get married.
10. Pedro watches TV to improve his English.
11. I remembered to bring my book to class.
12. Kim wrote to the university to ask for a catalog.
13. Sally touched my shoulder to get my attention.
14. Donna expects to graduate next spring.
15. Jerry needs to go to the bookstore to buy a spiral notebook.

EXERCISE 17:   Combine the given ideas to make sentences using infinitives of purpose. Begin each of your sentences with *"Yesterday I...."*

1. go shopping
   go downtown
   Yesterday I went downtown
   (in order) to go shopping.
2. call the dentist's office
   make an appointment
   Yesterday I. . . .
3. study for a test
   go to the library
4. get rid of my headache
   take an aspirin
5. go to the laundromat
   wash my clothes
6. have to run
   get to class on time
7. go to *(name of a place)*
   eat lunch
8. make a reservation
   call the travel agency

9. ask the teacher a question
   stay after class
10. write a letter to my parents
    ask them for some money
11. listen to a baseball game
    turn on the radio
12. call (. . .)
    invite him/her to my party
13. get a cup of coffee between
      classes
    borrow some money from (. . .)
14. stand in the doorway of a store
    get out of the rain while I was
      waiting for the bus

EXERCISE 18:   Study the examples.

(a) I went to the post office **for some stamps.** (b) I went to the post office **to buy some stamps.** (c) INCORRECT: I went to the post office for to buy some stamps. (d) INCORRECT: I went to the post office for buying some stamps.	**For** is also used to express purpose, but it is a preposition and is followed by a noun phrase, as in (a).

Complete the sentences by using **to** or **for.**

1. I went to Chicago ___for___ a visit.

2. I went to Chicago ___to___ visit my aunt and uncle.

3. I take long walks _____ relax.

4. I take long walks _____ relaxation.

5. I'm going to school _____ a good education.

6. I'm going to school _____ get a good education.

7. I'm not going to school just _____ have fun.

8. I'm not going to school just _____ fun.

9. I went to the store _____ some bread and milk.

10. I went to the store _____ get some bread and milk.

11. I turned on the radio _____ listen to the news.

12. I listened to the radio _____ news about the earthquake in Peru.

13. We wear coats in the winter _____ keep warm.

14. We wear coats in the winter _____ warmth.

EXERCISE 19—ORAL (BOOKS CLOSED):   Answer the questions in your own words. Show purpose by using an infinitive phrase or a "**for** phrase."

Example: Yesterday you turned on the TV. Why?
Response: Yesterday I turned on the TV (to listen to the news, for the latest news about the earthquake, etc.).

1. You went to the supermarket. Why?
2. You need to go to the bookstore. Why?
3. You went to the post office. Why?
4. You have to go to the library. Why?
5. You went to the health clinic. Why?
6. You reached into my pocket/purse. Why?
7. You came to this school? Why?
8. You borrowed some money from (. . .) Why?
9. You stopped at the service station. Why?
10. You play (*soccer, tennis, etc.*). Why?
11. You had to go out last night. Why?
12. You're going to go to (*Chicago*). Why?

7-9 USING INFINITIVES WITH *TOO* AND *ENOUGH*

	TOO + ADJECTIVE + (**FOR** SOMEONE) + INFINITIVE			Infinitives often follow expressions with **too**.
(a)	A piano is	**too heavy**		**to lift.**
(B)	That box is	**too heavy**	for me	**to lift.**
(c)	That box is	**too heavy**	for Bob	**to lift.**

Too comes in front of an adjective.

	ENOUGH + NOUN + INFINITIVE		
(d)	I don't have	**enough money**	**to buy** that car.
(e)	Did you have	**enough time**	**to finish** the test?

In the speaker's mind, the use of **too** implies a negative result. COMPARE:
> *The box is too heavy. I can't lift it.*
> *The box is very heavy, but I can lift it.*

	ADJECTIVE + **ENOUGH** + INFINITIVE		
(f)	Jimmy isn't	**old enough**	**to go** to school.
(g)	Are you	**hungry enough**	**to eat** three sandwiches?

Infinitives often follow expressions with **enough**.
Enough comes in front of a noun.*
Enough follows an adjective.

*__Enough__ can also follow a noun: *I don't have* **money enough** *to buy that car.*
In everyday English, **enough** usually comes in front of a noun.

EXERCISE 20:   Make sentences by putting the following in the correct order.

1. *time/to go to the park tomorrow/I don't have/enough*

   <u>I don't have enough time to go to the park tomorrow.</u>

2. *to touch the ceiling/too/I'm/short*

   _____

3. *to pay his bills/money/Tom doesn't have/enough*

   _____

4. *for me/this tea is/hot/to drink/too*

   _____

5. *to eat breakfast this morning/time/I didn't have/enough*

   _____

6. *enough/to stay home alone/old/Susie isn't*

   _____

7. *too/to stay home alone/young/Susie is*

   _____

8. *late/to go to the movie/for us/too/it's*

   _____

EXERCISE 21:   Make sentences by putting the following in the correct order.

1. *to finish/too/last night/I was/my homework/sleepy*

   <u>I was too sleepy to finish my homework last night.*</u>

2. *yesterday/time/downtown/I didn't have/to go/enough*

   _____

3. *to wear/for me/small/this jacket is/too*

   _____

4. *for us/cold/it's/today/too/to go swimming*

   _____

_____

*Time expressions such as **last night, yesterday, today** have three possible positions:

   Last night I was too sleepy to finish my homework.
   I was too sleepy **last night** to finish my homework.
   I was too sleepy to finish my homework **last night.**

5. *enough/a horse/I'm not/to lift/strong*

_____

6. *homework/our teacher never gives us/to do/enough*

_____

7. *busy/to the beach/too/last weekend/to go/Jack was*

_____

8. *to walk/I live/to class/far from school/too*

_____

9. *our homework/time/last night/our teacher didn't have/to correct/enough*

_____

10. *to the zoo/yesterday/tired/to go/too/I was*

_____

EXERCISE 22:   Complete the following sentences. *Use infinitives* in the completions.

1. The weather is too cold _____

2. Timmy is two years old. He's too young _____

3. Timmy isn't old enough _____

4. That suitcase is too heavy _____

5. Ann isn't strong enough _____

6. Last night I was too tired _____

7. Yesterday I was too busy _____

8. A Mercedes-Benz is too expensive _____

9. I don't have enough money _____

10. Yesterday I didn't have enough time _____

11. A teenager is old enough _____

12. This coffee is too hot _____

13. I know enough English _____

14. The test was too long _____

15. I'm too short _____

16. I'm not tall enough _____

EXERCISE 23—ERROR ANALYSIS: All of the following sentences contain mistakes. Find and correct the mistakes.

1. Do you enjoy to go to the zoo?
   (Correction: Do you enjoy going to the zoo?)
2. I went to the drug store for getting some toothpaste.
3. Did you go to shopping yesterday?
4. I usually go to the cafeteria for to get a cup of coffee in the morning.
5. Bob needed to went downtown yesterday.
6. We yesterday to the zoo went.
7. I want go to the beach tomorrow morning.
8. Is difficult to learn a second language.
9. It is important getting an education.
10. Timmy isn't enough old to get married.
11. Do you want go to swimming tomorrow?
12. I went to the bank for cashing a check.
13. I was to sleepy to finish my homework last night.
14. Is easy this exercise to do.
15. Last night too tired no do my homework.
16. Go to the zoo fun.

EXERCISE 24—WRITTEN: Write about your spare-time activities.

Think of several spare-time activities that you enjoy. What do you do? Where? When? Why? Mention some interesting experiences.

EXERCISE 25—PREPOSITIONS: Complete the sentences with prepositions. (See Appendix 4 for a list of preposition combinations.)

1. I apologized _____ Ann _____ stepping on her toe.

2. I thanked Sam _____ helping me fix my car.

3. My grandfather doesn't approve _____ gambling.

4. Please forgive me _____ forgetting your birthday.

5. My friend insisted _____ taking me to the airport.

6. Please excuse me _____ being late.

7. Children depend _____ their parents for love and support.

8. In my composition, I compared this city _____ my hometown.

9. Umbrellas protect people _____ rain.

10. We're relying _____ Jason to help us move into our new apartment.

chapter 8

Using Auxiliary Verbs; Using Two-Word Verbs

8-1 USING AUXILIARY VERBS AFTER *BUT* AND *AND*

(a) I **don't like** coffee, **but** my husband **does**. (b) I **like** tea, **but** my husband **doesn't**. (c) Mary **won't be** here tomorrow, **but** Alice **will**. (d) I**'ve** already **seen** that movie, **but** John **hasn't**. (e) He **isn't** here, **but** she **is**.*	After **but** and **and**, often a main verb is not repeated. Instead, only an auxiliary verb is used. The auxiliary is a substitute for the main verb phrase. The auxiliary after **but** and **and** has the same tense or modal as the main verb.
(f) I **don't like** coffee, **and** Bob **doesn't** either. (g) I **like** tea, **and** Mary **does** too. (h) Mary **won't be** here tomorrow, **and** John **won't** either. (i) I**'ve** already **seen** that movie, **and** Linda **has** too. (j) He **isn't** here, **and** Ann **isn't** either.	In (a): *. . . but my husband does = . . . but my husband likes coffee.* The auxiliary *does* (simple present) is the substitute for the main verb phrase (simple present).
	Notice in the examples: *negative* + **but** + *affirmative* *affirmative* + **but** + *negative* *negative* + **and** + *negative* *affirmative* + **and** + *affirmative*

*A verb is not contracted with a pronoun at the end of a sentence after **but** and **and**:

    CORRECT: *. . . but she is.*
    INCORRECT: *. . . but she's.*

EXERCISE 1:   Practice using auxiliary verbs after **but** and **and**.

1. Tom didn't study for the test, but Mary _____did_____ .

2. Alice doesn't come to class every day, but Julie _____ .

3. Jack went to the movie last night, but I _____ .

4. I don't live in the dorm, but Fred and Jim _____ .

5. Fred lives in the dorm, and Jim _____ too.

6. I don't live in the dorm, and Carol _____ either.

7. Jack went to the movie last night, and Greg _____ too.

8. My roommate was at home last night, but I _____ .

9. Ted isn't here today, but Alex _____ .

10. Ted isn't here today, and Linda _____ either.

11. The teacher was on time, and the students _____ too.

12. The teacher is listening to the tape, and the students _____ too.

13. Susan won't be at the meeting tonight, but I _____ .

14. Susan isn't going to go to the meeting tonight, but I _____ .

15. I'll be there, but she _____ .

16. I'll be there, and Tom _____ too.

17. I can speak French, and my wife _____ too.

18. I can speak French, but Al _____ .

19. I should study harder, and you _____ too.

20. I shouldn't smoke, and you _____ either.

21. I haven't finished my work yet, but Ann _____ .

22. I haven't finished my work yet, and Sally _____ either.

23. I didn't finish my work last night, but Ann _____ .

24. Tom has already written his composition, but Alex _____ .

25. Jane would like a cup of coffee, and I _____ too.

EXERCISE 2: Study the examples.

(a) I **haven't finished** studying yet, but Tom **has**.	In (a): **Have** is used as an auxiliary verb. The auxiliary after **but** is **has** because the main verb (**finish**) is present perfect.
(b) I **have** a car, but Dick **doesn't**.	In (b): **Have** is used as a main verb. The auxiliary after **but** is **does** because the main verb (**have**) is simple present.
(c) I **have to study** tonight, but Mary **doesn't**.	In (c): When **have to** is the auxiliary used with the main verb, a form of **do** is used after **but**.

Practice using auxiliary verbs after **but** and **and**.

1. I have a bicycle, but my sister _____ .

2. I have read that book, but my sister _____ .

3. I have to go to the library this evening, but my sister

   _____ .

4. I have to go to the library this evening, and my roommate

   _____ too.

5. I had to go to the libary last night, and my roommate _____
   too.

6. I had a good time at the party last Saturday, but my date

   _____ .

7. Bob has met my parents, but Tom _____ .

8. Janice had a lot of problems in high school, but her brother

   _____ .

9. You don't have to come to the meeting, but Alice _____ .

10. Ann didn't have to go to work yesterday, and Jack _____
    either.

11. Ann has a good job, and Jack _____ too.

12. Ann has worked for that company for a long time, and Jack

    _____ too.

EXERCISE 3:   Complete the sentences by using the names of your classmates and appropriate auxiliary verbs.

1. _____(Kunio)_____ has a mustache, but _____(Kutaiba) doesn't._____

2. _____(Maria)_____ doesn't have brown eyes, but _____(Yu-Tsu) does._____

3. _____ isn't in class today, but _____

4. _____ is here today, but _____

5. _____ can speak Spanish, but _____

6. _____ can't speak Arabic, but _____

7. _____ stayed home last night, but _____

8. _____ didn't come to class yesterday, but _____

9. _____ will be at home tonight, but _____

10. _____ won't be at the party tonight, but _____

11. _____ isn't wearing jeans today, but _____

12. _____ has long hair, but _____

13. _____ has met my brother, but _____

14. _____ lives in an apartment, but _____

15. _____ has curly hair, but _____

16. _____ doesn't have a car, but _____

17. _____ needs to go to the post office today, but _____

_____

18. _____ went to the post office yesterday, but _____

_____

EXERCISE 4:   Complete the sentences by using the names of your classmates. Add ***too*** (if the auxiliary verb is affirmative) or ***either*** (if the auxiliary verb is negative) to the end of the sentences.

1. _____(Carlos)_____ has a pen with blue ink, and _____(Yoko) does too._____

2. _____(Ali)_____ doesn't speak Chinese, and _____(Roberto) doesn't either._____

3. _____ isn't married, and _____

4. _____ sits in the same seat every day, and _____

5. _____ is wearing jeans today, and _____

6. _____ walked to class today, and _____

7. _____ was in class yesterday, and _____

8. _____ didn't call me last night, and _____

9. _____ isn't hungry right now, and _____

10. _____ comes to class every day, and _____

11. _____ has brown eyes, and _____

12. _____ has been here for over a month, and _____

    _____

13. _____ doesn't have a beard, and _____

14. _____ can't speak Arabic, and _____

15. _____ will be in class tomorrow, and _____

8-2   USING *AND* + *TOO, SO, EITHER, NEITHER*

| AND . . . TOO

AND SO . . . | (a) Sue likes milk,

  AND + S + *aux* + **TOO**
  ⌐and⌐ ⌐Tom⌐ ⌐does⌐ ⌐too.⌐

(b) Sue likes milk,

  AND + **SO** + *aux* + S
  ⌐and⌐ ⌐so⌐ ⌐does⌐ ⌐Tom.⌐ | (a) and (b) have the same meaning.
Notice in (b): After **and so** . . . , the auxiliary verb (*aux*) comes before the subject (S). |
| AND . . . EITHER

AND NEITHER . . . | (a) Mary doesn't like milk,

  AND + S + *aux* + **EITHER**
  ⌐and⌐ ⌐John⌐ ⌐doesn't⌐ ⌐either.⌐

(d) Mary doesn't like milk,

  AND + **NEITHER** + *aux* + S
  ⌐and⌐ ⌐neither⌐ ⌐does⌐ ⌐John.⌐ | (c) and (d) have the same meaning.
Notice in (d): After **and neither** . . . , the auxiliary verb comes before the subject.
Notice:
In (c): a negative auxiliary verb is used with **and . . . either**.
In (d): an affirmative auxiliary verb is used with **and neither** . . . . |

(e)	A: I'm hungry. B: **I am too.**	(f) A: I'm hungry. B: **So am I.**	**And** is usually not used when there are two speakers.
(g)	A: I don't like hot dogs. B: **I don't either.**	(h) A: I don't like hot dogs. B: **Neither do I.**	(e) and (f) have the same meaning. (g) and (h) have the same meaning.
(i)	A: I'm hungry. B: **Me too.** (*informal*)		**Me too** and **me neither** are often used in informal spoken English.
(j)	A: I don't like hot dogs. B: **Me neither.** (*informal*)		

EXERCISE 5: Complete the sentences by using the word in parentheses and an appropriate auxiliary.

1. (*Tom*)   Jack has a mustache, and so _____does Tom_____ .

   Jack has a mustache, and _____Tom does_____ too.

2. (*Fred*)   Alex doesn't have a mustache, and neither _____

   _____ .

   Alex doesn't have a mustache, and _____ either.

3. (*I*)   Mary was at home last night, and so _____ .

   Mary was at home last night, and _____ too.

4. (*Oregon*)   California is on the West Coast, and so _____

   _____ .

   California is on the West Coast, and _____ too.

5. (*Jean*)   I went to a movie last night, and so _____ .

   I went to a movie last night, and _____ too.

6. (*Jason*)   I didn't study last night, and neither _____ .

   I didn't study last night, and _____ either.

7. (*Dick*)   Jim can't speak Arabic, and neither _____ .

Jim can't speak Arabic, and _____ either.

8. (*Laura*)   I like to go to science fiction movies, and so _____

_____ .

I like to go to science fiction movies, and _____

_____ too.

9. (*Alice*)   I don't like horror movies, and neither _____

_____ .

I don't like horror movies, and _____
either.

10. (*porpoises*)   Whales are mammals, and so _____ .

WHALE   PORPOISE

Whales are mammals, and _____ too.

11. (*I*)   Karen hasn't seen that movie yet, and neither _____

_____ .

Karen hasn't seen that movie yet, and _____
either.

12. (*my brother*)   I have a car, and so _____ .

I have a car, and _____ too.

13. (*Mary*)   Bob won't be at the party, and neither _____

_____ .

Bob won't be at the party, and _____
either.

EXERCISE 6:   Complete the sentences by using the names of your classmates and appropriate auxiliaries.

1. _____(Maria)_____ wasn't in class yesterday, and neither ___was (Jin Won).___

2. _____ is wearing slacks today, and so _____

3. _____ lives in an apartment, and so _____

4. _____ can't speak Chinese, and neither _____

5. _____ stayed home and studied last night, and so _____

_____

6. _____ has curly hair, and so _____

7. _____ doesn't have a mustache, and neither _____

_____

8. _____ will be in class tomorrow, and so _____

9. _____ has already eaten breakfast/lunch, and so _____

_____

10. _____ didn't take the bus to school today, and neither

_____

11. _____ has to go downtown today, and so _____

12. _____ isn't married, and neither _____

13. _____ has dimples, and so _____

14. _____ isn't wearing a hat, and neither _____

EXERCISE 7: Complete the dialogues by agreeing with Speaker A's idea. Use **so** or **neither**. Use **I**.

1. A: I'm tired.

   B: _____So am I._____

2. A: I didn't enjoy the movie last night.

   B: _____Neither did I._____

3. A: I've never been in France.

   B: _____Neither have I.*_____

4. A: I always have a cup of coffee in the morning.

   B: _____

———————————

*Never makes a sentence negative.

5. A: I don't feel like going to class today.

    B: _____

6. A: I've never been in Brazil.

    B: _____

7. A: I need to go to the bank today.

    B: _____

8. A: I studied last night.

    B: _____

9. A: I can't go to Tom's party tomorrow night.

    B: _____

10. A: I should stay home and study tonight.

    B: _____

11. A: I have a roommate.

    B: _____

12. A: I've never visited Vancouver, British Columbia.

    B: _____

13. A: I don't have a car.

    B: _____

14. A: I have to go downtown this afternoon.

    B: _____

15. A: I watched TV last night.

    B: _____

EXERCISE 8: Complete the dialogues by agreeing with Speaker A's idea. Use **so** or **neither**. Use **I**.

1. A: I'm thirsty.

    B: _____

2. A: I did my homework last night.

    B: _____

3. A: I don't like sour oranges.

B: _____

4. A: I'm not married.

B: _____

5. A: I won't be in class tomorrow.

B: _____

6. A: I had a good night's sleep last night.

B: _____

7. A: I've been here for over six weeks.

B: _____

8. A: I have a digital watch.

B: _____

9. A: I'd like to go to the art museum.

B: _____

10. A: I like to go to museums.

B: _____

11. A: I wasn't at home last night.

B: _____

12. A: I didn't eat breakfast this morning.

B: _____

13. A: I'm hungry.

B: _____

14. A: I've never met Robert Smith.

B: _____

15. A: I can't speak German.

B: _____

A: But I can speak English.

B: _____

EXERCISE 9—ORAL (BOOKS CLOSED): Respond to the statements by using *so* or *neither*.

Example: Los Angeles is in California.
Response: So is (San Francisco).

1. (. . .) speaks (*language*).
2. (. . .) doesn't speak (*language*).
3. (. . .) has curly hair.
4. (. . .) doesn't have curly hair.
5. (. . .) is wearing (*clothing*) today.
6. (. . .) isn't wearing (*clothing*) today.
7. (. . .) came to class yesterday.
8. (. . .) has been in (*this city*) for (*time*).
9. I didn't go to a restaurant for dinner last night.
10. (. . .) can't speak (*language*).
11. (*A certain city*) is in (*this state/province*).
12. The United States is in North America.
13. (*A certain country*) is in (*Asia, Europe, Latin America, etc.*)
14. Texas is a big state.
15. Mercury is a planet.
16. A bicycle has two wheels.
17. Snakes don't have legs.
18. Chickens lay eggs.
19. Copper is a metal.
20. Soccer is a popular sport.
21. Boxing is a dangerous sport.
22. Paper burns.
23. The sun is a source of energy.
24. Pencils aren't expensive.
25. Airplanes have wings.
26. Niagara Falls is a famous landmark in North America.
27. Bananas are yellow.
28. Coffee contains caffeine.

8-3 USING AUXILIARY VERBS: TAG QUESTIONS

	AFFIRMATIVE	NEGATIVE	A tag question is a question that is added onto the end of a sentence. An auxiliary verb is used in a tag question.
(a)	**You know** Bob Wilson,	**don't you?**	
(b)	**Mary is** from Chicago,	**isn't she?**	In (a), (b), and (c): When the main verb is affirmative, the tag question is negative.
(c)	**Jerry can play** the piano,	**can't he?**	In (c), (d), and (e): When the main verb is negative, the tag question is affirmative.
	NEGATIVE	**AFFIRMATIVE**	
(d)	**You don't know** Jack Smith,	**do you?**	
(e)	**Mary isn't** from New York,	**is she?**	
(f)	**Jerry can't speak** Arabic,	**can he?**	

Notice in the following: I (the speaker) use a tag question because I expect you (the listener) to agree with me. I give my idea while asking a question at the same time.*

THE SPEAKER'S IDEA	THE SPEAKER'S QUESTION	THE EXPECTED ANSWER
(g) I think that you know Bob Wilson.	You know Bob Wilson, don't you?	Yes, I do.
(h) I think that you don't know Jack Smith.	You don't know Jack Smith, do you?	No, I don't.
(i) I think that Mary is from Chicago.	Mary is from Chicago, isn't she?	Yes, she is.
(j) I think that Mary isn't from New York.	Mary isn't from New York, is she?	Yes, she isn't.
(k) I think that Jerry can play the piano.	Jerry can play the piano, can't he?	Yes, he can.
(l) I think that Jerry can't speak Arabic.	Jerry can't speak Arabic, can he?	No, he can't.

*Compare: *A yes/no question:*

A: Do you know Bob Wilson? (*The speaker has no idea. The speaker is simply looking for information.*)
B: Yes, I do. OR: No, I don't.

A tag question:

A: You know Bob Wilson, don't you? (*The speaker believes that you know Bob Wilson. The speaker wants to make sure that his/her idea is correct.*)
B: Yes, I do. (*The speaker expects you to answer* **yes.** *You can, however, answer* **no** *if you do not know Bob Wilson.*)

EXERCISE 10:   Add tag questions and give the expected answers.

1. A: You are a student, _____aren't you?_____

   B: _____Yes, I am._____

2. A: Barbara lives in the dorm, _____

   B: _____

3. A: You don't live in the dorm, _____

   B: _____

4. A: Ted came to class yesterday, _____

   B: _____

5. A: Alice will be in class tomorrow, _____

   B: _____

6. A: Mr. Lee is at home now, _____

   B: _____

7. A: Our teacher didn't give us a homework assignment, _____

   B: _____

8. A: You can speak Spanish, _____

   B: _____

9. A: Tom and John can't speak Arabic, _____

   B: _____

10. A: You should write a letter to your father, _____

    B: _____

11. A: It snows a lot in Minneapolis, _____

    B: _____

12. A: You weren't at home last night around nine, _____

    B: _____

13. A: You've already read this morning's paper, _____

    B: _____

14. A: Mary has a car, _____

    B: _____

15. A: You don't have to go to the library tonight, _____

    B: _____

16. A: You used to live in Los Angeles, _____

    B: _____

17. A: This is your pen,* _____

    B: _____

---

*When *this* or *that* is used in the first part of the sentence, *it* is used in the tag question: *This is your book, isn't it?*

When *these* or *those* is used in the first part of the sentence, *they* is used in the tag question: *These are your shoes, aren't they?*

18. A: That is Mary's dictionary, _____

    B: _____

19. A: Those are your gloves, _____

    B: _____

20. A: These are Jean's glasses, _____

    B: _____

21. A: This isn't a hard exercise, _____

    B: _____

22. A: That was an easy test, _____

    B: _____

EXERCISE 11—ORAL (BOOKS CLOSED): Ask and answer tag questions.

Example: You think that someone in this room lives in an apartment.

Student A: (Ali), you live in an apartment, don't you?

Student B: Yes, I do. OR: No, I don't.

Example: You think that someone in this room lives in an apartment.

Student A: (Ali), (Maria) lives in an apartment, doesn't she?

Student B: Yes, she does. OR: No, she doesn't. OR: I don't know.

You think that someone in this room . . .

1. lives in the dorm
2. doesn't live in an apartment
3. lives in an apartment
4. doesn't live in the dorm
5. was in class yesterday
6. wasn't in class yesterday
7. came to class yesterday
8. didn't come to class yesterday
9. is married
10. isn't married
11. has been married for (*a certain number of*) years
12. has a car
13. doesn't have a bicycle
14. went downtown yesterday
15. didn't go downtown yesterday
16. has a digital watch
17. arrived in (*this city*) (*a certain number of*) weeks/months ago
18. has been in (*this city*) for (*a certain length of time*)

19. can speak (*language*)
20. is from (*country*)
21. can't speak (*language*)
22. isn't from (*country*)
23. likes to play (*name of a sport*)
24. will be in class tomorrow
25. has seen (*title of a current movie*)
26. can't play (*a musical instrument*)
27. has (*a certain number of*) children

28. has been to (*a notable place in this city*)
29. has already eaten breakfast/ lunch/dinner
30. usually eats lunch at the cafeteria
31. wasn't at home last night
32. can whistle
33. knows (*name of a person*)
34. wore blue jeans to class yesterday*

8-4 TWO-WORD VERBS (SEPARABLE)

(a)	We **put off** our trip.	In (a): ***put off*** = *a two-word verb.* *A two-word verb* = a verb and a preposition which together have a special meaning. For example, ***put off*** means *postpone*.
(b) (c) (d) (e)	We **put off** *our trip.* We **put** *our trip* **off.** I **turned on** *the light.* I **turned** *the light* **on.**	Many two-word verbs are *separable.*† In other words, a <u>noun</u> can either follow or come between (separate) the verb and the preposition. (b) and (c) have the same meaning. (d) and (e) have the same meaning.
(f) (g)	We **put** *it* **off.** I **turned** *it* **on.**	If a two-word verb is *separable*, a <u>pronoun</u> always comes between the verb and the preposition; a pronoun never follows the preposition. INCORRECT: We put off it. INCORRECT: I turned on it.

†Some two-word verbs are *nonseparable.* Chart 8–5 will discuss *nonseparable* two-word verbs. See Appendix 4 for a list of two-word verbs.

---

*To the teacher: As an extension of this exercise, ask the students to make sentences about their classmates which begin with "I think that . . . ," and then to change that supposition to a sentence with a tag question.

Example: Complete this sentence: I think (that) Juan . . . .
Student A: I think (that) Juan is from Venezuela.
Teacher: Ask Juan if your information is correct.
Student A: You are from Venezuela, aren't you?
Student B: Yes, I am. OR: No, I'm not.

SOME COMMON TWO-WORD VERBS (SEPARABLE)

figure out ......*find the solution to a problem*
hand in.........*give homework, test papers, etc. to a teacher*
hand out ....*give something to this person, then that person, then another person, etc.*
look up.........*look for information in a dictionary, a telephone directory, an encyclopedia, etc.*
make up........*invent a story*
pick up........*lift*
put down ....*stop holding or carrying*
put off ....*postpone*
put on ....*put clothes on one's body*
take off ....*remove clothes from one's body*
throw away
throw out } ...*put in the trash, discard*
turn off ....*stop a machine or a light*
turn on ....*start a machine or a light*
wake up ....*stop sleeping*
write down .....*write a note on a piece of paper*

EXERCISE 12:   Complete the sentences with the following prepositions: *away, down, in, off, on, out, up*.*

1. Before I left home this morning, I put _____ my coat.

2. When I got to class this morning, I took my coat _____ .

3. The students handed their homework _____ .

4. Johnny made a story _____ . He didn't tell the truth.

5. The weather was bad, so we put _____ the picnic until next week.

6. Alice looked a word _____ in her dictionary.

7. Alice wrote the definition _____ .

8. My roommate is messy. He never picks _____ his clothes.

9. The teacher handed the test papers _____ at the beginning of the class period.

10. A strange noise woke _____ the children in the middle of the night.

---

*To the teacher: Discuss alternate positions for the prepositions. In discussing the meaning of the two-word verbs, put the two-word verbs into other contexts (e.g., What did you put on before you left home this morning?).

11. I threw _____ yesterday's newspaper.

12. When some friends came to visit, John stopped watching TV. He turned the television set _____ .

13. It was dark when I got home last night, so I turned the lights

    _____ .

14. Peggy finally figured _____ the answer to the arithmetic problem.

15. When I was walking through the airport, my arms got tired. So I put my suitcases _____ for a minute and rested.

EXERCISE 13: Complete the sentences with pronouns and prepositions.

1. A: Did you postpone your trip to Puerto Rico?

   B: Yes, we did. We put ____it off____ until next summer.

2. A: Is Pat's phone number 322-4454 or 322-5545?

   B: I don't remember. You'd better look _____ .
   The telephone directory is in the kitchen.

3. A: Is Mary still asleep?

   B: Yes. I'd better wake _____ . She has a class at nine.

4. A: Do you want to keep these newspapers?

   B: No. Throw _____ .

5. A: I'm hot. This sweater is too heavy.

   B: Why don't you take _____ ?

6. A: Is that story true?

   B: No. I made _____ .

7. A: When does the teacher want our compositions?

    B: We have to hand _____ tomorrow.

8. A: I made an appointment with Dr. Armstrong for three o'clock next Thursday.

    B: You'd better write _____ so you won't forget.

9. A: Do you know the answer to this problem?

    B: No. I can't figure _____ .

10. A: Johnny, you're too heavy for me to carry. I have to put

    _____ .

    B: Okay.

11. A: Where are the letters I put on the kitchen table?

    B: I picked _____ and took them to the post office.

12. A: How does this tape recorder work?

    B: Push this button to turn _____ , and push that button to

    turn _____ .

13. A: I have some papers for the class. Ali, would you please hand

    _____ for me?

    B: I'd be happy to.

14. A: Timmy, here's your hat. Put _____ before you go out. It's cold outside.

    B: Okay, Dad.

8-5 TWO-WORD VERBS (NONSEPARABLE)

(a) I **ran into Bob** at the bank yesterday.
 (b) I saw Bob yesterday. I **ran into him** at the bank.
	If a two-word verb is *nonseparable*, a noun or pronoun follows (never precedes) the preposition.
	    INCORRECT: I ran Bob into at the bank.
	    INCORRECT: I ran him into at the bank.

SOME COMMON TWO-WORD VERBS (NONSEPARABLE)

call on......*ask to speak in class*
get over....*recover from an illness*
run into.....*meet by chance*

get on......*enter* ⎱
get off......*leave* ⎰ *a bus, an airplane, a train, a subway, a bicycle*

get in(to) ....*enter* ⎱
get out of ....*leave* ⎰ *a car, a taxi*

EXERCISE 14—TWO-WORD VERBS: Complete the sentences with prepositions. Discuss the meaning of the two-word verbs in the sentences.

1. When I raised my hand in class, the teacher called _____ me.

2. While I was walking down the street, I ran _____ an old friend.

3. Fred feels okay today. He got _____ his cold.

4. Last week I flew from Chicago to Miami. I got _____ the

   plane in Chicago. I got _____ the plane in Miami.

5. Sally took a taxi to the airport. She got _____ the taxi in front

   of her apartment building. She got _____ the taxi at the
   airport.

6. I take the bus to school every day. I get _____ the bus at the

   corner of First Street and Sunset Boulevard. I get _____ the
   bus just a block away from the classroom building.

EXERCISE 15—ORAL (BOOKS CLOSED):   Complete the sentences.

> *Example:*   Yesterday I cleaned my closet. I found an old pair of shoes that I
> don't ever wear anymore. I didn't keep the shoes. I threw. . .
> *Response:*   . . . them away/out.

1. The teacher gave us some important information in class yesterday. I didn't want to forget it, so I wrote. . . .

2. When I raised my hand in class, the teacher called. . . .

3. I was carrying a suitcase, but it was too heavy, so I put. . . .

4. I didn't know the meaning of a word, so I looked. . . .

5. I was sleepy last night, so I didn't finish my homework. I put. . . .

6. It was dark when I got home, so I turned. . . .

7. (. . .) isn't wearing his/her hat right now. When s/he got to class, s/he took. . . .

8. My pen just fell on the floor. Could you please pick. . . ?

9. I saw (. . .) at a concert last night. I was surprised when I ran. . . .

10. When you finish using a stove, you should always be careful to turn. . . .

11. When I finished my test, I handed. . . .

12. Is (. . .) sleeping?! Would you please wake. . . ?

13. What's the answer to this problem? Have you figured. . . ?

14. I don't need this piece of paper anymore. I'm going to throw. . . .
15. I had the flu last week, but now I'm okay. I got. . . .
16. I told a story that wasn't true. I made. . . .
17. Name some means of transportation that you get on.
18. Name some that you get in.
19. Name some that you get off.
20. Name some that you get out of.
21. Name some things that you turn on.
22. Name some things that you turn off.

chapter 9

Passive Sentences

9-1 ACTIVE SENTENCES AND PASSIVE SENTENCES

(a)	ACTIVE:	**Bob mailed the package.**
(b)	PASSIVE:	**The package was mailed by Bob.**
(c)	ACTIVE:	**The teacher corrects our homework.**
(d)	PASSIVE:	**Our homework is corrected by the teacher.**
(e)	ACTIVE:	**Mr. Lee has taught this class.**
(f)	PASSIVE:	**This class has been taught by Mr. Lee.**
(g)	ACTIVE:	**Bob will mail the package.**
(h)	PASSIVE:	**The package will be mailed by Bob.**

(a) and (b)
(c) and (d)
(e) and (f)
(g) and (h) } have the same meaning.

Notice: The object of an active sentence becomes the subject of a passive sentence:

$$\begin{array}{ccc} S & V & O \\ \lceil Bob \rceil & \lceil mailed \rceil & \lceil \textbf{the package.} \rceil \end{array}$$

$$\begin{array}{ccc} S & V & \textit{"by phrase"} \\ \lceil \textbf{The package} \rceil & \lceil was\ mailed \rceil & \lceil by\ Bob. \rceil \end{array}$$

Notice: The subject of an active sentence becomes part of the "*by* phrase" in a passive sentence.

$$\begin{array}{ccc} S & V & O \\ \lceil \textbf{Bob} \rceil & \lceil mailed \rceil & \lceil the\ package. \rceil \end{array}$$

$$\begin{array}{ccc} S & V & \textit{"by phrase"} \\ \lceil The\ package \rceil & \lceil was\ mailed \rceil & \lceil \textbf{by Bob.} \rceil \end{array}$$

9-2   FORMING PASSIVE VERBS

To make a verb passive, use a form of **be** (e.g., *am, is, are, was, were, has been, have been, will be, to be*) and the past participle (e.g., *mailed, corrected, taught, surprised*).

TENSE	ACTIVE		PASSIVE $\left(BE + \begin{array}{c} PAST \\ PARTICIPLE \end{array} \right)$		
SIMPLE PRESENT	The news	**surprises** me.	I	**am surprised**	by the news.
	The news	**surprises** Sam.	Sam	**is surprised**	by the news.
	The news	**surprises** us.	We	**are surprised**	by the news.
SIMPLE PAST	The news	**surprised** me.	I	**was surprised**	by the news.
	The news	**surprised** us.	We	**were surprised**	by the news.
PRESENT PERFECT	Bob	**has mailed** the letter.	The letter	**has been mailed**	by Bob.
	Bob	**has mailed** the letters.	The letters	**have been mailed**	by Bob.
FUTURE	Bob	**will mail** the letter.	The letter	**will be mailed**	by Bob.
	Bob	**is going to mail** the letter.	The letter	**is going to be mailed**	by Bob.

EXERCISE 1:   Change the active verbs to passive verbs. Write the subject of the passive sentence.

1. SIMPLE PRESENT

   (a) The teacher *helps* **me**.　　　　(a) ____I____ __am helped__ by the teacher.

   (b) The teacher *helps* **John**.　　　(b) _____ _____ by the teacher.

   (c) The teacher *helps* **us**.　　　　(c) _____ _____ by the teacher.

2. SIMPLE PAST

   (a) The teacher *helped* **me**.　　　(a) _____ _____ by the teacher.

   (b) The teacher *helped* **them**.　　(b) _____ _____ by the teacher.

3. PRESENT PERFECT

   (a) The teacher *has helped* **Mary**.　(a) _____ _____ by the teacher.

   (b) The teacher *has helped* **us**.　　(b) _____ _____ by the teacher.

4. FUTURE

   (a) The teacher *will help* **me**.　　　(a) _____ _____ by the teacher.

   (b) The teacher *is going to help* **me**.   (b) _____ _____ by the teacher.

(c) The teacher *will help* **Bob**.   (c) _____ _____ by the teacher.

(d) The teacher *is going to help* **Bob**.   (d) _____ _____ by the teacher.

EXERCISE 2: Change the verbs to the passive. Do not change the tense.

		BE	+	PAST PARTICIPLE	
1. Bob *mailed* the package.	The package	was	+	mailed	by Bob.
2. Mr. Catt *delivers* our mail.	Our mail	_____		_____	by Mr. Catt.
3. The children *have eaten* the cake.	The cake	_____		_____	by the children.
4. Linda *wrote* that letter.	That letter	_____		_____	by Linda.
5. The jeweler *is going to fix* my watch.	My watch	_____		_____	by the jeweler.
6. Ms. Bond *will teach* our class tomorrow.	Our class	_____		_____	by Ms. Bond tomorrow.
7. That company *employs* many people.	Many people	_____		_____	by that company.
8. That company *has hired* Sue.	Sue	_____		_____	by that company.
9. The secretary *is going to type* the letters.	The letters	_____		_____	by the secretary.
10. A high school student *bought* my old car.	My old car	_____		_____	by a high school student.
11. Mr. Adams *will do* the work.	The work	_____		_____	by Mr. Adams.
12. The janitor *washed* the windows.	The windows	_____		_____	by the janitor.

EXERCISE 3:   Change the sentences from active to passive.

1. Columbus discovered the New World.

    The New World was discovered by Columbus.

2. Thomas Edison invented the phonograph.

3. Water surrounds an island.

4. A maid will clean our hotel room.

5. A plumber is going to fix the leaky faucet.

6. A doctor has examined the sick child.

7. The police arrested James Swan.

8. A large number of people speak Spanish.

9. The secretary is going to type the letter.

10. The teacher's explanation confused Carlos.

11. My mistake embarrassed me.

12. Helicopters fascinate children.

13. Shakespeare wrote *Hamlet.* *

_____

14. This news will amaze you.

_____

EXERCISE 4:   Change the active sentences to passive sentences that have the same meaning and tense.

	ACTIVE	PASSIVE	
1. (a)	The news surprised John.	John was surprised	by the news.
(b)	The news didn't surprise me.	I wasn't surprised	by the news.
(c)	Did the news surprise you?	Were you surprised	by the news?
2. (a)	The news surprises Henry.	_____	by the news.
(b)	The news doesn't surprise us.	_____	by the news.
(c)	Does the news surprise you?	_____	by the news?
3. (a)	The news will shock Steve.	_____	by the news.
(b)	The news won't shock Jean.	_____	by the news.
(c)	Will the news shock Pat?	_____	by the news?
4. (a)	Mary wrote that report.	_____	by Mary.
(b)	Don didn't write it.	_____	by Don.
(c)	Did Fred write it?	_____	by Fred?
5. (a)	Bob has signed the petition.	_____	by Bob.
(b)	Paul hasn't signed it.	_____	by Paul.
(c)	Has Jim signed it yet?	_____	by Jim yet?
6. (a)	Sue is going to sign it.	_____	by Sue.

_____

*Notice that *Hamlet,* the title of a play, is printed in italics. In handwritten or typed sentences, the title of a book or a play is underlined.

    Printed: Tolstoy Wrote *War and Peace.*
Handwritten: *Tolstoy wrote War and Peace.*
    Typed: Tolstoy wrote War and Peace.

PETITION

We, the undersigned, believe that the house at 3205 Tree Street is an historic building. We believe that it should not be destroyed in order to build a fast-food restaurant at that location.

Robert E. Miller _____   *Wm. H. Brock* _____

Elizabeth J. Wilson _____   *Ms. Catherine Ann Jackson* _____

James Walsh _____   *An Binh Nguyen* _____

Alicia Alvarez _____   _____

(b) John isn't going to sign it.   _____ by John.

(c) Is Carol going to sign it?   _____ by Carol?

EXERCISE 5:   Change the sentences from active to passive.

1. A thief stole Ann's purse.

   _____ Ann's purse was stolen by a thief. _____

2. Did a cat kill the bird?

   _____

3. My cat didn't kill the bird.

   _____

4. A squirrel didn't bite the jogger.

   _____

5. A dog bit the jogger.

   _____

6. Do a large number of people speak English?

_____

7. Did Johnny break the window?

_____

8. Is the janitor going to fix the window?

_____

9. More than 100 people have signed the petition.

_____

10. Did Shakespeare write *A Midsummer Night's Dream?*

_____

11. Ernest Hemingway didn't write *A Midsummer Night's Dream.*

_____

12. Will a maid clean our hotel room?

_____

13. Does the hotel provide clean towels?

_____

14. Sometimes my inability to understand spoken English frustrates me.

_____

EXERCISE 6:   Study the examples.

TRANSITIVE VERBS
  ACTIVE: Bob mailed the letter.
  PASSIVE: The letter was mailed by Bob.
 	
INTRANSITIVE VERBS
  ACTIVE: An accident happened.
  PASSIVE: (*not possible*)
	A transitive verb is a verb that is followed by an object. Examples:
	  S **V** **O**
	  Bob mailed the letter.
	  Mr. Lee signed the check.
	  A cat killed the bird.

	An intransitive verb is a verb that is not followed by an object. Examples:
	  S **V**
	  An accident happened.
	  John came to my party.
	  I slept well last night.

	An intransitive verb cannot be used in the passive. Only transitive verbs can be used in the passive.

Change the sentences to the passive if possible.

1. Jack walked to school yesterday. _____(no change is possible)_____

2. We stayed in a hotel. _____

3. Susie broke the window. _____

4. The leaves fell to the ground. _____

5. I slept at my friend's house last night. _____

6. The second baseman caught the ball. _____

7. Ann's cat died last week. _____

8. That book belongs to me. _____

9. The airplane arrived twenty minutes late. _____

10. The teacher announced a quiz. _____

11. I agree with George. _____

12. Do you agree with me? _____

13. Dick went to the doctor's office. _____

14. An accident happened at the corner of Third and Main. _____

15. An accident occurred at the corner of Third and Main. _____

16. Many people saw the accident. _____

9-3 USING THE "*BY* PHRASE"

(a) This sweater **was made** *by my aunt.*	The "*by* phrase" is used in passive sentences when it is important to know who performs an action. In (a): *by my aunt* is important information.
(b) That sweater **was made** in Korea. (*by someone*) (c) Spanish **is spoken** in Colombia. (*by people*) (d) That house **was built** in 1940. (*by someone*) (e) Rice **is grown** in many countries. (*by people*)	Usually there is no "*by* phrase" in a passive sentence. The "*by* phrase" is not used when it is not known or not important to know exactly who performs an action. In (b): The exact person (or people) who made the sweater is not known and is not important to know, so there is no "*by* phrase" in the passive sentence.

EXERCISE 7: Change the sentence from active to passive. Include the "**by** phrase" only if necessary.

1. Bob Smith built that house.

    That house was built by Bob Smith.

2. Someone built this house in 1904.

    This house was built in 1904. (*by someone = unnecessary*)

3. People grow rice in India.

    _____

4. People speak Spanish in Venezuela.

    _____

5. Do people speak Spanish in Peru?

    _____

6. Alexander Graham Bell invented the telephone.

    _____

7. When did someone invent the wheel?

    _____

8. People sell hammers at a hardware store.

    _____

9. People use hammers to pound nails.

    _____

10. The president has cancelled the meeting.

    _____

11. Someone has cancelled the soccer game.

    _____

12. Someone will list my name in the new telephone directory.

    _____

13. Charles Darwin wrote *The Origin of Species*.

    _____

14. Someone published *The Origin of Species* in 1859.

    _____

15. Someone serves beer and wine at that restaurant

    _____

16. Has anyone ever hypnotized you?

_____

17. Something confused me in class yesterday.

_____

18. Something embarrassed me yesterday.

_____

19. Someone filmed many of the Tarzan movies in the rain forest in Puerto Rico.

_____

20. Someone has changed the name of this street from Bay Avenue to Martin Luther King Way.

_____

EXERCISE 8—ORAL: Change the sentences from active to passive. Include the "**by** phrase" only if it contains important information.

>   *Example:*   Someone has invited us to a party.
>   *Response:*   We have been invited to a party.

Example: No one has invited John to the party.
Response: John hasn't been invited to the party.

1. Someone established the Red Cross in 1864.
2. When did someone establish this school?
3. Someone collects the garbage on Thursdays.
4. No one will collect the garbage tomorrow.
5. People spell "writing" with one "t."
6. People don't spell "writing" with two "t's."
7. People spell "written" with two "t's."
8. Someone is going to build a new hospital next year.
9. When did someone build the Suez Canal?
10. Jack wrote that composition.
11. The University of Minnesota has accepted me.
12. People don't teach calculus in elementary school.
13. People held the 1984 Summer Olympics in Los Angeles.
14. No one delivers the mail on holidays.
15. Will someone deliver the mail tomorrow?
16. Someone made my tape recorder in Japan.
17. Where did someone make your tape recorder?
18. My grandfather made that table.
19. No one has ever hypnotized me.
20. Did my directions confuse you?

EXERCISE 9: Complete the sentences with the correct form of the verb (active or passive) in parentheses.

1. Yesterday our teacher *(arrive)* _____arrived_____ five minutes late.

2. The morning paper *(read)*_____ by over 200,000 people every day.

3. Last night my favorite TV program *(interrupt)* _____ by a special news bulletin.

4. That's not my coat. It *(belong)* _____ to Louise.

5. Our mail *(deliver)* _____ before noon every day.

6. The "b" in "comb" *(pronounce, not)* _____ . It is silent.

7. A bad accident *(happen)* _____ on Highway 95 last night around midnight.

8. When I *(arrive)* _____ at the airport yesterday, I *(meet)* _____ by my cousin and a couple of her friends.

9. Yesterday I *(hear)* _____ about Margaret's divorce. I *(surprise)* _____ by the news. Janice *(shock)* _____

10. A new house *(build)* _____ next to ours next year.

11. Roberto *(write)* _____ this composition last week. That one *(write)* _____ by Abdullah.

12. Radium *(discover)* _____ by Marie and Pierre Curie in 1898.

13. A: Do you understand the explanation in the book?

    B: No, I don't. I *(confuse)* _____ by it.

14. A: Where are you going to go to school next year?

    B: I *(accept)* _____ by Shoreline Community College.

15. A: I think football is too violent.

    B: I *(agree)* _____ with you. I *(prefer)* _____ baseball.

16. A: When *(your bike, steal)* _____ ?

    B: Two days ago.

17. A: *(you, pay)* _____ your electric bill yet?

    B: No, I haven't, but I'd better pay it today. If I don't, my electricity *(shut off)* _____ by the power company.

18. A: Did you hear about the accident?

    B: No. What *(happen)* _____ ?

    A: A bicyclist *(hit)* _____ by a taxi in front of the dorm.

    B: *(the bicyclist, injure)* _____ ?

    A: Yes. Someone *(call)* _____ an ambulance. The bicyclist *(take)* _____ to City Hospital and *(treat)* _____ in the emergency ward for cuts and bruises.

    B: What *(happen)* _____ to the taxi driver?

A: He *(arrest)* _____ for reckless driving.

He's lucky that the bicyclist *(kill, not)* _____ .

EXERCISE 10:   Complete the sentences with the verbs (active or passive) in parentheses. Use any appropriate tense.

1. At the soccer game yesterday, the winning goal *(kick)* _____ by Luigi. Over 100,000 people *(attend)* _____ the soccer game.

2. The bombing of the embassy *(report)* _____ on TV last night. Fortunately, no one *(kill)* _____ in the explosion, but several people *(injure)* _____ .

3. Horses originated in North America. They *(cross)* _____ a land bridge into Asia. That land bridge *(exist, not)* _____ anymore. Before the Indians *(arrive)* _____ in North America, horses *(become)* _____ extinct there, but they *(survive)* _____ _____ in Asia. The horses were wild. They *(domesticate)** _____ by central Asian nomads. At first, horses *(use)* _____ in hunting and war. Oxen *(use)* _____ for farming. Horses *(reintroduce)* _____ into America by Europeans after the New World *(discover)* _____ .

4. The Eiffel Tower *(be)* _____ in Paris, France. It *(visit)*

_____
*People domesticate (tame) animals.

_____ by millions of people every year. It *(design)* _____

_____ by Alexandre Eiffel (1832–1923). It *(erect)* _____

_____ in 1889 for the Paris exposition. Since that time it *(be)*

_____ the most famous landmark in Paris. Today it *(recognize)*

_____ by people throughout the world.

EXERCISE 11:   Study the examples.

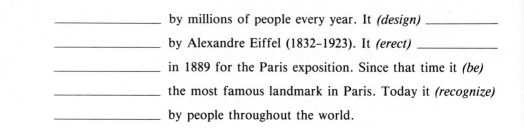

ACTIVE	PASSIVE	Passive form of the present progressive:
The secretary **is typing** some letters.	(a) Some letters **are being typed** by the secretary.	**am** ⎱ **is** ⎰ + **being** + *past participle* **are**
Someone **is building** a new hospital.	(b) A new hospital **is being built**.	
The secretary **was typing** some letters.	(c) Some letters **were being typed** by the secretary.	Passive form of the past progressive: **was** ⎱ **were** ⎰ + **being** + *past participle*
Someone **was building** a new hospital.	(d) A new hospital **was being built**.	

Change the sentences from active to passive. Include the "**by** phrase" only if it contains important information.

1. Someone is building a new house on Elm Street.

   _____

2. The Smith Construction Company is building that house.

   _____

3. Yoko is reading this sentence.

   _____

4. We can't use our classroom today because someone is painting it.

   We can't use our classroom today because _____

5. We couldn't use our classroom yesterday because someone was painting it.

   We couldn't use our classroom yesterday because _____

6. We can't use the language lab today because someone is fixing the equipment.

   We can't use the language lab today because _____

7. We couldn't use the language lab yesterday because someone was fixing the equipment.

We couldn't use the language lab yesterday because _____

8. Someone is repairing my shoes.

_____

9. Someone was repairing my shoes.

_____

10. Someone is organizing a student trip to the art museum.

_____

EXERCISE 12:   Study the examples.

ACTIVE MODAL AUXILIARIES	PASSIVE MODAL AUXILIARIES $\left(\text{MODAL} + \textbf{\textit{BE}} + \substack{\text{PAST} \\ \text{PARTICIPLE}}\right)$		
Bob **will mail** it.	It	**will be mailed**	by Bob.
Bob **can mail** it.	It	**can be mailed**	by Bob.
Bob **should mail** it.	It	**should be mailed**	by Bob.
Bob **ought to mail** it.	It	**ought to be mailed**	by Bob.
Bob **must mail** it.	It	**must be mailed.**	by Bob.
Bob **has to mail** it.	It	**has to be mailed**	by Bob.
Bob **may mail** it.	It	**may be mailed**	by Bob.
Bob **might mail** it.	It	**might be mailed**	by Bob.

Change the sentences from active to passive. Include the "**by** phrase" only if it contains important information.

1. A doctor can prescribe medicine.   Medicine can be prescribed by a doctor.

2. Someone has to send this letter by special delivery. _____ _____

_____

3. People cannot sell beer to minors. _____

_____

4. Mr. Hook must sign this report. _____

_____

5. Someone may build a new post office on First Street. _____

_____

6. For best results, people should plant tomatoes in early June. _____

_____

7. People can reach me at 555-3815. _____

_____

8. Someone has to fix our car before we drive to Chicago. _____

_____

9. Someone ought to paint that fence. _____

_____

10. Someone might cancel our English class. _____

_____

11. Someone has to pay this bill before the 19th. _____

_____

12. People cannot control the weather. _____

_____

13. People have to place stamps in the upper right-hand corner of an envelope.

_____

14. All of the students must do the assignment. _____

_____

15. People have to return income tax forms by April 15. _____

_____

9-4   SUMMARY: PASSIVE VERB FORMS

ACTIVE			PASSIVE			
Dr. Gray **helps**	Tom.	Tom		**is helped**	by Dr. Gray.	Reminder: To
Dr. Gray **is helping**	Tom.	Tom		**is being helped**	by Dr. Gray.	make a verb
Dr. Gray **has helped**	Tom.	Tom		**has been helped**	by Dr. Gray.	passive, use a
Dr. Gray **helped**	Tom.	Tom		**was helped**	by Dr. Gray.	form of **be** and
Dr. Gray **had helped**	Tom.	Tom		**had been helped**	by Dr. Gray.	the past par-
Dr. Gray **is going to help**	Tom.	Tom	**is going to be helped**		by Dr. Gray.	ticiple.

Dr. Gray **will help**	Tom.	Tom	**will be helped**	by Dr. Gray.
Dr. Gray **can help**	Tom.	Tom	**can be helped**	by Dr. Gray.
Dr. Gray **should help**	Tom.	Tom	**should be helped**	by Dr. Gray.
Dr. Gray **ought to help**	Tom.	Tom	**ought to be helped**	by Dr. Gray.
Dr. Gray **must help**	Tom.	Tom	**must be helped**	by Dr. Gray.
Dr. Gray **has to help**	Tom.	Tom	**has to be helped**	by Dr. Gray.
Dr. Gray **may help**	Tom.	Tom	**may be helped**	by Dr. Gray.
Dr. Gray **might help**	Tom.	Tom	**might be helped**	by Dr. Gray.

EXERCISE 13:   Complete the sentences with the correct form of the verbs (active or passive) in parentheses.

1. This letter *(have to mail)* _____ today.

2. Those letters *(mail)* _____ yesterday.

3. That letter *(should mail)* _____ tomorrow.

4. These letters *(be going to mail)* _____ tomorrow.

5. That letter *(ought to send)* _____ by special delivery.

6. This letter *(must send)* _____ today.

7. Those letters *(arrive)* _____ yesterday.

8. Right now some letters *(type)* _____ by the secretary.

9. When I walked into the office yesterday, some letters *(type)* _____ by the secretary.

10. The letters *(type, already)* _____ by the secretary. She *(type)*_____ them yesterday.

11. That letter is important. It *(ought to type)* _____ on letterhead stationery.

12. These letters *(can mail)* _____ at the corner. There's a mailbox there.

EXERCISE 14—ORAL (BOOKS CLOSED): Practice using passive forms.

Example: Someone will paint this room.
Response: This room will be painted.

I. *Someone . . .*
   1. should paint this room.
   2. ought to paint this room.
   3. must paint this room.
   4. will paint this room.
   5. is going to paint this room.
   6. may paint this room.
   7. is painting this room.
   8. was painting this room.
   9. has painted this room.
   10. painted this room last year.
   11. should return this book to the library.
   12. must return this book.
   13. can return this book.
   14. will return this book.
   15. is going to return this book.
   16. has to return this book.
   17. has already returned that book.
   18. returned that book yesterday.

II. *Someone . . .*
   19. must solve this problem.
   20. is preparing dinner.
   21. has to pay this bill.
   22. should eat this food.
   23. will mail the package.
   24. may raise the price of gas.
   25. has made a mistake.
   26. ought to wash the windows.

III. 27. No one has washed the dishes yet.
   28. Someone should wash them soon.
   29. No one has sent that package yet.
   30. Someone should send it soon.
   31. No one has solved that problem yet.
   32. Someone must solve it soon.
   33. Did someone wash this sweater in hot water?
   34. No one should wash this sweater in hot water.
   35. No one invited me to the party.
   36. Did someone invite you to the party?
   37. Someone built the Suez Canal in the nineteenth century.
   38. No one built the Suez Canal in the twentieth century.
   39. When did someone build the Panama Canal?

40. Should someone return this book to the library?

41. Did someone return that book to the library?

42. No one has returned it to the library yet.

43. Has someone paid that bill yet?

44. No one has paid it yet.

45. Someone should pay it soon.

46. Millions of people visit the Eiffel Tower every year.

47. Alexandre Eiffel designed it.

48. Someone erected it in 1889.

9-5 USING PAST PARTICIPLES AS ADJECTIVES (STATIVE PASSIVE)

<table>
<tr>
<td>
BE + ADJECTIVE
(a) Paul   is   young.
(b) Paul   is   tall.
(c) Paul   is   hungry.

BE + PAST PARTICIPLE
(d) Paul   is   married.
(e) Paul   is   tired.
(f) Paul   is   frightened.
</td>
<td>
Be can be followed by an adjective. The adjective describes or gives information about the subject of the sentence.
Be can be followed by a past participle (the passive form). The past participle is often like an adjective. The past participle describes or gives information about the subject of the sentence. Past participles are used as adjectives in many common, everyday expressions.
</td>
</tr>
<tr>
<td>
(g) Paul   <i>is married to</i>   Susan.
(h) Paul   <i>was excited about</i>   the game.
(i) Paul   <i>will be prepared for</i>   the exam.
</td>
<td>
Often the past participles in these expressions are followed by particular prepositions + an object. For example:
married is followed by to (+ an object)
excited is followed by about (+ an object)
prepared is followed by for (+ an object)
</td>
</tr>
</table>

SOME COMMON EXPRESSIONS WITH *BE* **+ PAST PARTICIPLE**

1. be acquainted (with)
2. be bored (with, by)
3. be broken
4. be closed
5. be crowded (with)
6. be devoted (to)
7. be disappointed (in, with)
8. be divorced (from)
9. be done (with)
10. be drunk (on)
11. be engaged (to)
12. be excited (about)
13. be exhausted (from)
14. be finished (with)
15. be frightened (of, by)
16. be gone (from)
17. be hurt
18. be interested (in)
19. be involved (in)
20. be located in, near, south of, etc.
21. be lost
22. be made of
23. be married (to)
24. be opposed (to)
25. be prepared (for)
26. be qualified (for)
27. be related (to)
28. be satisfied (with)
29. be scared (of, by)
30. be shut
31. be spoiled
32. be terrified (of, by)
33. be tired (of, from)*
34. be worried (about)

*I'm **tired of** the cold weather. = *I've had enough cold weather. I want the weather to get warm.*
I'm **tired from** working hard all day. = *I'm exhausted because I worked hard all day.*

EXERCISE 15:   Complete the sentences with the expressions in the list. Use *the simple present tense.*

be acquainted	be located	be satisfied
be broken	be lost	be scared
be crowded	be made	be spoiled
be disappointed	be qualified	✔ be worried
be exhausted	be related	

1. Dennis isn't doing well in school this semester. He _____is worried_____ about his grades.

2. My shirt _____ of cotton.

3. I live in a three-room apartment with four other people. Our apartment

    _____ .

4. Vietnam _____ in Southeast Asia.

5. I'm going to go straight to bed tonight. It's been a hard day. I

    _____ .

6. I _____ to Jessica Adams. She's my cousin.

7. Excuse me, sir, but I think I _____ . Could you please tell me how to get to the bus station from here?

8. My tape recorder doesn't work. It _____ .

9. We leave a light on in our son's bedroom at night because he

    _____ of the dark.

10. Alice thinks her boss should pay her more money. She _____

    not _____ with her present salary.

11. The children _____ . I had promised to take them to the beach today, but now we can't go because it's raining.

12. _____ you _____ with Mrs. Novinsky? Have you ever met her?

13. According to the job description, an applicant must have a Master's degree and at least five years of teaching experience. Unfortunately, I

    _____ not _____ for that job.

14. This milk doesn't taste right. I think it _____ . I'm not going to drink it.

EXERCISE 16: Complete the sentences with appropriate prepositions.

1. The day before Christmas, the stores are crowded _____with_____ last-minute shoppers.

2. Are you qualified _____ that job?

3. Mr. Heath loves his family very much. He is devoted _____ them.

4. Our dog runs under the bed during storms. He's terrified _____ thunder.

5. My sister is married _____ a law student.

6. Are you prepared _____ the test?

7. I'll be finished _____ my work in another minute or two.

8. The children are excited _____ going to the circus.

9. Senator Wilson is opposed _____ the President's new tax plan.

10. Jane isn't satisfied _____ her present apartment. She's looking for a new one.

11. I failed the test because I didn't study. I'm disappointed _____ myself.

12. Janet doesn't take good care of herself. I'm worried _____ her health.

13. The marathon runners were exhausted _____ running for 26 miles.

14. I'm tired _____ this rainy weather. I hope the sun shines tomorrow.

15. In terms of evolution, a hippopotamus is related _____ a horse.

16. The students are involved _____ many extracurricular activities.

17. Are you acquainted _____ this author? I think her books are excellent.

18. When will you be done _____ your work?

19. I'm starving! Right now I'm interested _____ only one thing: food.

20. The children want some new toys. They're bored _____ their old ones.

21. Sam is engaged _____ his childhood sweetheart.

22. Our daughter is scared _____ dogs.

EXERCISE 17—ORAL (BOOKS CLOSED): Supply appropriate prepositions + *some-one* or *something*.

Example: I'm worried. . . .
Response: about someone/something.

1. I'm interested. . . .
2. I'm married. . .
3. I'm scared. . . .
4. I'm related. . . .
5. I'm disappointed. . . .
6. I'm qualified. . . .
7. I'm satisfied. . . .
8. I'm prepared. . . .
9. I'm acquainted. . . .
10. I'm opposed. . . .
11. I'm frightened. . . .
12. I'm excited. . . .
13. I'm engaged. . . .
14. I'm exhausted. . . .
15. I'm tired. . . .
16. I'm finished. . . .
17. I'm done. . . .
18. I'm involved. . . .

(To the teacher: Repeat the exercise. Use only the past participles as cues and ask the students to make their own sentences.)

Example: worried
Response: I'm worried about my brother./The teacher is worried about my grades./We are worried about the next test./etc.

EXERCISE 18: Complete the sentences with the words in parentheses. Use *the passive form, simple present or simple past.* Include *prepositions where necessary.*

1. (*close*)   When we got to the post office, it _____was closed_____ .

2. (*make*)   My earrings _____are made of_____ gold.

3. (*divorce*)   Sally and Tom were married for six years, but now they

                                          _____ .

4. (*relate*)   Your name is Tom Hood. _____ you

                                          _____ Mary Hood?

5. (*spoil*)   This fruit _____ . I think I'd better throw it out.

6. (*exhaust*)   Last night I _____ , so I went straight to bed.

7. (*involve*)   Last week I _____ a three-car accident.

8. (*locate*)   The University of Washington _____ Seattle.

9. (*drink*)   Ted _____ . He's making a fool of himself.

10. (*interest*)   I _____ learning more about that subject.

11. (*devote*)   Linda loves her job. She _____ her work.

12. (*lose*)   What's the matter, little boy? _____ you

                                          _____ ?

13. (*terrify*)   Once when we were swimming at the beach, we saw a shark. All of us _____ .

14. (*acquaint*)   _____ you _____ Sue's roommate?

15. (*qualify*)   I was interviewed for the job, but I didn't get it. The interviewer said that I _____ not _____ it.

16. (*disappoint*)   My daughter brought home a report card with all D's and F's. I can't understand it. I _____ her.

17. (*do*)   At last, I _____ my homework. Now I can go to bed.

18. (*crowd*)   There are too many students in our class. The classroom

                                          _____ .

19. (*shut*)   It's starting to rain. _____ all of the windows

                                          _____ ?

20. (*go*)   Where's my wallet? It _____ ! Did you take it?

EXERCISE 19:   Study the examples.

		-ING	*-ED*
(a)	**The book interests** me.	It **is interesting.**	I **am interested.**
(b)	**The book bores** me.	It **is boring.**	I **am bored.**
(c)	**Mr. Lee confuses** me.	He **is confusing.**	I **am confused.**
(d)	**The news surprises** me.	It **is surprising.**	I **am surprised.**
(e)	**The game excites** Tom.	It **is exciting.**	Tom **is excited.**

Circle the correct form, *-ing* or *-ed*, of the words in parentheses.

1. Our classes are (*interesting,* *interested*).
2. The students are (*interesting, interested*) in learning more about the subject.
3. Ms. Green doesn't explain things well. The students are (*confusing, confused*).
4. Have you heard the latest news? It's really (*exciting, excited*).
5. I don't understand these directions. I'm (*confusing, confused*).
6. I read an (*interesting, interested*) article in the newspaper this morning.
7. I heard some (*surprising, surprised*) news on the radio.
8. I'm (*boring, bored*). Let's do something. How about going to a movie?
9. Mr. Sawyer bores me. I think he is a (*boring, bored*) person.
10. Mr. Ball fascinates me. I think he is a (*fascinating, fascinated*) person.
11. Most young children are (*fascinating, fascinated*) by animals.
12. Young children think that animals are (*fascinating, fascinated*).

13. I was very (*embarrassing, embarrassed*) yesterday when I spilled my drink on the dinner table.
14. That was an (*embarrassing, embarrassed*) experience.
15. I read a (*shocking, shocked*) report yesterday.

16. The children went to a circus. For them, the circus was (*exciting, excited*). The (*exciting, excited*) children jumped up and down.

9-6 *GET* + **ADJECTIVE**; *GET* + **PAST PARTICIPLE**

***GET* + ADJECTIVE** (a) I **am getting** *hungry.* Let's eat. ***GET* + PAST PARTICIPLE** (b) Tom and Sue **got** *married* last month.	Sometimes *get* is followed by an adjective. **Get** expresses the same idea as *become.* (See the list below for common expressions with *get* + *adjective*.) Sometimes *get* is followed by a past participle. (See the list below.)*

COMMON EXPRESSIONS WITH *GET* + **ADJECTIVE**		COMMON EXPRESSIONS WITH *GET* + **PAST PARTICIPLE**
1. *get angry*	10. *get hungry*	19. *get arrested*
2. *get bald*	11. *get late*	20. *get bored*
3. *get busy*	12. *get nervous*	21. *get confused*
4. *get cold*	13. *get old*	22. *get dressed*
5. *get dark*	14. *get rich*	23. *get drunk*
6. *get dizzy*	15. *get sick*	24. *get hurt*
7. *get fat*	16. *get sleepy*	25. *get lost*
8. *get full*	17. *get thirsty*	26. *get married*
9. *get hot*	18. *get well*	27. *get tired*
		28. *get worried*

*This chart contains only a few common expressions with *get* + *past participle*. **Get** can be used with many verbs, especially in informal spoken English. Some other common expressions: *get* + *acquainted, crowded, divorced, done, engaged, excited, finished, frightened, interested, invited, involved, killed, scared.*

EXERCISE 20:   Complete the sentences. Use each word in the list only one time.

angry	dressed	lost
arrested	drunk	married
bald	full	rich
bored	hot	sick
✔ cold	hungry	sleepy
confused	hurt	tired
dizzy	late	

1. In winter, the weather gets _____cold_____ .

2. In summer, the weather gets _____ .

3. This food is delicious, but I can't eat any more. I'm getting

    _____ .

4. I overslept this morning. When I finally woke up, I jumped out of bed, got

    _____ , picked up my books, and ran to class.

5. Mom and Dad are going to celebrate their 50th wedding anniversary next

    month. They got _____ fifty years ago.

6. When Jane gave us directions to her house, I got _____ . So
    I asked her to explain again how to get there.

7. I didn't understand Jane's directions very well, so on the way to her house

    last night I got _____ . I couldn't find her house.

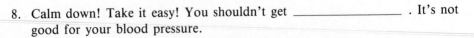

8. Calm down! Take it easy! You shouldn't get _____ . It's not
    good for your blood pressure.

9. Mr. Anderson is losing some of his hair. He's getting _____ .

10. I didn't like the movie last night. It wasn't interesting. I got

    _____ and wanted to leave early.

11. When's dinner? I'm getting _____ .

12. We should leave for the concert soon. It's getting _____ . We should leave in the next five minutes if we want to be on time.

13. I want to make a lot of money. Do you know a good way to get

_____ quick?

14. Julius got _____ for speeding yesterday. He has to go to court next week.

15. Was it a bad accident? Did anyone get _____ ?

16. When I turned around and around in a circle, I got _____ .

17. I don't feel very good. I think I'm getting _____ . Maybe I should see a doctor.

18. My friends got _____ at the party Saturday night, so I drove them home in my car. They were in no condition to drive.

19. I think I'll go to bed. I'm getting _____ .

20. Let's stop working and take a break. I'm getting _____ .

EXERCISE 21: Complete the sentences with an appropriate form of **get**.

1. Shake a leg! Step on it! _____Get_____ busy. There's no time to waste.

2. Tom and Sue _____got_____ married last month.

3. Let's stop working for a while. I _____am getting_____ tired.

4. I don't want _____to get_____ old, but I guess it happens to everybody.

5. I _____ interested in biology when I was in high school, so I decided to major in it in college.

6. My father started _____ bald when he was in his twenties. I'm in my twenties, and I'm starting _____ bald. It must be in the genes.

7. Brrr. It _____ cold in here. Maybe we should turn on the furnace.

8. When I was in the hospital, I got a card from my aunt and uncle. It said, " _____ well soon."

9. When I went downtown yesterday, I _____ lost. I didn't remember to take my map of the city with me.

10. A: Why did you leave the party early?

    B: I _____ bored.

11. A: I _____ hungry. Let's eat soon.
    B: Okay.

12. A: What happened?

    B: I don't know. Suddenly I _____ dizzy, but I'm okay now.

13. A: Do you want to go for a walk?

    B: Well, I don't know. It _____ dark outside right now.
    Let's wait and go for a walk tomorrow.

14. I always _____ nervous when I have to give a speech.

15. A: Where's Bud? He was supposed to be home two hours ago. He always

    calls when he's late. I _____ worried. Maybe we should
    call the police.
    B: Relax. He'll be home soon.

16. A: Hurry up and _____ dressed. We have to leave in ten
    minutes.
    B: I'm almost ready.

17. A: I'm going on a diet.
    B: Oh?

    A: See? This shirt is too tight. I _____ fat.

18. A: Janice and I are thinking about _____ married in June.
    B: That's a nice month for a wedding.

EXERCISE 22—ERROR ANALYSIS: Find and correct the errors in the following
sentences.

> *Example:*   I am agree with him.
> *Correction:* I agree with him.

1. An accident was happened at the corner yesterday.
2. This is belong to me.
3. I am very surprise by the news.
4. I'm interesting in that subject.
5. He is marry with my cousin.
6. Vietnam is locate in Southeast Asia.
7. Mary's dog was died last week.

8. Were you surprise when you saw him?

9. When I went downtown, I get lost.

10. Last night I very tire.

11. The bus was arrived ten minutes late.

12. When are you going to get marry?

13. I am agree with you.

14. We are not agree with him.

9-7 USING *BE USED/ACCUSTOMED TO* AND *GET USED/ACCUSTOMED TO*

(a) I **am used to** hot weather. (b) I **am accustomed to** hot weather. (c) I am used **to living** in a hot climate. (d) I am accustomed **to living** in a hot climate.	(a) and (b) have the same meaning: Living in a hot climate is usual and normal for me. I'm familiar with what it is like to live in a hot climate. Hot weather isn't strange or different to me.
	Notice in (c) and (d): *to* (a preposition) is followed by the *-ing* form of a verb (a gerund).*
(e) I just moved from Florida to Alaska. I have never lived in a cold climate before, but I **am getting used to (accustomed to)** the cold weather here.	In (e): *I'm getting used to/accustomed to* = something is beginning to seem usual and normal to me.

COMPARE:
*To express the habitual past (see 2–4), the infinitive form follows *used*: I *used to live* in Chicago, but now I live in New York. However, *be used to* is followed by a gerund: I *am used to living* in a big city.
NOTE: In both *used to* (habitual past) and *be used to,* the "d" is not pronounced in "used."

EXERCISE 23: Complete the sentences with *be used to*, affirmative or negative.

1. Juan is from Mexico. He ____is used to____ hot weather. He

   ____isn't used to____ cold weather.

2. Alice was born and raised in Chicago. She _____ living in a big city.

3. My hometown is New York City, but this year I'm going to school in a

   town with a population of 10,000. I _____ living in a small

   town. I _____ living in a big city.

4. We do a lot of exercises in class. We _____ doing exercises.

Complete the sentences with *be accustomed to,* affirmative or negative.
NOTICE: *accustomed* is spelled with two "c's" and one "m."

5. Spiro is from Greece. He _____ eating Greek food.

   He _____ eating American food.

6. I always get up around 6:00 a.m. I _____ getting up early.

   I _____ sleeping late.

7. Our teacher always gives us a lot of homework. We _____
   having a lot of homework every day.

8. We rarely take multiple choice tests. We _____ taking that
   kind of test.

EXERCISE 24—ORAL (BOOKS CLOSED): Talk about yourself. Use *be used/accustomed to.*

   Example: cold weather
   Response: I am (OR: I am not) used/accustomed to cold weather.

   1. hot weather
   2. cold weather
   3. living in a warm climate
   4. living in a cold climate
   5. living in a big city
   6. living in a small town

   7. getting up early
   8. sleeping late
   9. eating a big breakfast
   10. drinking coffee in the morning
   11. American food
   12. being on my own*

EXERCISE 25—ORAL (BOOKS CLOSED): Answer the questions.

   Example: What time are you accustomed to getting up?
   Response: I'm accustomed to getting up (at 7:30).

   1. What time are you accustomed to getting up?
   2. What time are you used to going to bed?
   3. Are you accustomed to living in (*name of this city*)?
   4. Are you accustomed to living in a big city?

To be on one's own is an idiom. It means to be away from one's family and responsible for oneself.

5. Are you used to speaking English every day?

6. Who lives with a roommate? Are you accustomed to that?

7. Who lives alone? Are you accustomed to that?

8. What are you accustomed to eating for breakfast?

9. Our weather right now is hot/cold/humid/cold and wet/etc. Are you used to this kind of weather?

10. How are you used to getting to school every day?

11. Where are you accustomed to eating lunch?

12. What time are you accustomed to eating dinner?

13. What kind of food are you accustomed to eating?

14. Who lives in a dorm? Are you used to the noise in a dorm?

15. Are you used to speaking English everyday, or does it seem strange to you?

EXERCISE 26: Complete the sentences with your own words.

You are living in a different country. Living in a foreign country requires adjustments. Write about some of these adjustments.

1. I'm getting used to _____

2. I'm also getting accustomed to _____

3. I have gotten accustomed to _____

4. I haven't gotten used to _____

5. I can't get used to _____

6. Do you think I will ever get accustomed to _____

9-8 USING BE SUPPOSED TO

(a) John **is supposed to call** me tomorrow. (IDEA: I expect John to call me tomorrow.)	**Be supposed to** is used to talk about an activity or event that is expected to occur.
(b) We **are supposed to write** a composition. (IDEA: The teacher expects us to write a composition.)	In (a): The idea of **is supposed to** is that John is expected (by me) to call. I asked him to call me. He promised to call me. I expect him to call me.
(c) It **is supposed to rain** today. (IDEA: People expect it to rain today.)	
(d) Alice **was supposed to be** home at ten. (IDEA: Someone expected Alice to be home at ten.)	NOTE: The present form of **be** is used for both future expectations and present expectations.

EXERCISE 27: Make sentences with a similar meaning by using *be supposed to.*

1. The teacher expects us to be on time for class.

   <u>We are supposed to be on time for class.</u>

2. People expect the weather to be cold tomorrow. _____

   _____

3. People expect the plane to arrive at 6:00. _____

   _____

4. I expect Tom to call me. _____

5. My boss expects me to work late tonight. _____

6. I expect the mail to arrive at noon. _____

7. Someone expected me to return this book to the library yesterday, but I
   didn't. _____

8. Our professor expects us to read Chapter 9 before class tomorrow.

   _____

9. Someone expected me to go to a party last night, but I stayed home.

   _____

10. The teacher expects us to do Exercise 10 for homework. _____

    _____

11. The weather bureau has predicted rain for tomorrow. According to the
    weather bureau, it _____

12. The directions on the pill bottle say, "Take one pill every six hours."
    According to the directions on the bottle, I _____

    _____

13. My mother expects me to dust the furniture and (to) vacuum the carpet.

    _____

EXERCISE 28—ORAL: Read the dialogues and then answer the questions. Use *be supposed to.*

1. **Tom's boss:** Mail this package.
         Tom: Yes, sir.
   What is Tom supposed to do? (He is supposed to mail a package.)

2. **Mary:** Call me at nine.
   Ann: Okay.
   What is Ann supposed to do?

3. **Ms. Martinez:** Please make your bed before you go to school.
   Johnny: Okay, Mom.
   What is Johnny supposed to do?

4. **Mr. Takada:** Put your dirty clothes in the laundry basket.
   Susie: Okay, Dad.
   What is Susie supposed to do?

5. **Mrs. Wilson:** Bobby, pick up your toys and put them away.
   Bobby: Okay, Mom.
   Mrs. Wilson: Annie, please hang up your coat.
   Annie: Okay, Mom.
   What are the children supposed to do?

6. **Dr. Kettle:** You should take one pill every eight hours.
   Patient: All right, Dr. Kettle. Anything else?
   Dr. Kettle: Drink plenty of fluids.
   What is the patient supposed to do?

7. **Prof. Larson:** Read Chapter 10 and answer the questions at the end of the chapter.
   Students: (*no response*)
   What are the students supposed to do?

8. **Prof. Thompson:** Read the directions carefully, use a No. 2 pencil, and raise your hand if you have any questions.
   Students: (*no response*)
   What are the students supposed to do?

EXERCISE 29—WRITTEN: You have been in this country for _____ months/years. Write about some of the things you have learned about this country, about other people, and about yourself. Assume that your reader knows very little about this country.

chapter 10

Adjective Clauses

10-1 ADJECTIVE CLAUSES: INTRODUCTION

ADJECTIVES	ADJECTIVE CLAUSES*
An *adjective* modifies a noun. *Modify* means to change a little. An adjective gives a little different meaning to a noun. It describes or gives information about a noun.	An *adjective clause* modifies a noun. It describes or gives information about a noun.
An *adjective* usually comes in front of a noun.	An *adjective clause* follows a noun.

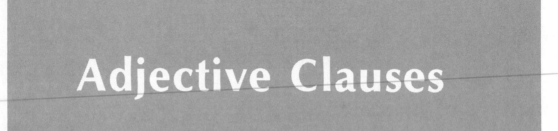

(a) I met a **kind man.** *adjective + noun*

(b) I met an **old man.** *adjective + noun*

(c) I met a **man** **who is kind to animals.** *noun + adjective clause*

(d) I met a **man** **who is five years older than my father.** *noun + adjective clause*

(e) I met a **man** **who lives in Chicago.** *noun + adjective clause*

*A clause is a structure that has a subject and a verb.
There are two kinds of clauses: independent and dependent.
   An *independent clause* is a main clause. It can stand alone as a sentence.
   A *dependent clause* must be connected to an independent clause. A dependent clause cannot stand alone as a sentence. An adjective clause is a dependent clause.
   I met a man = *an independent clause*
   who is kind to animals = *a dependent clause*

10-2   USING *WHO* AND *WHOM* IN ADJECTIVE CLAUSES

(a) The man is friendly.	**S V** **He** lives next to me. ↓ **who** ↓ **S V** **who** lives next to me	In (a): **He** is a subject pronoun. **He** refers to **the man.** To make an adjective clause, we can change **he** to **who. Who** is a subject pronoun. **Who** refers to **the man.**
(b) The man **who lives next to me** is friendly.		In (b): An adjective clause immediately follows the noun it modifies. INCORRECT: *The man is friendly who lives next to me.*
(c) The man was friendly.	**S V O** I met **him.** ↓ **whom** **O S V** **whom** I met	In (c): **Him** is an object pronoun. **Him** refers to the **the man.** To make an adjective clause, we can change **him** to **whom. Whom** is an object pronoun. **Whom** refers to **the man.*** **Whom** comes at the beginning of an adjective clause.
(d) The man **whom I met** was friendly.		In (d): An adjective clause immediately follows the noun it modifies. INCORRECT: *The man was friendly whom I met.*

*In informal English, **who** is often used as an object pronoun instead of **whom:**

FORMAL: The man *whom* I met was friendly.
INFORMAL: The man *who* I met was friendly.

EXERCISE 1:   Combine the two sentences into one sentence. Make (b) an adjective clause. Use **who** or **whom.**

1. (a) Do you know the people? (b) They live in the white house.
   Do you know the people who live in the white house?
2. (a) The woman gave me some information. (b) I called her.
   The woman whom I called gave me some information.
3. (a) The policeman was friendly. (b) He gave me directions.
4. (a) The waitress was friendly. (b) She served us dinner.
5. (a) I don't know the man. (b) He is talking to Mary.
6. (a) The people were very nice. (b) I met them at the party last night.
7. (a) The woman thanked me. (b) I helped her.
8. (a) Do you like the mechanic? (b) He fixed your car.
9. (a) Mr. Polanski is a mechanic. (b) You can trust him.

10. (a) The people have three cars. (b) They live next to me.
11. (a) I talked to the woman. (b) She was sitting next to me.
12. (a) I talked to the people. (b) They were sitting next to me.
13. (a) The woman was walking her dog. (b) I saw her.
14. (a) The people were playing football. (b) I saw them at the park.

EXERCISE 2:   Complete the sentences in Column A with the adjective clauses in Column B. Consult your dictionary if necessary.

Example: A Bostonian is someone who lives in Boston.

COLUMN A

1. A Bostonian is someone. . .
2. A pilot is a person. . .
3. A procrastinator is someone. . .
4. A botanist is a scientist. . .
5. An insomniac is somebody. . .
6. A revolutionary is someone. . .
7. A misanthrope is a person. . .
8. A meteorologist is a person. . .
9. A jack-of-all-trades is someone. . .
10. An expert can be defined as a person. . .

COLUMN B

(a) who has trouble sleeping.
(b) who seeks to overthrow the government.
(c) who flies an airplane.
(d) who studies weather phenomena.
✔ (e) who lives in Boston.
(f) who hates people.
(g) who always puts off doing things.
(h) who knows a lot about a little and a little about a lot.
(i) who has many skills.
(j) who studies plants.

EXERCISE 3:   Complete the sentences with your own words. Consult your dictionary if necessary.

1. A baker is a person who _____

2. A mechanic is someone who _____

3. A bartender is a person who _____

4. A philatelist is someone who _____

5. A spendthrift is somebody who _____

6. An astronomer is a scientist who _____

7. A carpenter is a person who _____

8. A miser is someone who _____

10-3   USING *WHO, WHOM,* **AND** *THAT* **IN ADJECTIVE CLAUSES**

	In addition to **who,** we can use **that** as the subject of an adjective clause.
(a) The man is friendly. [S / He → who / that] lives next to me.	
(b) The man **who** lives next to me is friendly. (c) The man **that** lives next to me is friendly. S V	(b) and (c) have the same meaning.
(d) The man was friendly. I met [O / him. → whom / that]	In addition to **whom,** we can use **that** as the object in an adjective clause.
(e) The man **whom** I met was friendly. (f) The man **that** I met was friendly. O S V	(e) and (f) have the same meaning.
(g) The man I met was friendly.	An object pronoun can be omitted from an adjective clause. (e), (f), and (g) have the same meaning.
	NOTE: A subject pronoun cannot be omitted: INCORRECT: *The man lives next to me is friendly.* CORRECT: *The man who/that lives next to me is friendly.*

EXERCISE 4: Change *that* to *who* or *who(m)*.* Also, omit *that* if possible.

1. The woman that I met last night was interesting.
   The woman who(m) I met last night was interesting.
   The woman I met last night was interesting.
2. The man that answered the phone was polite.
3. The people that Ann is visiting live on Elm Street.
4. Do you like the boy that is talking to Eleanor?
5. The students that came to class late missed the quiz.
6. I didn't know any of the people that John invited to his party.
7. The woman that I saw in the park was feeding the pigeons.
8. The woman that was feeding the pigeons had a sackful of bread crumbs.
9. I like the barber that usually cuts my hair.
10. The person that I admire most is my grandmother.

10-4 USING *WHICH* AND *THAT* IN ADJECTIVE CLAUSES

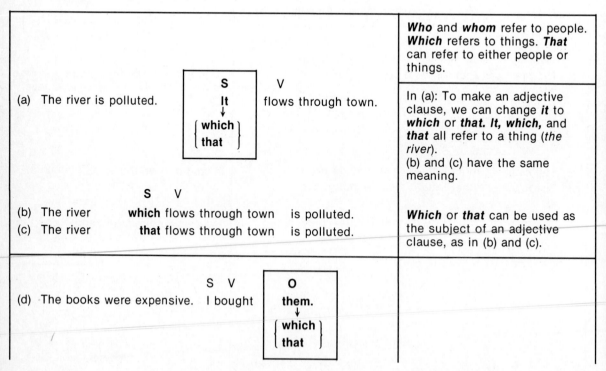

		Who and *whom* refer to people. *Which* refers to things. *That* can refer to either people or things.
(a) The river is polluted.	**S** / **It** → {which / that} **V** flows through town.	In (a): To make an adjective clause, we can change *it* to *which* or *that*. *It, which,* and *that* all refer to a thing (*the river*). (b) and (c) have the same meaning.
(b) The river (c) The river	**S V** **which** flows through town is polluted. **that** flows through town is polluted.	*Which* or *that* can be used as the subject of an adjective clause, as in (b) and (c).
(d) The books were expensive.	**S V** I bought **O** them. → {which / that}	

---

*The parentheses around the "m" indicate that sometimes (in everyday informal usage) *who* is used as an object pronoun instead of *whom*.

	O	**S**	**V**	
(e)	The books	**which**	I bought	were expensive.
(f)	The books	**that**	I bought	were expensive.
(g)	The books		I bought	were expensive.

Which or *that* can be used as an object in an adjective clause, as in (e) and (f).

An object pronoun can be omitted from an adjective clause, as in (g). (e), (f), and (g) have the same meaning.

EXERCISE 5:   Combine the two sentences into one sentence. Make (b) an adjective clause. Give all the possible forms.

1. (a) The pill made me sleepy. (b) I took it.
    The pill which I took made me sleepy.
    The pill that I took made me sleepy.
    The pill I took made me sleepy.

2. (a) The soup was too salty. (b) I had it for lunch.

3. (a) I have a class. (b) It begins at 8:00 a.m.

4. (a) I know a man. (b) He doesn't have to work for a living.

5. (a) My daughter asked me a question. (b) I couldn't answer it.

6. (a) All of the people can come. (b) I asked them to my party.

7. (a) I lost the scarf. (b) I borrowed it from my roommate.

8. (a) A lion is an animal. (b) It lives in Africa.

9. (a) The woman predicted my future. (b) She read my palm.

10. (a) A globe is a ball. (b) It has a map of the world on it.

11. (a) Where can I catch the bus? (b) It goes downtown.

12. (a) The bus is always crowded. (b) I take it to school every morning.

13. (a) I have some valuable antiques. (b) I found them in my grandmother's attic.

14. (a) The notes helped me a lot. (b) I borrowed them from you.

EXERCISE 6:   Complete the sentences in Column A with the adjective clauses in Column B.

Example: A quart is a liquid measure that equals two pints.

COLUMN A

1. A quart is a liquid measure. . .
2. A puzzle is a problem. . .
3. Cake is a dessert. . .
4. A passport is a special paper. . .
5. A hammer is a tool. . .
6. A barometer is an instrument. . .
7. A coin is a piece of metal. . .
8. A pyramid is a structure. . .

COLUMN B

(a) that is difficult to solve.
(b) that measures air pressure.
✔ (c) that equals two pints.
(d) that is used to pound nails.
(e) that is square at the bottom and has four sides that come together at the top in a point.
(f) that is used as money.
(g) that permits a citizen to travel in other countries.
(h) that is made of flour, eggs, milk, and sugar.

EXERCISE 7:   Study the examples.

(a) I know *the man* **who is** sitting over there.	In (a): The verb in the adjective clause (**is**) is singular because **who** refers to a singular noun.
(b) I know *the people* **who are** sitting over there.	In (b): The verb in the adjective clause (**are**) is plural because **who** refers to a plural noun.

Circle the correct word in parentheses.

1. The students who (*is, are*) in my class come from many countries.
2. I met some people who (*knows, know*) my brother.
3. The student who (*is, are*) talking to the teacher is from Peru.
4. I talked to the men who (*was, were*) sitting near me.
5. Do you know the people that (*lives, live*) in that house?
6. Biographies are books which (*tells, tell*) the stories of people's lives.

7. A book that (*tells, tell*) the story of a person's life is called a biography.

8. The woman that (*was, were*) sitting in front of me at the movie was wearing a big hat.

9. The people who (*was, were*) standing in line to get into the theater were cold and wet.

10. Water is a chemical compound that (*consists, consist*) of oxygen and hydrogen.

10-5 USING PREPOSITIONS IN ADJECTIVE CLAUSES

(a) The man was helpful. I talked **PREP** **to** **O** **him**.	**Whom, which,** and **that** can be used as the object of a preposition in an adjective clause. **Reminder:** An object pronoun can be omitted from an adjective clause, as in (d) and (i).
(b) The man **whom** I talked **to** was helpful.	
(c) The man **that** I talked **to** was helpful.	
(d) The man I talked **to** was helpful.	
(e) The man **to whom** I talked was helpful.	In very formal English, a preposition often comes at the beginning of an adjective clause, as in (e) and (j). The preposition is followed by either **whom** or **which** (not **that**) and the pronoun cannot be omitted.
(f) The chair is comfortable. I am sitting **PREP** **in** **O** **it**.	
(g) The chair **which** I am sitting **in** is comfortable.	
(h) The chair **that** I am sitting **in** is comfortable.	(b), (c), (d), and (e) have the same meaning.
(i) The chair I am sitting **in** is comfortable.	
(j) The chair **in which** I am sitting is comfortable.	(g), (h), (i), and (j) have the same meaning.

EXERCISE 8: Combine the two sentences in each pair. Use (b) as an adjective clause. Give all the possible forms of the adjective clauses.

1. (a) The movie was interesting. (b) We went to it.
    The movie which we went to was interesting.
    The movie that we went to was interesting.
    The movie we went to was interesting.
    The movie to which we went was interesting.

2. (a) The woman pays me a fair salary. (b) I work for her.
3. (a) The man is over there. (b) I told you about him.
4. (a) I want to tell you about the party. (b) I went to it last night.
5. (a) The person is sitting at that desk. (b) You should talk to her about your problem.
6. (a) Alicia likes the family. (b) She is living with them.
7. (a) The picture is beautiful. (b) Tom is looking at it.
8. (a) I enjoyed the music. (b) We listened to it after dinner.

EXERCISE 9—ORAL: Combine the sentences, using the second sentence as an adjective clause. Practice omitting the object pronoun (*whom, which, that*).

Example: The hill was steep. I climbed it.
Response: The hill I climbed was steep.

1. I met the people. You told me about them.
2. The bananas were too ripe. My husband bought them.
3. The market has fresh vegetables. I usually go to it.
4. I couldn't understand the woman. I talked to her on the phone.
5. The scrambled eggs were cold. I had them for breakfast at the cafeteria.
6. The office is on Main Street. Amy works in it.
7. I had a good time on the trip. I took it to Glacier National Park.
8. The blouse is made of silk. Mary is wearing it.
9. The doctor prescribed some medicine for my sore throat. I went to him yesterday.
10. The cream was spoiled. I put it in my coffee.
11. The fast forward button on the tape recorder doesn't work. I bought it last month.
12. Here is the brochure. You asked me about it.
13. The man is tall, dark, and handsome. My sister goes out with him.
14. The university is in New York. I want to go to it.
15. The plane leaves at 7:08 p.m. I'm taking it to Denver.
16. I'm going to call about the want ad. I saw it in last night's paper.

10-6 USING *WHOSE* IN ADJECTIVE CLAUSES

(a) The man called the police.	**His car** → **whose car** was stolen.	***Whose*** shows "possession." In (a): We can change ***his car*** to ***whose car*** to make an adjective clause.

(b) The man **whose car was stolen** called the police.	In (b): *whose car was stolen* = an adjective clause.
(c) I know a girl. ⎡ **Her brother** ↓ **whose brother** ⎤ is a movie star. (d) I know a girl **whose brother is a movie star.**	In (c): We can change *her brother* to *whose brother* to make an adjective clause.
(e) The people are moving to Hawaii. We bought ⎡ **their house.** ↓ **whose house** ⎤ (f) The people **whose house we bought** are moving to Hawaii.	In (e): We can change *their house* to *whose house* to make an adjective clause.
	Notice: *whose* comes immediately after the noun it modifies.

EXERCISE 10: Combine the two sentences into one sentence. Make (b) an adjective clause. Use *whose.*

You and your friend are at a party. You are telling your friend about the people at the party.

1. (a) There is the man. (b) His car was stolen.
   There is the man whose car was stolen.
2. (a) There is the woman. (b) Her cat died.
3. (a) Over there is the man. (b) I'm dating his daughter.
4. (a) Over there is the woman. (b) You met her husband yesterday.
5. (a) There is the professor. (b) I'm taking her course.
6. (a) That is the man. (b) His son is an astronaut.
7. (a) That is the girl. (b) I borrowed her camera.
8. (a) There is the boy. (b) His mother is a famous musician.

9. (a) They are the people. (b) We visited their house last month.
10. (a) That is the couple. (b) Their apartment was burglarized.

EXERCISE 11—ORAL (BOOKS CLOSED):   Combine the sentences. Use **whose.**

   Example: The man called the police. His car was stolen.
   Response: The man whose car was stolen called the police.

1. The woman was sad. Her cat died.
2. The man is friendly. I'm dating his daughter.
3. The woman is my teacher. You met her husband.
4. The professor gives hard tests. I'm taking her course.
5. The man is an engineer. His son is an astronaut.
6. The girl is a good friend of mine. I borrowed her camera.
7. The boy wants to be a violinist. His mother is a famous musician.
8. The people were very nice. We visited their house.
9. The couple bought new locks. Their apartment was burglarized.

10. I have a friend. Her brother is a policeman.
11. I have a neighbor. His dog barks all day long.
12. I like the people. We went to their house.
13. I thanked the woman. I borrowed her dictionary.
14. The woman shouted "Stop! Thief!" Her purse was stolen.
15. The man is famous. His picture is in the newspaper.

EXERCISE 12:   Complete the following sentences with **who, whom, which, whose,**
or **that.** Discuss all the possible completions. Discuss the possibility of omitting the
pronoun.

1. People ___who OR: that___ live in New York City are called New Yorkers.

2. George Washington is the president _____ picture is on a
   one-dollar bill.

3. I like the people with _____ I work.

4. Have you seen the movie _____ is playing at the Fox
   Theater?

5. A stenographer is a person _____ can write in shorthand.

6. Do you know the woman _____ John is engaged to?

7. I have a friend _____ father is a famous artist.

8. The camera _____ I bought has a zoom lens.

9. Students _____ have part-time jobs have to budget their time very carefully.

10. Mary likes the present _____ I gave her for her birthday.

11. The person to _____ you should send your application is the Director of Admissions.

12. That's Tom Jenkins. He's the boy _____ parents live in Switzerland.

13. A thermometer is an instrument _____ measures the temperature.

14. A high-strung person is someone _____ is always nervous.

15. The man _____ I told you about is standing over there.

EXERCISE 13—ORAL (BOOKS CLOSED): Add adjective clauses to the main sentence.

I. MAIN SENTENCE: The man was nice. (*written on the board*)

   Example: I met him yesterday.
   Response: The man (whom/that) I met yesterday was nice.

   1. You introduced me to him.
   2. He helped me yesterday.
   3. I spoke to him on the phone.
   4. I called him.
   5. He answered the phone.
   6. I had dinner with him last week.
   7. He opened the door for me.
   8. I told you about him.
   9. Mary went to a movie with him last night.
   10. He gave me directions to the post office.
   11. Bob roomed with him.
   12. He visited our class yesterday.
   13. We visited his house.

14. He helped us at the hardware store.
15. I borrowed his pen.
16. I met him at the party last night.

II.   MAIN SENTENCE: Do you know the woman? (*written on the board*)

Example: She is standing over there.
Response: Do you know the woman who/that is standing over there?

1. Mary is talking to her.
2. Her car was stolen.
3. Fred married her.
4. (. . .) is talking about her. ,
5. She is waving at us.
6. Her apartment was burglarized.
7. She works in that office.
8. She is sitting over there.
9. My brother is engaged to her.
10. Her son was arrested by the police.

III. MAIN SENTENCE: The movie was good. (*written on the board*)

Example: I saw it yesterday.
Response: The movie (which/that) I saw yesterday was good.

1. We went to it.
2. I watched it on TV last night.
3. John told me about it.
4. It was playing at (*name of a local theater.*)
5. (. . .) saw it.
6. It starred (*name of an actor/actress*).

EXERCISE 14—ERROR ANALYSIS: All of the following sentences contain mistakes. Can you find the mistakes and correct them?

1. The book which I bought it at the bookstore yesterday was very expensive.
2. The woman was nice that I met yesterday.
3. The people which live next to me are friendly.
4. I met a woman who her husband is a famous lawyer.

5. Do you know the people who lives in that house?

6. The professor teaches Chemistry 101 is very good.

7. I wrote a thank-you note to the people who I visited their house on Thanksgiving Day.

8. The people who I met them at the party last night were interesting.

9. I enjoyed the music which we listened to it.

10. The man was very angry whose bicycle was stolen.

EXERCISE 15—WRITTEN: Complete the sentences with your own words. (Use your own paper.)

1. My friend told me about a man who. . . .

2. I have a friend whose. . . .

3. I returned the book which. . . .

4. The woman who. . . .

5. The people I. . . .

6. Do you know the man that. . .?

7. The movie we. . . .

8. The people whose. . . .

9. The book I. . . .

10. The person to whom. . . .

EXERCISE 16—WRITTEN: Imagine that you are in a roomful of people. You know everyone who is there. I (your reader) know no one. Tell me who these people are. Write your description of these people.

Begin your composition with: I'm glad you came to the party. Let me tell you about the people who are here. The woman who. . . .

EXERCISE 17:   Complete the sentences with your own words.

1. One of the things I like best _____is* hot and spicy food._____

2. One of the places I want to visit someday _____

3. One of the people I admire most in the world _____

4. Some of the cities I would like to visit _____are*_____

5. Some of the places I hope to visit someday _____

---

*Notice: **One of the** + *plural noun* (+ *adjective clause*) + *singular verb*.
   Some of the + *plural noun* (+ *adjective clause*) + *plural verb*.

6. One of the cities I would like to visit while I'm in this country _____

_____

7. One of the programs I like to watch on TV _____

8. One of the subjects I would like to know more about _____

9. Some of the things I like best in life _____

EXERCISE 18: Study the examples and then complete the sentences. Notice the superlative form (*-est/most*) of the adjectives in the list:

bad – worst	*good – best*
beautiful – most beautiful	*hard – hardest*
easy – easiest	*interesting – most interesting*
fascinating – most fascinating	*kind – kindest*

1. I've read a lot of good books.

    One of the <u> best books I've ever read is *Tom Sawyer* by Mark Twain. </u>

2. I've been in a lot of beautiful cities.

    <u> San Francisco is </u> one of the <u> most beautiful cities I've ever been in. </u>

3. I've visited a lot of interesting places.

    One of the _____

4. I've known a lot of kind people.

    _____ one of the _____

5. I've taken a lot of hard courses.

    _____ one of the _____

6. I've talked to a lot of interesting people.

    One of the _____

7. I've had a lot of easy classes.

    One of the _____

8. I've read a lot of good books.

    _____ one of the _____

9. I've seen a lot of good movies.

    One of the _____

10. I've seen some bad movies.

_____ one of the _____

11. I've met some fascinating people.

One of the _____

12. I've had some good teachers

One of the _____

10-7   MORE TWO-WORD VERBS (SEPARABLE)*

ask out	*ask someone to go on a date*
call back	*return a telephone call*
call off	*cancel*
call up	*make a telephone call*
give back	*return something to someone*
hang up	*(1) hang on a hanger or a hook; (2) end a telephone call*
pay back	*return money to someone*
put away	*put something in its usual or proper place*
put back	*return something to its original place*
put out	*extinguish (stop) a fire, a cigarette, a cigar*
shut off	*stop a machine or light, turn off*
try on	*put on clothing to see if it fits*
turn down	*decrease the volume*
turn up	*increase the volume*

*See 8-4 and 8-5 for more information about two-word verbs.

EXERCISE 19—TWO-WORD VERBS: Complete the sentences with pronouns and prepositions.

1. A: Could you lend me a couple of bucks?
    B: Sure.

    A: Thanks. I'll pay _____you back_____ tomorrow.

2. A: The radio is too loud. Could you please turn _____ ?
    B: Sure.

3. A: I can't hear the TV. Could you please turn _____ ?
    B: I'd be glad to.

4. A: Have you heard from Jack lately?

   B: Yes. He called _____ last night.*

5. A: Someone's at the door. Can I call _____ in a few minutes?
   B: Sure.
6. A: Where's my coat?

   B: I hung _____ .

7. A: This is a nice-looking coat. Why don't you try _____ ?
   B: How much does it cost?
8. A: Is the oven on?

   B: No. I shut _____ .

---

*There is no difference in meaning between *He called me last night* and *He called me up last night*.

9. A: May I borrow your small calculator tonight?

   B: Sure.

   A: I'll give _____ to you tomorrow.

   B: Okay.

10. A: You can't smoke that cigarette in the auditorium. You'd better put

   _____ before we go in.

   B: Okay.

11. A: Do you have any plans for Saturday night?

   B: Yes. I have a date. Jim Olsen asked _____ .

12. A: Did you take my eraser off of my desk?

   B: Yes, but I put _____ on your desk when I was finished.

   A: Oh? It's not here.

   B: Look under your notebook.

   A: Ah. There it is. Thanks.

13. A: Your toys are all over the floor, kids. Before you go to bed, be sure to

   put _____ .

   B: Okay, Daddy.

14. A: Did you go to Kathy's party last night?

   B: She didn't have a party. She called _____ .

chapter *11*

Count/Noncount Nouns and Articles

EXERCISE 1—PRETEST (BOOKS CLOSED): This is a spelling test. Write the plural forms of the given words. (Use your own paper.)

> *Example:* one chair, two. . .
> *Response (written):* chairs

1. glass
2. problem
3. church
4. bush
5. animal
6. sex
7. library
8. monkey
9. family
10. wife
11. shelf
12. roof
13. hero
14. radio
15. zero
16. foot
17. mouse
18. sheep

11-1 PLURAL FORMS OF NOUNS

	SINGULAR	PLURAL	
(a)	one bird one street one rose	two birds two streets two roses	To make most nouns plural, add **-s.**
(b)	one dish one match one class one box	two dishes two matches two classes two boxes	Add **-es** to nouns ending in **-sh, -ch, -ss,** and **-x.**

(c)	one baby one city	two babies two cities	If a noun ends in a consonant + **-y,** change the **y** to **i** and add **es.** (NOTE: If **-y** is preceded by a vowel, add only **-s:** *boys, days, keys.*)
(d)	one knife one shelf	two knives two shelves	If a noun ends in **-fe** or **-f,** change the ending to **-ves.** (Exceptions: *beliefs, chiefs, roofs, cuffs.*)

(e)	one tomato
	one zoo
	one zero
		two tomatoes
		two zoos
		two zeroes/zeros
			The plural form of nouns that end in **-o** is sometimes **-oes** and sometimes **-os:**
			  -oes: *tomatoes, potatoes, heroes, echoes, mosquitoes*
			  os: *zoos, radios, studios, pianos, solos, sopranos, photos, autos*
			  -oes or **-os:** *zeroes/zeros, volcanoes/volcanos, tornadoes/tornados*

(f)	one child one foot one goose one man one mouse one tooth one woman ———	two children two feet two geese two men two mice two teeth two women two people	Some nouns have irregular plural forms.
(g)	one deer one fish one sheep	two deer two fish two sheep	The plural form of some nouns is the same as the singular form.

EXERCISE 2: Write the plural forms of the nouns.

1. one potato, two ____potatoes____

2. a dormitory, many _____

3. one child, two _____

4. a leaf, a lot of _____

5. a wish, many _____

6. one fish, two _____

7. an opinion, many _____

8. a mouse, several _____

9. a sandwich, some _____

10. a man, many _____

11. one woman, two _____

12. a flash, three _____

13. one tomato, a few _____

14. one tooth, two _____

15. one half, two _____

16. a tax, a lot of _____

17. a possibility, several _____ 24. a mosquito, a lot of _____

18. a thief, many _____ 25. one sheep, two _____

19. a volcano, many _____ 26. a wolf, some _____

20. a goose, a lot of _____ 27. one stitch, two _____

21. an attorney, a few _____ 28. one foot, three _____

22. a butterfly, several _____ 29. one piano, two _____

23. one category, two _____ 30. a belief, many _____

11-2   COUNT AND NONCOUNT NOUNS

	SINGULAR	PLURAL	
COUNT NOUN	a chair one chair	chairs two chairs three chairs some chairs several chairs a lot of chairs many chairs a few chairs	Some nouns are called *count nouns*: (1) In the singular, they can be preceded by *a/an* or *one*. (2) They have a plural form: *-s* or *-es*.
NONCOUNT NOUN	furniture some furniture a lot of furniture much furniture a little furniture		Some nouns are called *noncount nouns*: (1) They are not immediately preceded by *a/an* or *one*. (2) They do not have a plural form (no final *-s* is added).

EXERCISE 3:   Notice the expressions of quantity (*two, some, a lot of, etc.*) that are used with count nouns and with noncount nouns in chart 11-2. In the following, draw a line through the expressions of quantity that *cannot* be used to complete the sentences.

NONCOUNT NOUNS

   fruit

   mail

   traffic

COUNT NOUNS

   apples

   letters

   cars

Example: I ate _____ fruit.
(a) some
~~(b) several~~
(c) a little
~~(d) a few~~

1. I ate _____ fruit.
(a) some
(b) several
(c) a little
(d) a few
(e) too many
(f) too much
(g) a lot of
(h) two

4. I get _____ letters every day.
(a) a lot of
(b) some
(c) a little
(d) a few
(e) too much
(f) too many
(g) several
(h) three

2. I ate _____ apples.
(a) some
(b) several
(c) a little
(d) a few
(e) too many
(f) too much
(g) a lot of
(h) two

5. There is _____ traffic in the street.
(a) several
(b) some
(c) too many
(d) a little
(e) a lot of
(f) a few
(g) too much
(h) five

3. I get _____ mail every day.
(a) a lot of
(b) some
(c) a little
(d) a few
(e) too much
(f) too many
(g) several
(h) three

6. There are _____ cars in the street.
(a) several
(b) some
(c) too many
(d) a little
(e) a lot of
(f) a few
(g) too much
(h) five

11-3   NONCOUNT NOUNS

(a) I bought **some furniture.**
(b) I got **some mail** yesterday.
	A noncount noun is not preceded by ***a/an,*** ***one, two, three,*** etc.
	    (INCORRECT: *I bought a furniture.*)
	A noncount noun does not have a plural form.
	    (INCORRECT: *I bought some furnitures.*)

INDIVIDUAL PARTS (COUNT NOUNS)	THE WHOLE (A NONCOUNT NOUN)	
(c) chairs tables beds etc.	furniture	Noncount nouns usually refer to a whole group of things that is made up of many individual parts, a whole category made up of different varieties. For example, some common noncount nouns are: *furniture, mail, money, fruit,* and *jewelry.*

(d) letters
postcards
bills
etc.
	mail	A language is not always logical. For instance:
		    (a) *I had some* ***corn*** *for dinner.* (noncount)
		    (b) *I had some* ***peas*** *for dinner.* (count)
		Both ***corn*** and ***peas*** express a larger whole made up of smaller parts, but ***corn*** is a noncount noun and ***pea*** is a count noun.

(e) pennies nickels dollars etc.	money	(a) ***Vegetables*** *are good for you.* (count) (b) ***Fruit*** *is good for you.* (noncount)
(f) apples bananas oranges etc.	fruit	Both ***vegetables*** and ***fruit*** describe whole categories of food, but one is count and the other noncount.

(g) rings
bracelets
necklaces
etc.
	jewelry	Logically, you can count furniture. But in grammar, you cannot count furniture. For example: *I see a table and a bed.*
		    CORRECT: *I see some furniture.*
		    INCORRECT: *I see two furnitures.*

*A noncount noun is also sometimes called *a mass noun.*

SOME COMMON NONCOUNT NOUNS: WHOLE GROUPS MADE UP OF INDIVIDUAL PARTS

A. *clothing*
   equipment
   food*(1)
   fruit
   furniture
   garbage
   hardware
   jewelry
   machinery
   mail
   makeup
   money
     cash
     change
   postage
   scenery
   stuff
   traffic

B. *homework*
   housework
   work(2)

C. *advice*
   information
   gossip(3)
   news
   noise(4)

D. *history*
   literature
   music
   poetry
   psychology, engineering, biology,
     chemistry, physics, etc. (names
     of academic fields)

E. *English, Arabic, Chinese*, etc.
     (names of languages)
   grammar
   slang
   vocabulary

F. *corn*
   dirt
   dust
   flour
   grass
   hair(5)
   pepper(6)
   rice
   salt
   sugar
   wheat

---

*Some nouns can be used either as a count noun or as a noncount noun. Nouns in the list that are frequently used as count nouns as well as noncount nouns are followed by a number in parentheses. Examples of usage are given below.

(1) *noncount:* I bought **some food** at the grocery store.
    count: Vegetables and meat are **foods** (*kinds of food*).

(2) *noncount:* I have **some work** to do tonight.
    count: That painting is **a work** of art.

(3) *noncount:* I don't listen to **gossip**.
    count: Chris is **a gossip** (*a person who gossips*).

(4) *noncount:* I can't hear you. There's **too much noise.**
    count: I heard **some** funny **noises** in the kitchen.

(5) *noncount:* Jane has brown **hair.**
    count: There is **a hair** on my jacket.

(6) *noncount:* I added **some pepper** to the soup.
    count: I bought **a green pepper** at the store.

EXERCISE 4:   Complete the sentences with the correct form, *singular or plural,* of the given nouns. When necessary, choose the correct word in parentheses in some of the sentences.

1. *chair*   I bought some ____chairs_____ .

2. *furniture*   I bought some ____furniture_____ .

3. *fruit*   There (ⓘs, are) a lot of ____fruit_____ on the table.

4. *vegetable*   There (is, ⓐre) a lot of ____vegetables__ on the table.

5. *clothing*   I have a lot of _____ in my closet.

6. *dress*   Mary has a lot of _____ in her closet.

7. *information*   There (is, are) a lot of _____ in an encyclopedia.

8. *fact*   There (is, are) a lot of _____ in an encyclopedia.

9. *grammar*   I know a lot of _____ .

10. *vocabulary*   I'm learning a lot of new _____ .

11. *word*   I'm learning a lot of new _____ .

12. *slang*   I want to learn some American _____ .

13. *idiom*   I know a lot of English _____ .

14. *traffic*   There (is, are) a lot of _____ in the street.

15. *car*   There (is, are) a lot of _____ on the road.

16. *literature*   I like to read good _____ .

17. *novel*   I like to read good _____ .

18. *poem*   I like to read _____ .

19. *poetry*   I like to read _____ .

20. *mail*   Did you get any _____ today?

21. *letter*   Did you get any _____ today?

22. *sand*   I got some _____ in my shoes at the beach.

23. *dust*   There (is, are) a lot of _____ under the bed.

24. *homework*   I have a lot of _____ to do tonight.

25. *assignment*   The teacher gives us a lot of _____ .

26. *penny*   Tommy had four _____ in his pocket.

27. *money*   He has some _____ in his pocket.

28. *quarter*   I need two _____ for the vending machine. I want to get a can of soda pop.

29. *change*   I need some _____ for the vending machine.

30. *thing*   Whose _____ (is, are) (this, these)?

31. *stuff*   Whose _____ (is, are) (this, these)?

32. *corn*   Janice had some _____ for dinner.

33. *pea*   Jack had some _____ with his dinner.

34. *makeup*   When Alice went to the drug store, she bought some

                   _____ .

35. *garbage*   The street is very dirty. There (is, are) some

                   _____ in the street.

EXERCISE 5: Complete the sentences with the *singular or plural form* of the given nouns. When necessary, choose the correct word in parentheses in some of the sentences.

1. *machinery*   It takes a lot of _____ to build a road.

2. *machine*   There (is, are) a lot of washing _____ in a laundromat.

3. *equipment*   There (is, are) a lot of _____ in the chemistry lab.

4. *tool*   There (is, are) a lot of _____ in the garage.

5. *hardware*   That store sells a lot of _____ .

6. *ring, bracelet* Marie wears a lot of _____ and

                   _____ .

7. *jewelry*   Marie wears a lot of _____ .

8. *jewel*   A crown has a lot of _____ .

9. *suggestion*   Can you give me some _____ ?

10. *advice*   Can you give me some _____ ?

11. *gossip*   I refuse to listen to _____ .

12. *news*   There (isn't, aren't) any interesting _____
                     in today's paper.

13. *lake, mountain* We saw a lot of _____ and

                     _____ on our vacation.

14. *scenery*   We saw a lot of beautiful _____ on our
                     vacation.

15. *plant*   Ann has a lot of _____ in her apartment.

16. *grass*   When we went on a picnic, we sat on the

                     _____ .

17. *chemistry*   I like to learn about _____ .

18. *English*   Ahmed's children know a lot of _____ .

19. *hair*   My wife has dark _____ and green eyes.

20. *hair*   Bob brushed a couple of _____ off the
                     shoulder of his blue suit coat.

21. *work*   Rodin's statue of "The Thinker" is one of my favorite

                     _____ of art.

22. *work*   I have a lot of _____ to do tomorrow.

23. *job*   I have a lot of small _____ to do around
                     the house tomorrow.

24. *song*   The children learned a lot of new _____
                     in nursery school.

25. *music*   I enjoy listening to _____ .

11-4 MORE NONCOUNT NOUNS

A. LIQUIDS (e.g., water), SOLIDS (e.g., ice), and GASES (e.g., steam)

LIQUIDS		SOLIDS		GASES
beer*(1)	milk	bread	cement	air
blood	oil	butter	chalk	fog
coffee(2)	shampoo	cheese	copper	hyrdogen
cream	soup	ice	cotton	oxygen
gasoline	tea	ice cream	glass(4)	pollution
honey	water	lettuce	gold	smog
juice	wine	margarine	iron(5)	smoke
		meat	paper(6)	steam
		bacon	rubber	
		beef	silver	
		chicken(3)	soap	
		fish(3)	tin	
		ham	toothpaste	
		lamb(3)	wood(7)	
		pork	wool	
		toast		

*The words in the list that are followed by a number in parentheses can also be used as count nouns.

(1) *noncount:* Tom bought **some beer** for the party.
    count: Would you like **a beer** *(a glass/can/bottle of beer)?*

(2) *noncount:* I had **some coffee** after dinner.
    count: **Two coffees,** please.

(3) *noncount:* I had **some chicken/fish/lamb** for dinner.
    count: She drew a picture of **a chicken/a fish/a lamb.**

(4) *noncount:* Windows are made of **glass.**
    count: I drank **a glass** of water.
    count: Mary wears **glasses** when she reads.

(5) *noncount:* **Iron** is a metal.
    count: I pressed my shirt with **an iron.**

(6) *noncount:* I need **some paper** to write a letter.
    count: I wrote **a paper** *(a long composition)* for Professor Lee.
    count: I bought **a paper** *(a newspaper).*

(7) *noncount:* The table is made of **wood.**
    count: I like to walk in **the woods** *(a place with many trees.).*

B. NATURAL PHENOMENA (things that occur in nature)

weather	lightning	darkness	electricity
dew	rain	light(8)	fire(9)
fog	sleet	daylight	gravity
hail	snow	moonlight	
heat	thunder	sunlight	
humidity	wind	sunshine	

(8) *noncount:* I opened the curtain to let in **some light.**
    count: Please turn off **the lights** (e.g., lamps).

(9) *noncount:* **Fire** is hot.
    count: We made **a fire** in the fireplace.

C. **ABSTRACTIONS** *(An abstraction is something that has no physical form. A person cannot touch it.)*

anger	enjoyment	happiness	ignorance	luck	recreation
beauty	entertainment	hate	intelligence	patience	space(13)
confidence	experience(11)	health	justice	peace	stupidity
courage	fun	help	knowledge	poverty	time(14)
cowardice	generosity	honesty	laughter	pride	violence
education(10)	greed	hospitality	love(12)	progress	wealth

(10) *noncount:* **Education** is important.
     count: You can get a good **education** at that school.

(11) *noncount:* Tom can't cook very well. He hasn't had **much experience** in the kitchen.
     count: I had **many** interesting **experiences** on my trip.

(12) *noncount:* Children need **a lot of love.**
     count: Sailing is **one of** Bob's greatest **loves.**

(13) *noncount:* I don't have **enough space** in my apartment for a piano.
     count: There is **a space** between each word in a sentence.

(14) *noncount:* **How much time** do you need to finish your work?
     count: **How many times** have you been in Mexico?

EXERCISE 6: Complete the sentences with the correct form, *singular or plural,* of the given nouns. When necessary, choose the correct word in parentheses in some of the sentences.

1. *snow*   It's winter. There (is, are) a lot of ____snow____ on the ground.

2. *knowledge*   Professor Nash has a lot of _____ about that subject.

3. *weather*   There (is, are) a lot of cold _____ in Alaska.

4. *sunlight*   _____ (is, are) a source of vitamin D.

5. *fun*   We had a lot of _____ on the picnic.

6. *luck*   I want to wish you good _____ .

7. *idea*   Bob has a lot of good _____ .

8. *milk*   I bought some _____ at the store.

9. *intelligence*   I admire Barbara for her _____ .

10. *gold*   My earrings are made of _____ .

11. *sandwich*   Do you like _____ ?

12. *entertainment*   What do you do for _____ on weekends?

13. *generosity*   Thank you for your _____ .

14. *help*   Could you give me some _____ with this?

15. *game*   Children like to play _____ .

16. *patience*   Teaching children to read requires _____ .

17. *confidence*   I'm sure you can do it. I have _____ in you.

18. *progress*   Irene's English is improving. She's making a lot of

                     _____ .

19. *courage*   Be brave. You must have _____ .

20. *pollution*   Automobiles are a source of _____ .

21. *time*   It took me a lot of _____ to write my composition.

22. *time*   I really liked that movie. I saw it three

                     _____ .

23. *hospitality*   Thank you for your _____ .

24. *beef*   The _____ we had for dinner last night (was, were) very good.

EXERCISE 7: Study the examples.

(a) I had **some coffee**. (b) I had **two cups of coffee**. (c) I bought **some butter**. (d) I bought **a pound of butter**. (e) I ate **some toast**. (f) I ate **a piece of toast**.	When a speaker wants to mention a specific quantity, s/he often uses expressions such as *two cups of, a pound of, a piece of* with noncount nouns.

On the following page, use the words in the list to complete the sentences. Use the plural form if necessary. Some sentences have more than one possible completion.

bar	*loaf*
bottle	*piece*
bowl	*pound*
cup	*quart*
gallon	*tube*
glass	

1. I drank a ____cup____ of coffee.

2. I bought two ____pounds____ of cheese.

3. I bought a _____ of milk at the supermarket.

4. I drank a _____ of orange juice.

5. I had a _____ of toast and an egg for breakfast.

6. I put ten _____ of gas in my car.

7. I had a _____ of soup for lunch.

8. I need a _____ of chalk.

9. I drank a _____ of beer.

10. I bought a _____ of margarine.

11. There is a _____ of fruit on the table.

12. I used two _____ of bread to make a sandwich.

13. I bought one _____ of bread at the store.

14. I need to buy a new _____ of toothpaste.

15. There is a _____ of soap in the bathroom.

16. Let me give you a _____ of advice.

EXERCISE 8:   Study the examples.

(a) **How many apples** did you buy? (b) **How much fruit** did you buy?	**Many** is used with count nouns. **Much** is used with noncount nouns.

Complete the sentences by using **many** or **much** and the given noun. Use the plural form of the noun if necessary. Choose the correct word in parentheses as necessary.

1. *apple*   How ___many apples___ did you buy?

2. *fruit*   How ___much fruit___ did you buy?

3. *mail*   How _____ did you get yesterday?

4. *letter*   How _____ did you get yesterday?

5. *postage*   How _____ do I need for this package?

6. *stamp*   How _____ did you buy?

7. *English*   Anna's husband doesn't know _____ .

8. *slang*   Sometimes I can't understand my roommate because he

   uses too _____ .

9. *word*   How _____ (is, are) there in your dictionary?

10. *coffee*   Louise drinks too _____ .

11. *sandwich*   Tommy has a stomach ache. He ate too _____

   _____ .

12. *sugar*   You shouldn't eat too _____ .

EXERCISE 9:   Complete the sentences with *much* or *many* and the *singular or plural form* of the noun. Choose the correct word in parentheses as necessary.

1. *course*   How _____ are you taking this semester?

2. *homework*   How _____ do you have to do tonight?

3. *news*   There (isn't, aren't) _____ in the paper today.

4. *article*   How _____ (is, are) there on the front page of today's paper?

5. *fun*   I didn't have _____ at the party. It was boring.

6. *star*   How _____ (is, are) there in the universe?

7. *sunshine*   There (isn't, aren't) _____ in Seattle in the winter.

8. *pollution*   (Is, Are) there _____ in Miami?

9. *luck*   We didn't have _____ when we went fishing.

10. *kind*   There (is, are) _____ of flowers.

11. *violence*   I think there (is, are) too _____ on TV.

12. *makeup*   I think that Mary wears too _____ .

EXERCISE 10—ORAL (BOOKS CLOSED):   Ask and answer questions with **how much** and **how many.**

> *Example:*   Mary has two children.
> *Student A:* How many children does Mary have?
> *Student B:* Two.

1. I invited ten people to my party.
2. There are 50 states in the United States
3. I drink two cups of coffee every day.*
4. I bought one pound of butter.
5. I bought ten gallons of gas(oline).
6. There are ten provinces in Canada.
7. There are 345 pages in this book.
8. I have twenty dollars.
9. I cooked two cups of rice.
10. There are (around 25) desks in this room.
11. I use very little salt on my food.
12. I know very few students in my chemistry class.
13. A round-trip ticket from here to (Chicago) costs $430.
14. I bought two pounds of cheese.
15. There are 9,000 different kinds of birds in the world.
16. I know a lot of English vocabulary.

EXERCISE 11:   Study the examples.

(a) I bought **a few apples.** (b) I bought **a little fruit.**	**A few** is used with count nouns. **A little** is used with noncount nouns.

———————

*There are two possible questions:

> *How much coffee do you drink every day?*
> *How many cups of coffee do you drink every day?*

Complete the sentences by using *a little* or *a few* and the given noun. Use the plural form of the noun when necessary.

1. *music*   I feel like listening to ___a little music___ tonight.

2. *song*   We sang ___a few songs___ at the party.

3. *desk*   We need ___a few___ more ___desks___ in our classroom.

4. *time*   I'm not finished with my work. I need ___a little___ more ___time___ .

5. *help*   Do you need _____ with that?

6. *advice*   I need _____ .

7. *fruit*   I bought _____ at the market.

8. *apple*   I bought _____ at the market.*

9. *chicken*   I'm still hungry. I think I'll have _____ more _____ .

10. *chicken*   When I was a child, we raised _____ in our back yard.

11. *money*   If I accept that job, I'll make _____ more _____ .

12. *penny*   Annie put _____ in her pocket.

13. *information*   Could you give me _____ ?

14. *hour*   Don's plane will arrive in _____ more _____ .

15. *clothes†*   Sally bought _____ yesterday.

16. *clothing*   Ted bought _____ and some books.

---

*I bought a few apples. = I bought a small number of apples.
I bought a little apple. = I bought one apple and it was small, not large.
†**Clothes** and **clothing** have the same meaning. **Clothes** is always plural.
  Clothing is a noncount noun.

11-5 GUIDELINES FOR ARTICLE USAGE

	USING *A* OR ∅ (NO ARTICLE)		USING *A* OR *SOME*
SINGULAR COUNT NOUNS	(a) **A dog** makes a good pet. (b) **A banana** is yellow. (c) **A pencil** contains lead.	A speaker uses *a* with a singular count noun when s/he is making a generalization. In (a): The speaker is talking about any dog, all dogs, dogs in general.	(j) I saw **a dog** in my yard. (k) Mary ate **a banana.** (l) I need **a pencil.**
PLURAL COUNT NOUNS	(d) ∅ **Dogs** make good pets. (e) ∅ **Bananas** are yellow. (f) ∅ **Pencils** contain lead.	A speaker uses no article (∅) with a plural count noun when s/he is making a generalization.* In (d): The speaker is talking about any dog, all dogs, dogs in general. Note: (a) and (d) have the same meaning.	(m) I saw **some dogs** in my yard. (n) Mary bought **some bananas.** (o) Bob has **some pencils** in his pocket.
NONCOUNT NOUNS	(g) ∅ **Fruit** is good for you. (h) ∅ **Coffee** contains caffeine. (i) I like ∅ **music.**	A speaker uses no article (∅) with a noncount noun when s/he is making a generalization.* In (g): The speaker is talking about any fruit, all fruit, fruit in general.	(p) I bought **some fruit.** (q) Bob drank **some coffee.** (r) Would you like to listen to **some music?**

*Sometimes a speaker uses an expression of quantity (e.g., *almost all, most, some*) when s/he makes a generalization: *Almost all dogs make good pets. Most dogs are friendly. Some dogs have short hair.*

	USING *THE*	

A speaker uses **a** with a singular count noun when s/he is talking about one thing (or person) that is not specific.
In (j): The speaker is saying, "I saw one dog (not two dogs, some dogs, many dogs). It wasn't a specific dog (e.g., your dog, the neighbor's dog, that dog). It was only one dog out of the whole group of animals called dogs."
	(s) Did you feed **the dog**?
	(t) I had a banana and an apple.
	      I gave **the banana** to Mary.
	(u) **The pencil** on that desk is Jim's.
	(v) **The sun** is shining.
	(w) Please close **the door.**
	(x) Mary is in **the kitchen.**
		The is used in front of:
		    singular count nouns:
		      the dog
		    plural count nouns:
		      the dogs
		    noncount nouns:
		      the fruit
		
		A speaker uses **the** (not **a**, ∅, or **some**) when the speaker and the listener are thinking about the same specific thing(s) or person(s).
		In (s): The speaker and the listener are thinking about the same specific dog. The listener knows which dog the speaker is talking about: the dog that they own, the dog that they feed every day. There is only one dog that the speaker could possibly be talking about.
		In (t): A speaker uses **the** when s/he mentions a noun the second time. First mention: *I had a banana.* . . . Second mention: *I gave the banana.* . . . In the second mention, the listener now knows which banana the speaker is talking about: the banana the speaker had (not the banana John had, not the banana in that bowl).

A speaker often uses **some**† with a plural count noun when s/he is talking about things (or people) that are not specific. In (m): The speaker is saying, "I saw more than one dog. They weren't specific dogs (e.g., your dogs, the neighbor's dogs, those dogs). The exact number of dogs isn't important (two dogs, five dogs), so I'm simply saying that I saw an indefinite number of dogs."	(y) Did you feed **the dogs**? (z) I had some bananas and some apples. I gave **the bananas** to Mary. (aa) **The pencils** on that desk are Jim's. (bb) Please turn off **the lights.**	
A speaker often uses **some**† with a noncount noun when s/he is talking about something that is not specific. In (p): The speaker is saying, "I bought an indefinite amount of fruit. The exact amount isn't important information (e.g., two pounds of fruit, four bananas, and two apples). And I'm not talking about specific fruit (e.g., that fruit, the fruit in that bowl)."	(cc) **The fruit** in this bowl is ripe. (dd) I drank some coffee and some milk. **The coffee** was hot. (ee) I can't hear you. **The music** is too loud. (ff) **The air** is cold today.	

†In addition to **some,** a speaker might use **several, a few, a lot of,** etc. with a plural count noun, or **a little, a lot of,** etc. with a noncount noun. (See 11–2.)

EXERCISE 12:   Discuss Speaker A's use of articles in the following dialogues. Why does Speaker A use *a, some, the,* or ∅? Discuss what both A and B are thinking about.

DIALOGUE 1:

A: **A dog** makes a good pet.   B: I agree.

DIALOGUE 2:

A: I saw **a dog** in my yard.

DIALOGUE 4:

A: **Dogs** make good pets.   B: I agree.

DIALOGUE 5:

A: I saw **some dogs** in my yard.

DIALOGUE 7:

A: **Fruit** is good for you.   B: I agree.

DIALOGUE 8:

A: I ate **some fruit.**

DIALOGUE 3:

B: Oh?

A: Did you feed **the dog**?

B: Yes.

DIALOGUE 6:

B: Oh?

A: Did you feed **the dogs**?

B: Yes.

DIALOGUE 9:

B: Oh?

A: **The fruit** in this bowl is ripe.

B: Good.

EXERCISE 13: Here are some conversations. Try to decide whether the speakers would probably use **the** or **a/an**.* Are the speakers thinking about the same objects or persons?

1. A: Do you have _____a_____ car?

    B: No. But I have _____a_____ bicycle.

2. A: Do you need _____the_____ car today, honey?

    B: Yes. I have a lot of errands to do. Why don't I drive you to work today?

    A: Okay. But be sure to fill _____the_____ car up with gas sometime today.

3. A: Did you have a good time at _____ party last night?

    B: Yes.

    A: So did I. I'm glad that you decided to go with me.

4. A: What did you do last night?

    B: I went to _____ party.

    A: Oh? Where was it?

5. A: I bought _____ table yesterday.

    B: Oh? I didn't know you went shopping for furniture.

6. A: Have you seen my keys?

    B: Yes. They're on _____ table next to _____ front door.

7. A: Is Mr. Jones _____ graduate student?

    B: No. He's _____ professor.

8. A: Where's _____ professor?

    B: She's absent today.

9. A: Would you like to go to _____ zoo this afternoon?

    B: Sure. Why not?

10. A: Does San Diego have _____ zoo?

    B: Yes. It's world famous.

_____

*A is used in front of nouns that begin with a consonant: *a book, a dog, a pencil.* *An* is used in front of nouns that begin with a vowel or a vowel sound: *an apple, an elephant, an idea, an opinion, an uncle, an hour.*

11. A: Where do you live?

   B: We live on _____ quiet street in the suburbs.

12. A: I'm hungry and I'm tired of walking. How much farther is it to

   _____ restaurant?

   B: Just a couple of blocks. Let's cross _____ street here.
   A: Are you sure you know where you're going?

13. A: Did Bob find _____ job?

   B: Yes. He's working at _____ restaurant.
   A: Oh? Which one?

14. A: Did you feed _____ cat?
   B: Yes. I fed him a couple of hours ago.

15. A: Does Jane have _____ cat?

   B: No, she has _____ dog. She doesn't like cats.

16. A: Where's Dennis?

   B: He's in _____ kitchen.

17. A: Do you like your new apartment?

   B: Yes. It has _____ big kitchen.

EXERCISE 14: Complete the sentences with the given nouns. Use **the** for specific statements. Do not use **the** for general statements.

1. *flowers*   (a) ___The flowers___ in that vase are beautiful.

             (b) ___Flowers___ are beautiful.

2. *mountains*   (a) _____ are beautiful.

             (b) _____ in Colorado are beautiful.

3. *water*   (a) _____ consists of hydrogen and oxygen.
             (b) I don't want to go swimming today.

             _____ is too cold.

4. *information*   (a) _____ in that book is inaccurate.

             (b) An encyclopedia is a source of _____ .

5. *health*   (a) _____ is more important than money.

                          (b) Doctors are concerned with _____ of their patients.

6. *men, women*   (a) _____ have stronger muscles than

                          _____ .

                          (b) At the party last night, _____ sat on one side of the room and _____ sat on the other.

7. *problems*   (a) Everyone has _____ .

                          (b) Irene told me about _____ she had with her car yesterday.

8. *happiness*   (a) I can't express _____ I felt when I heard the good news.

                          (b) Everyone seeks _____ .

9. *vegetables*   (a) _____ are good for you.

                          (b) _____ we had for dinner last night were overcooked.

10. *gold*   (a) _____ is a precious metal.

                          (b) _____ in Mary's ring is 24 karats.

EXERCISE 15: Add *the* if necessary. Otherwise, make the symbol ∅ to show that no article is necessary.

1. Please pass me _____the_____ butter.

2. _____∅_____ butter is a dairy product.

3. John, where's _____ milk? Is it in _____ refrigerator or on _____ table?

4. _____ milk comes from cows and goats.

5. Tom usually has _____ wine with dinner.

6. Dinner's ready. Shall I pour _____ wine?

7. I'm studying _____ English. I'm studying _____ grammar.

8. _____ grammar in this chapter isn't easy.

9. _____ chemistry is my favorite subject.

10. Do you like _____ weather in this city?

11. _____ copper is used in electrical wiring.

12. _____ air is free.

13. _____ air is humid today.

14. _____ windows are closed. Please open them.

15. _____ windows are made of _____ glass.

16. We usually have _____ meat for dinner.

17. _____ meat we had for dinner last night was tough.

18. People used to use _____ candles for _____ light, but now they use _____ electricity.

EXERCISE 16:   Use **a/an/some** or **the** in the following. Reminder: Use **the** when a noun is mentioned for the second time.

1. Yesterday I saw _____a_____ dog and _____a_____ cat.

   _____The_____ dog was chasing _____the_____ cat.

   _____THE_____ cat was chasing _____THE_____ mouse.

   _____THE_____ mouse ran into _____THE_____ hole, but

   _____THE_____ hole was very small. _____THE_____ cat couldn't

   get into _____THE_____ hole, so it ran up _____THE_____ tree.

   _____ dog tried to climb _____ tree too, but it

   couldn't.

2. Yesterday I bought _____ clothes. I bought _____

   suit, _____ shirt, and _____ tie.

   _____ suit is gray and comes with a vest. _____

   shirt is pale blue, and _____ tie has black and gray stripes.

3. Yesterday I saw _____ man and _____ woman.
   They were having _____ argument. _____ man
   was yelling at _____ woman, and _____
   woman was shouting at _____ man. I don't know what
   _____ argument was about.

4. I had _____ soup and _____ sandwich for
   lunch. _____ soup was too salty, but _____
   sandwich was pretty good.

5. A: I saw _____ accident yesterday.
   B: Oh? Where?
   A: On Grand Avenue. _____ man in _____
      Volkswagen drove through a stop sign and hit _____ bus.
   B: Was anyone hurt in _____ accident?
   A: I don't think so. _____ man who was driving
      _____ Volkswagen got out of his car and seemed to be
      okay. His car was only slightly damaged. No one in _____
      bus was hurt.

6. A: What did you do last weekend?
   B: I went on _____ picnic Saturday and saw
      _____ movie Sunday.
   A: Did you have fun?
   B: _____ picnic was fun, but _____ movie was
      boring.

EXERCISE 17: Complete the sentences with **a, an, some, the,** or ∅.

1. A: Do you like _____∅_____ fruit?
   B: Very much.

2. A: I'm hungry.
   B: Would you like _____ fruit? How about
      _____ apple?

3. A: _____ fruit we bought at the market was fresh.
   B: That's the best place to buy _____ fruit.

4. _____ gas is expensive nowadays.

5. _____ gas at Mack's Service Station is cheaper than

_____ gas at the Shell Station.

6. I need _____ gas. Let's stop at the next service station.

7. Kathy bought _____ radio. She likes to listen to

_____ music when she studies.

8. A: Would you please turn _____ radio down?

_____ music is too loud.

B: No problem.

9. A: Do you see _____ man who is standing next to Janet?
B: Yes. Who is he?

A: He's _____ president of this university.

10. A one-dollar bill has the picture of _____ president of the
United States.

11. A: What did you buy when you went shopping?

B: I bought _____ blouse and _____ jewelry.

A: What color is _____ blouse?
B: Red.

12. A: Where's my bookbag?

B: It's on _____ floor. Over there. In _____

corner next to _____ sofa.

13. We need to buy _____ furniture. I'd like to get

_____ sofa and _____ easy chair.

14. _____ furniture is expensive these days.

15. _____ vegetarian doesn't eat _____ meat.

16. Last week I read _____ book about _____ life
of Gandhi.

17. I enjoy _____ life.

18. A: Let's go swimming in _____ lake today.

B: That sounds like _____ good idea.

19. _____ lake is a body of _____ water that is

smaller than _____ sea but larger than _____

pond. _____ ocean is larger than _____ sea.

20. During our vacation in Florida, we walked along _____

beach in front of our hotel and looked at _____ ocean.

EXERCISE 18—ERROR ANALYSIS: All of the following sentences contain mistakes. Can you find the mistakes and correct them?

1. There are a lot of informations in that book.
2. The oil is a natural resource.
3. Lions are wild animal.
4. I was late because there were too many traffics.
5. I caught two fishes.
6. Our teacher gives us too many homeworks.
7. Ann knows a lot of vocabularies.
8. I had a egg for breakfast.
9. There is many kind of trees in the world.
10. I'm studying the English.
11. I'm living in United State.
12. Only twelve student were in class yesterday.
13. I need some advices.
14. We all have a few problem in the life.

EXERCISE 19—WRITTEN: Write about one (or both) of the following topics.

1. Look around your room, apartment, house. Tell your reader what you see. Indicate quantity (*some, a lot of, two, etc.*) and position (*in the corner, next to the bed, etc.*).
2. Think of someone you admire. Tell your reader why you admire this person.

11-6   MORE TWO-WORD VERBS (SEPARABLE)*

cross out	draw a line through
do over	do again
fill in	complete a sentence by writing in a blank
fill out	write information in a form (e.g., an application form)
fill up	fill completely with gas, water, coffee, etc.
find out	discover information
give up	quit doing something or quit trying
leave out	omit
start over	start again
tear down	destroy a building
tear off	detach, tear along a dotted or perforated line
tear out of	remove a piece of paper from a book or notebook
tear up	tear into small pieces

*See 8-4 and 8-5 for more information about two-word verbs.

EXERCISE 20—TWO-WORD VERBS: Complete the sentences with prepositions.

1. Maria Alvarez's name is supposed to be on this list, but it isn't. Someone probably left it _CROSS, OUT_ by mistake.

2. I can't solve this math problem. I give _UP_ .

3. I'm not satisfied with my composition. I think I'll do it _OVER_ .

4. Dick had trouble figuring out what to say in his letter to his girlfriend. He started the letter _START OVER_ three times.

5. A: Good news! I've been accepted at the University of Tennessee.

   B: Great. When did you find _OUT_ ?
   A: I got a letter in the mail today.

6. A: My roomate moved last week. He went to the post office before he left and filled out a change-of-address card, but I'm still getting some of his mail. What should I do?

   B: Cross _OUT_ the old address on a letter and write in his new one. Also write "please forward" on the letter. You don't have to use another stamp.

7. How much does it cost to fill _____ your gas tank?

8. We're doing an exercise. We're filling _____ blanks with prepositions.

9. When I went to Dr. Green's office for the first time, I had to fill _____ a long form about my health history.

10. I made a mistake on the check I was writing, so I tore it _____ and wrote another check.

11. An old building was in the way of the new highway through the city, so they tore the old building _____ .

12. John tore a piece of paper _____ _____ his spiral notebook.

13. When I pay my Master Card bill, I have to tear _____ the top portion of the bill along the perforated line and send it back with my check.

11-7 MORE TWO-WORD VERBS (NONSEPARABLE)*

(a) Last night some friends **dropped in**.	In (a): *drop in* is not followed by an object.
(b) Let's **drop in on** *Alice* this afternoon. Let's **drop in on** *her* this afternoon.	In (b): *drop in on* is followed by an object.
	Some two-word verbs are actually three-word verbs (*verb + two prepositions*) when they are followed by an object. These verbs are nonseparable.

drop in (on) . . . .*visit without calling first or without an invitation*
drop out (of) . . . .*stop attending (school)*
fool around (with) . . . .*have fun while wasting time*
get along (with) . . . .*have a good relationship with*
get back (from) . . . .*return from (a trip)*
get through (with) . . . .*finish*
grow up (in) . . . .*become an adult*
look out (for) . . . .*be careful*
run out (of) . . . .*finish the supply of (something)*
watch out (for) . . . .*be careful*

*See 8-4 and 8-5 for more information about two-word verbs.

EXERCISE 21—TWO-WORD VERBS: Complete the sentences with prepositions.

1. Look _____out_____ ! There's a car coming!

2. Look _____out_____ . _____for_____ that car!

3. Where did you grow _____ ?

4. I grew _____ _____ Springfield.

5. I couldn't finish the examination. I ran _____ _____ time.

6. A: What did you do yesterday?

    B: Nothing much. I just fooled _____ .

7. A: Hi, Chris! What's up? I haven't seen you in a long time. Where have you been?
    B: I went to California last week to visit my brother.

    A: Oh? When did you get _____ _____ California?
    B: Just yesterday.

8. A: Where's Jack? He hasn't been in class for at least two weeks.

    B: He dropped _____ _____ school.

9. A: Watch _____ _____ that truck!
    B: What truck?

10. A: What time do you expect to get _____ _____ your homework?
    B: In about an hour, as soon as I finish reading this chapter.

11. A: I haven't seen the Grants for a long time. Let's drop

    _____ _____ them this evening.

    B: We'd better call first. They may not like unexpected company.

12. A: I want to change my room in the dorm.
    B: Why?

    A: I don't get _____ _____ my roommate.

chapter *12*

Noun Clauses

12-1 NOUN CLAUSES: INTRODUCTION

(a) S V O I know his address. (*noun phrase*)	Verbs are often followed by objects. The object is usually a noun phrase,* as in (a): ***his address*** is a noun phrase; ***his address*** is the object of the verb ***know***.
(b) S V O I know where he lives. (*noun clause*)	Some verbs can be followed by noun clauses.* A noun clause has a subject and a verb: In (b): ***where he lives*** is a noun clause; ***he*** is the subject of the clause and ***lives*** is the verb of the clause.
	A noun clause can be used in the same way as a noun phrase; e.g., as the object of a verb. In (b): the noun clause (*where he lives*) is the object of the verb ***know***.
(c) I know **where he lives.** (*noun clause*)	A noun clause can begin with a question word. (See 12-2.)

*Grammar terminology:
   A *phrase* is a group of related words. It does not contain a subject and a verb.
   A *clause* is a group of related words. It contains a subject and a verb.
A noun clause is a dependent clause and cannot stand alone as a sentence. It must be connected to an independent clause (a main clause).

(d) I don't know **if he is married.** *(noun clause)*	A noun clause can begin with *if* or ***whether***. (See 12-3.)
(e) I know **that the world is round.** *(noun clause)*	A noun clause can begin with ***that***. (See 12-4.)

12-2 NOUN CLAUSES WHICH BEGIN WITH A QUESTION WORD

INFORMATION QUESTION	NOUN CLAUSE	
		Notice in the examples: Question word order is not used in a noun clause.
(a) Where does he live?	(b) I don't know **where he lives.** ⌐S⌐ ⌐V⌐ ⌐O⌐	INCORRECT: *I know where does he live.* CORRECT: *I know where he lives.*
(c) When did they leave?	(d) Do you know **when they left?**	
(e) What did she say?	(f) Please tell me **what she said.**	
(g) Why is Tom absent today?	(h) I don't understand **why Tom is absent today.**	The following question words can be used to introduce a noun clause: ***when, where, why, how, who, whom, what, which, whose***

EXERCISE 1:   Complete the sentences by changing the questions to noun clauses.

1. *Where did John go?* I don't know ____where John went.____

2. *How old is Mary?* I don't know _____

3. *Why did Bob leave?* I don't know _____

4. *When did Bob leave?* I don't know _____

5. *Where did he go?* I don't know _____

6. *Where is he?* I don't know _____

7. *Where does he live?* I don't remember _____

8. *What did he say?* I didn't hear _____

9. *Where is the post office?* Could you please tell me _____

10. *What time is it?*   Could you please tell me _____

11. *How much does this*   Could you please tell me _____
    book cost?

12. *What does this word*   Could you please tell me _____
    mean?

13. *What country is Anna*   Do you know _____
    from?

14. *Why was Kathy absent*   Do you know _____
    yesterday?

15. *How far is it to*   I wonder _____
    Chicago?

16. *When does the*   Can you tell me _____
    semester end?

17. *What is Sue talking*   I don't understand _____
    about?

18. *When did David arrive?*   I don't know _____

19. *When is he going*   Do you know _____
    to leave?

20. *Where can I buy a*   Do you know _____
    good radio?

EXERCISE 2:   Complete the sentences by changing the questions to noun clauses.

1. *Who(m) did you see at*   Tell me __who(m) you saw at the party.__
   the party?

2. *Who came to the party?*   Tell me __who came to the party.*__

3. *Who(m) did Helen talk to?* Do you know _____

4. *Who lives in that*   Do you know _____
   apartment?

5. *What happened?*   Tell me _____

6. *What did he say?*   Tell me _____

7. *What kind of car does*   I can't remember _____
   Jackie have?

---

*Usual question word order is not used when the question word (e.g., *who* or *what*) is the subject of a
question (see 5–2). In this case, the word order in the noun clause is the same as the word order in the
question.

8. *How old are their children?* I can't ever remember _____

9. *Why did you say that?* I don't understand _____

10. *Where can I catch the bus?* Could you please tell me _____

_____

11. *Who broke the window?* Do you know _____

12. *How long has Ted been living here?* Do you know _____

13. *What time is flight 677 supposed to arrive?* Can you tell me _____

14. *Who did Ellen invite to her party?* I don't know _____

15. *Why is Tommy crying?* Do you know _____

16. *Why is Mary angry?* Do you know _____

17. *Who teaches that class?* Can you tell me _____

18. *Who did you meet at the party?* Tell me _____

EXERCISE 3: Study the examples.

QUESTION	NOUN CLAUSE
V **S**	**S** **V**
(a) Who is that boy?	(b) I don't know who **that boy is.**
V **S**	**S** **V**
(c) Whose pen is this?	(d) I don't know whose pen **this is.**

Complete the sentences by changing the questions to noun clauses.

1. *Who is she?* I don't know _____

2. *Who are they?* I don't know _____

3. *What is that?* Do you know _____

4. *What are those?* Can you tell me _____

5. *Whose book is that?* I don't know _____

6. *Whose books are those?* Do you know _____

7. *What is a wrench?*   Do you know _____

8. *Who is that woman?*   I wonder _____

9. *Whose house is that?*   I wonder _____

10. *What is an elephant?*   Don't you know _____

11. *What is in that drawer?*   I don't know   what is in that drawer.* _____

12. *Who is in that room?*   I don't know _____

13. *Whose car is in the driveway?*   Do you know _____

14. *Whose car is that?*   Do you know _____

15. *What is on TV tonight?*   I wonder _____

16. *What is a carrot?*   Do you know _____

17. *Whose glasses are those?*   Could you tell me _____

18. *Who am I?*   He doesn't know _____

EXERCISE 4—ORAL (BOOKS CLOSED): Change the questions to noun clauses. Begin your response with *"I don't know. . . ."*

Example: Where does (. . .) live?
Response: I don't know where (. . .) lives.

1. Where did (. . .) go yesterday?
2. What did (. . .) buy yesterday?
3. Why did (. . .) go downtown yesterday?
4. When did (. . .) get home last night?
5. What time did (. . .) go to bed last night?
6. Where does (. . .) live?
7. Where does (. . .) eat lunch?
8. What time does (. . .) eat dinner?
9. Why does (. . .) go downtown every day?
10. What time does (. . .) usually get up?
11. Why is (. . .) absent?
12. Where is (. . .)?
13. What time is it?
14. How old is (. . .)?
15. What is (. . .)'s last name?
16. How long has (. . .) been living here?

_____

*A prepositional phrase (e.g., *in that drawer*) does not precede *be* in a noun clause.

17. Who broke that window?
18. Who did (. . .) call last night?
19. What happened in France yesterday?
20. What did (. . .) eat for breakfast?
21. Who wrote *War and Peace*?
22. Who did (. . .) see yesterday?
23. What caused the earthquake in (Iran)?
24. What causes earthquakes?
25. Who is that girl?
26. Who are those people?
27. Whose (*backpack*) is that?
28. Whose (*gloves*) are those?
29. What kind of tree is that?
30. What kind of car does (. . .) have?
31. What is a range?
32. What does "range" mean?
33. How many meanings does "range" have?
34. How long has (. . .) been living here?
35. Where is (*name of a restaurant*)?
36. Where did (. . .) use to live?
37. Who is (*the mayor of this city*)?

EXERCISE 5—ORAL (BOOKS CLOSED):   Change the questions to noun clauses. Begin your response with *"Could you please tell me. . . ."*

    Example   Where does (. . .) live?
    Response: Could you please tell me where (. . .) lives?

1. What time is it?
2. Where is the post office?
3. Where is the library?
4. Where is the rest room?
5. How much does this pen cost?
6. How much does this book cost?
7. How much do these shoes cost?
8. What does this word mean?
9. What does "complex" mean?
10. What does "steam" mean?
11. Where is the nearest hospital?
12. Why were you late for class?
13. Where can I buy a garden hose?
14. What is a garden hose?
15. Whose pen is this?
16. Whose papers are those?

EXERCISE 6—ORAL (BOOKS CLOSED):   Practice using noun clauses while reviewing irregular verbs. Begin your response with *"I don't know. . . ."*

    Example: What did (. . .) find?
    Response: I don't know what he/she found.

1. Where did (. . .) sit yesterday?
2. What did (. . .) wear yesterday?
3. When did (. . .) wake up?
4. What did (. . .) buy?

5. Where did (. . .) lose his/her umbrella?

6. How did (. . .) tear his shirt/her blouse?

7. Who did (. . .) speak to yesterday?

8. How long did (. . .) sleep last night?

9. What did (. . .) make for dinner last night?

10. What did (. . .) give (. . .) for his/her birthday?

11. Why did (. . .) fly to New York?

12. What did (. . .) steal?

13. How much money did (. . .) lend (. . .)?

14. Why did (. . .) fall down?

15. Which book did (. . .) choose?

16. When did (. . .) quit smoking?

17. What did (. . .) see?

18. Why did (. . .) shake his/her head?

19. Why did (. . .) bring his/her radio to class?

20. Why did (. . .) take your dictionary?

21. Why did (. . .) draw a picture?

22. Who did (. . .) write a letter to?

23. How did (. . .) meet his wife/her husband?

24. Why did (. . .) bite his/her lip?

25. When did this (*term, session, semester, etc.*) begin?

26. How did (. . .) break his/her arm?

27. How did (. . .) catch a cold?

28. When did (. . .) get married?

29. When did (. . .) do his/her homework?

30. Where did (. . .) grow up?

12-3 NOUN CLAUSES WHICH BEGIN WITH *IF* OR *WHETHER**

YES/NO QUESTION	NOUN CLAUSE	
	S V O	When a yes/no question is changed to a noun clause, **if** is used to introduce the clause. (NOTE: *I wonder = I want to know; I'm asking myself this question.*)
(a) Is John at home?	(b) I don't know **if John is at home.**	
(c) Does the bus stop here?	(d) Do you know **if the bus stops here?**	
(e) Did Alice go to Chicago?	(f) I wonder **if Alice went to Chicago.**	
(g) I don't know **if** John is at home **or not.**		When **if** introduces a noun clause, the expression **or not** frequently comes at the end of the clause, as in (g).

*See 13–5 for the use of *if* and **whether** with **ask** in reported speech.

(h) I don't know **whether** John is at home. (i) I don't know **whether** John is at home **or not**. (j) I don't know **whether or not** John is at home.	In (h): **Whether** has the same meaning as **if.** In (i): **Or not** can come at the end of the noun clause. In (j): **Or not** can come immediately after **whether.** (NOTE: **Or not** cannot come immediately after **if.**)
	NOTE: **If** and **whether** have the same meaning when they are used to introduce noun clauses. Both of them are used in spoken English and informal writing. In formal English, **whether** is usually more appropriate than **if.** In informal English, **if** is more common than **whether.**

EXERCISE 7—ORAL: Complete the sentences by changing the yes/no questions to noun clauses. Introduce the noun clause with **if** or **whether.** Practice using **or not.**

1. *Is Mary at the library?*

I don't know

if Mary is at the library.

if Mary is at the library or not.

whether Mary is at the library.

whether Mary is at the library or not.

whether or not Mary is at the library.

2. *Does Bob live in an apartment?*   I don't know _____

3. *Did Joe go downtown?*   I don't know _____

4. *Will Ann be in class tomorrow?*   I wonder _____

5. *Is Tom at home?*   Do you know _____

EXERCISE 8:   Change the questions to noun clauses.

1. *Did Steve go to the bank?*   I don't know _____if (whether) Steve_____

_____went to the bank._____

2. *Where did Steve go?*   I don't know _____where Steve went._____

3. *Is Karen at home?*   Do you know _____

4. *Where is Karen?*   Do you know _____

5. *How is Pat feeling today?*   I wonder _____

6. *Is Pat feeling better today?*   I wonder _____

7. *Does the bus stop here?*   Do you know _____

8. *Where does the bus stop?*   I wonder _____

9. *Why is Elena absent today?*   The teacher wants to know _____

_____

10. *Is Elena going to be absent again tomorrow?*   I wonder _____

11. *Where did Janet go last night?*   Do you know _____

12. *Should I buy that book?*   I wonder _____

13. *Which book should I buy?*   I wonder _____

14. *Can Jerry speak French?*   I don't know _____

15. *How much does that book cost?*   Do you know _____

16. *Where is the nearest drug store?*   I wonder _____

17. *Is Jane Dawkins married?*   Sam wants to know _____

18. *Is there life on other planets?*   No one knows _____

19. *Are we going to have a test tomorrow?*   Let's ask the teacher _____

20. *Is there a Santa Claus?*   The little boy wants to know _____

_____

21. *Who is that man?*   I'm going to ask Jackie _____

22. *Is that man a teacher?*   I'm going to ask Jackie _____

EXERCISE 9—ORAL (BOOKS CLOSED):   Make sentences with noun clauses. Begin your response with *"I wonder...."*

    Example: Did (. . .) go to the bank?
    Response: I wonder if (. . .) went to the bank.

    Example: Where did (. . .) go?
    Response: I wonder where (. . .) went.

1. Why is (. . .) absent today?
2. Where is (. . .)?
3. Is (. . .) sick?
4. Will it snow tomorrow?
5. Will the weather be nice tomorrow?
6. Is (. . .) going to be in class tomorrow?
7. How long has (. . .) been living here?
8. How far is it to St. Louis?
9. How much does a Rolls Royce cost?
10. Does (. . .) have a car?
11. Who lives in that house?
12. Who is that woman?
13. Is that woman a teacher?
14. Whose book is that?
15. Whose gloves are those?
16. Whose pen is that?
17. Whose papers are those?
18. Did (. . .) study last night?
19. Where did (. . .) go last night?
20. Did (. . .) go to the library last night?

EXERCISE 10:   Change the questions to noun clauses.

1. *Will it rain tomorrow?*   I wonder _____

2. *What is an amphibian?*   Do you know _____

3. *Is a frog an amphibian?*   Can you tell me _____

4. *What's on TV tonight?*   I wonder _____

5. *What is the speed of sound?*   Do you know _____

6. *Does sound travel faster than light?*   Do you know _____

7. *Are dogs color-blind?* Do you know _____

8. *Is there a pot of gold at the end of the rainbow?* The little girl wants to know _____

_____

9. *Do animals have the same emotions as human beings?* The little boy wants to know _____

_____

10. *Why is the sky blue?* Annie wants to know _____

11. *Does that store accept credit cards?* Do you know _____

12. *When will the next earthquake occur in California?* No one knows _____

13. *Will there be another earthquake in California this year?* No one knows _____

14. *How do dolphins communicate with each other?* Do scientists know _____

15. *Will people be able to communicate with dolphins someday?* I wonder _____

16. *Have beings from outer space ever visited the earth?* I wonder _____

EXERCISE 11—ORAL (BOOKS CLOSED): Make sentences with noun clauses.

STUDENT A: Ask a question beginning with *"Do you know. . .?"*
STUDENT B: Answer *"no."* Give a short answer and then a full answer.

Example: Does (. . .) live in the dorm?
Student A: Do you know if (. . .) lives in the dorm?
Student B: No, I don't. I don't know whether or not (. . .) lives in the dorm.

Example: Where does (. . .) live?
Student A: Do you know where (. . .) lives?
Student B: No, I don't. I don't know where (. . .) lives.

1. Does (. . .) have a car?
2. What kind of car does (. . .) have?
3. Is there a pay phone in this building?
4. What does "gossip" mean?
5. What time does the mail come?
6. Is the mail here yet?
7. Does (. . .) have a job?
8. Is (. . .) married?
9. Why is (. . .) absent today?
10. Is the library open on Sundays?
11. What time does the bookstore close?
12. Does (. . .) speak (*language*)?
13. Who is that woman?
14. Is (. . .) planning to take another English course?
15. Can (. . .) sing?

12-4 NOUN CLAUSES WHICH BEGIN WITH *THAT*

(a) I think **that Mr. Jones is a good teacher.** S V O	A noun clause can be introduced by the word **that**. In (a): . . . *that Mr. Jones is a good teacher* = a noun clause. It is the object of the verb *think*.
(b) I hope **that you can come to my party.** (c) Mary realizes **that she should study harder.** (d) I dreamed **that I was on the top of a mountain.**	"That clauses" are frequently used as the objects of verbs which express mental activity. (See the list below.)
(e) I think **that Mr. Jones is a good teacher.** (f) I think **Mr. Jones is a good teacher.**	The word **that** is often omitted, especially in speaking. (e) and (f) have the same meaning.

COMMON VERBS FOLLOWED BY "*THAT* CLAUSES"*

assume that	*hope that*	*realize that*
believe that	*know that*	*suppose that*
discover that	*learn that*	*suspect that*
dream that	*notice that*	*think that*
guess that	*predict that*	
hear that	*prove that*	

*The verbs in the above list are those which are emphasized in the exercises. Some other common verbs that can be followed by "*that* clauses" are:

agree that	*find out that*	*recall that*
conclude that	*forget that*	*recognize that*
decide that	*imagine that*	*regret that*
demonstrate that	*indicate that*	*remember that*
doubt that	*observe that*	*reveal that*
fear that	*presume that*	*show that*
feel that	*pretend that*	*teach that*
figure out that	*read that*	*understand that*

See 14–1 for the use of "*that* clauses" after **wish**. See 13–2 for the use of "*that* clauses" in reported speech.

EXERCISE 12:   Complete the sentences with the clauses in the list or with your own words. Use *that* to introduce the clause, or omit *that* if you wish.

> *All people are equal.*
> *Flying in an airplane is safer than riding in a car.*
> *He always twirls his mustache when he's nervous.*
> *High school students in the United States don't study as hard as the students in my country do.*
> *A huge monster was chasing me.*
> *I should study tonight.*
> *I will get married someday.*
> ✓ *I will have a peanut butter sandwich.*
> *John "Cat Man" Smith stole Mrs. Adams' jewelry.*
> *Over half of the people in the world go hungry every day.*
> *People are pretty much the same everywhere.*
> *There will be more than 6½ billion people in the world by the year 2000.*
> *They are getting a divorce.*

1. I'm hungry. I guess __(that) I will have a peanut butter sandwich.__

2. I have a test tomorrow. I suppose _____ ,
   but I'd rather go to a movie.

3. Why are you afraid to fly in an airplane? Read this report. It proves

_____

4. Right now I'm single. I can't predict my future exactly, but I assume

_____

POPULATION EXPLOSION

5. The earth is experiencing a population explosion. Scientists predict

_____

6. Last night I had a bad dream. In fact, it was a nightmare. I dreamed

_____

7. The police are investigating the burglary. They don't have much evidence,

but they suspect _____

8. My neighbors, Mr. and Mrs. Freeman, don't get along with each other.
They argue all the time. I'm not one to gossip,* but I've heard

_____

9. My cousin feels that people in the United States are unfriendly, but I

disagree with him. I've discovered _____

10. I've learned many things about life in the United States since I came here.

For example, I've learned _____

11. I always know when Paul is nervous. Have you ever noticed _____

_____

12. I believe that it is wrong to judge another person on the basis of race,

religion, or sex. I believe _____

13. World hunger is a serious problem. Do you realize _____

_____

EXERCISE 13—WRITTEN: Complete the following sentences with your own words.
Omit the word *that* if you wish. (Use your own paper.)

1. I believe that. . . .

2. I assume that. . . .

3. Do you realize that. . . ?

4. I can prove that. . . .

_____

*I'm not one to gossip = I'm not a person who gossips; I usually don't gossip.

5. I predict that. . . .

6. I've heard that. . . .

7. I guess that. . . . *

8. I suppose that. . . . *

9. Have you ever noticed that. . . ?

10. I suspect that. . . .

11. I hope that. . . .

12. Do you think that. . . ?

13. I've discovered that. . . .

14. Did you know that. . . ?

15. Last night I dreamed that. . . .

12-5 SUBSTITUTING *SO* FOR A "*THAT* CLAUSE" IN CONVERSATIONAL RESPONSES

(a) A: Is Pedro from Mexico? B: **I think so.** (*I think that Pedro is from Mexico.*)	***Think, believe,*** and ***hope*** are frequently followed by ***so*** in conversational English in response to a yes/no question. They are alternatives to answering *yes, no,* or *I don't know.**
(b) A: Does Judy live in an apartment? B: **I believe so.** (*I believe that Judy lives in an apartment.*)	
(c) A: Did you pass the test? B: **I hope so.** (*I hope that I passed the test.*)	
	So replaces a "*that* clause." In (a): ***so*** = *that Pedro is from Mexico.*
(d) A: Is Ali from Egypt? B: **I don't think so.** (*I don't think that Ali is from Egypt.*)	Negative usage of ***think so*** and ***believe so:*** *I don't think so.* *I don't believe so.*
(e) A: Is Jack married? B: **I don't believe so.** (*I don't believe that Jack is married.*)	
(f) A: Did you fail the test? B: **I hope not.** (*I hope that I didn't fail the test.*)	Negative usage of ***hope*** in conversational responses: *I hope not.*

*In addition to expressions with ***think, believe,*** and ***hope,*** the following expressions are commonly used in conversational responses: *I guess so, I guess not, I suppose so, I suppose not, I'm afraid so, I'm afraid not.*

EXERCISE 14—ORAL: Give the full idea of Speaker B's answers to A's questions by using a "***that*** clause."

1. A: Is Karen going to be home tonight?
   B: I think so. (*I think that Karen is going to be home tonight.*)
2. A: Is the library open on Sunday evenings?
   B: I believe so.

———

*****Guess*** and ***suppose*** can give the idea of ***think . . . probably.***
  I guess I should study tonight. = I think I probably should study tonight.
  I suppose I should study tonight. = I think I probably should study tonight.

3. A: Does Ann speak Spanish?
   B: I don't think so.
4. A: Are we going to have a test in grammar tomorrow?
   B: I don't believe so.
5. A: Will Bob be at the party tonight?
   B: I hope so.
6. A: Will your plane ticket cost more than $300?
   B: I hope not.

EXERCISE 15—ORAL (BOOKS CLOSED):   Answer the questions by using *think so* or *believe so* if you are not sure, or *yes* or *no* if you are sure.

> *Example:*   Does this book have more than 300 pages?
> *Response:*   I think/believe so. OR: I don't think/don't believe so. OR: Yes, it does. OR: No, it doesn't.

1. Does (. . .) have a car?
2. Are we going to have a test tomorrow?
3. Is there a fire extinguisher in this building?
4. Is Chicago farther north than New York City?
5. Does the word "patient" have more than one meaning?
6. Does the word "dozen" have more than one meaning?
7. Is your left foot bigger than your right foot?
8. Do gorillas eat meat?
9. Do spiders have eyes?
10. Don't look at your watch. Is it (*10:45*) yet?
11. Is the nearest post office on (*Pine Street*)?
12. Is next (*Tuesday*) the (*24th*)?
13. Are cats color-blind?
14. Can I buy a window fan at (*name of a local store*)?
15. Can you jog five miles without stopping?
16. Do any English words begin with the letter "x"?
17. In terms of evolution, is a pig related to a horse?
18. Is a tomato a vegetable?
19. Have I asked you more than 20 questions in this exercise?
20. Do you know what a noun clause is?
21. Is (. . .) planning to get married soon?
22. Does (. . .) usually use chopsticks when he/she eats at home?

12-6 OTHER USES OF "*THAT* CLAUSES"

(a) **I'm sure that** the bus stops here. (b) **I'm glad that** you're feeling better today. (c) **I'm sorry that** I missed class yesterday. (d) I **was disappointed that** Mary couldn't come to my party.	"*That* clauses" can follow certain expressions with **be** + *adjective* or **be** + *past participle*. The word "*that*" can be omitted with no change in meaning: *I'm sure the bus stops here.*

(e) **It is true that** the world is round.
(f) **It is a fact that** the world is round.
	Two very common expressions followed by "*that* clauses" are:
	   it is true (that)
	   it is a fact (that)

COMMON EXPRESSIONS FOLLOWED BY "*THAT* CLAUSES"*

be afraid that *be aware that* *be certain that* *be convinced that* *be disappointed that* *be glad that*	*be happy that* *be pleased that* *be sorry that* *be sure that* *be surprised that*	*It is true that . . . .* *It is a fact that . . . .*

*The above list contains expressions emphasized in the exercises. Some other common expressions with **be** that are frequently followed by "*that* clauses" are:

be amazed that *be angry that* *be ashamed that* *be astounded that* *be delighted that*	*be fortunate that* *be furious that* *be horrified that* *be lucky that* *be positive that*	*be proud that* *be shocked that* *be terrified that* *be thrilled that* *be worried that*

EXERCISE 16—ORAL: Complete the sentences. Use any appropriate verb form in the "*that* clause." (Notice the various verb forms used in the example.) Omit ***that*** if you wish.

Example: I'm glad that . . . .

Responses: I'm glad that { the weather is nice today.
I passed the test.
Sam is going to come to my party.
I've already finished my homework.
I can speak English.

1. I'm pleased that . . . .
2. I'm sure that . . . .
3. I'm surprised that . . . .
4. Are you certain that . . . ?
5. I'm very happy that . . . .
6. I'm sorry that . . . .

7. I'm not sorry that . . . .

8. I'm afraid that . . . .*

9. Are you aware that . . . ?

10. I'm disappointed that . . . .

11. I'm convinced that . . . .

12. It is true that . . . .

13. It is a fact that . . . .

14. It's not true that . . . .

EXERCISE 17—WRITTEN: Complete the following with your own words. Use noun clauses. (Use your own paper.)

1. My friend and I agree that . . . .

2. I regret that . . . .

3. I wonder if . . . .

4. You are lucky that . . . .

5. I'm delighted that . . . .

6. Do you know where . . . ?

7. The little boy is ashamed that . . . .

8. I can't remember what . . . .

9. It is a fact that . . . .

10. I doubt that . . . .

11. I'm amazed that . . . .

12. Do you know whether or not . . . ?

13. I want to know why . . . .

14. I feel that . . . .

15. I'm worried that . . . .

16. Are you certain that . . . ?

17. I don't know when . . . .

18. I don't know if . . . .

EXERCISE 18—ORAL (BOOKS CLOSED)   Review separable two-word verbs by completing the sentences with pronouns and prepositions.

> *Example:*   I wanted to be sure to remember (. . .)'s phone number,
>   so I wrote . . .
> *Response:*   . . . it down.

1. I can't hear the tape. Could you please turn . . . ?

2. I have an application form for (*name of a school*). I have to fill . . . .

3. I dropped my book. Could you please pick . . . ?

4. This is a hard problem. I can't figure . . . .

5. I bought these shoes a few days ago. Before I bought them, I tried . . . .

6. Where's your homework? Did you hand . . . ?

---

*Sometimes **be afraid** expresses fear:
  I don't want to go near that dog. I'm afraid that it will bite me.*
Sometimes **be afraid** expresses polite regret:
  I'm afraid you have the wrong number. = I'm sorry, but I think you have the wrong number.
  I'm afraid I can't come to your party. = I'm sorry, but I can't come to your party.

7. (. . .) asked (. . .) to go to a movie with him. He asked . . . .
8. We postponed the picnic. We put . . . .
9. I misspelled a word on my composition, so I crossed . . . .
10. I didn't know the meaning of a word, so I looked . . . .
11. We don't need that light. Would you please turn . . . ?
12. My coat was too warm to wear inside, so I took . . . .
13. That music is too loud. Could you please turn . . . ?
14. These papers are for the class. Could you please hand . . . ?
15. (. . .) was going to have a party, but s/he cancelled it. S/he called . . . .
16. I was thirsty, but my glass was empty. So I filled . . . .
17. My coat is in the closet. I hung. . . .
18. The story I told wasn't true. I made . . . .
19. When I wrote a check, I made a mistake. So I tore . . . .
20. I was cold. So I reached for my sweater and put . . . .
21. (. . .) fell asleep in class, so I woke . . . .
22. I was finished with the tools, so I put . . . .
23. I don't need these papers, so I'm going to throw . . . .
24. Let's listen to the radio. Would you please turn . . . ?

chapter *13*

Quoted Speech and Reported Speech

13-1 QUOTED SPEECH

SPEAKER	THE SPEAKER'S EXACT WORDS	QUOTING THE SPEAKER'S WORDS	Sometimes we want to quote a speaker's words—to write a speaker's exact words.* When we quote a speaker's words, we use quotation marks.
Ann:	The door is open.	(a) Ann said, "The door is open."	**HOW TO WRITE QUOTATIONS:**
Bob:	I need my pen.	(b) Bob said, "I need my pen."	1. Put a comma after *said*.
			2. Put quotation marks.†
			3. Capitalize the first word of the quotation.
			4. Write the quotation.
			5. Put a period at the end of the quotation.
			6. Put quotation marks after the period.

*Exact quotations are frequently used in many kinds of writing, such as newspaper articles, stories and novels, and academic papers.

†NOTE: Be sure to put the quotation marks above the line, not on the line.

WRONG: *Ann said, ,, My book is on the table.,,*

RIGHT: *Ann said, " My book is on the table."*

Tom:	I'm tired. I'm going to bed.	(c) Tom said, "I'm tired. I'm going to bed."	When there are two (or more) sentences in a quotation, put quotation marks at the beginning of the first sentence and after the second (or last) sentence.

EXERCISE 1: Write sentences in which you quote the speaker's exact words. Use *said*. Punctuate carefully.

1. *Ann*: My sister is a student.

    Ann said, "My sister is a student."

2. *Mike:* The library is closed.

   _____

3. *Alice:* I'm hungry.

   _____

4. *Alice:* I'm hungry. I want something to eat.

   _____

5. *Alice:* I'm hungry. I want something to eat. Let's go to a restaurant.

   _____

6. *The police officer:* Do you have a driver's license?*

   _____

7. *The police officer:* Stop or I'll shoot!*

   _____

8. *Hamlet:* To be or not to be: that is the question.

   _____

9. *John F. Kennedy:* Ask not what your country can do for you. Ask what you can do for your country.

   _____

_____

*Put quotation marks after a question mark and after an exclamation mark:
   Tom said, "What time is it?"
   My friend said, "Watch out!"

10. *The fox:* I'm going to eat you.*

_____

The rabbit: You have to catch me first!

_____

EXERCISE 2—ORAL/WRITTEN (BOOKS CLOSED): Practice writing quoted speech.

(To the teacher:
1) Say something and then ask the students to quote you exactly in writing.
2) Ask a student to say something and then ask the class to quote it exactly in writing.
3) Have a very brief conversation with one of the students and then ask the class to write the conversation using quoted speech. Discuss beginning a new paragraph each time the speaker changes.
4) Ask the students to have brief conversations with each other and then to write their conversations using quoted speech.)

EXERCISE 3—WRITTEN: Write a composition. Choose one of the following topics.

Topic 1:   Write a folk tale from your country in which animals speak. Use quotation marks.

Topic 2:   Write a children's story that you learned when you were young. When the characters in your story speak, use quotation marks.

Topic 3:   Make up a children's story. When the characters in your story speak, use quotation marks.

Topic 4:   Make up any kind of story. When the characters in your story speak, use quotation marks.

Topic 5:   Write a joke in which at least two people are talking to each other. Use quotation marks when the people are talking.

_____

*In folk tales, animals are frequently given the ability to speak.

13-2 QUOTED SPEECH VS. REPORTED SPEECH*

QUOTED SPEECH:	Quoted speech refers to reproducing a speaker's exact words. Quotation marks are used.
REPORTED SPEECH:	Reported speech refers to reproducing the idea of a speaker's words. Not all of the speaker's exact words are used: verb forms and pronouns may change. Quotation marks are not used.

QUOTED SPEECH	REPORTED SPEECH	
(a) Ann said, **"I am hungry."**	(b) Ann said **that she was hungry.**	QUOTED SPEECH: Use quotation marks. Use the speaker's exact words.
(c) Tom said, **"I need my pen."**	(d) Tom said **that he needed his pen.**	REPORTED SPEECH: Do not use quotation marks. Report the idea of the speaker's words in a noun clause. Notice in the examples: The verb forms and pronouns change from quoted speech to reported speech.

Quoted speech is also called *direct speech*. *Reported speech* is also called *indirect speech*.

13-3 VERB FORM USAGE IN REPORTED SPEECH: FORMAL SEQUENCE OF TENSES

FORMAL: If the main verb of the sentence is in the past (e.g., *said*), the verb in the noun clause is usually also in a past form.* Notice the verb form changes in the examples below.

QUOTED SPEECH	REPORTED SPEECH
(a) He said, "I **work** hard." ⟶	He said (that) he **worked** hard.
(b) He said, "I **am working** hard." ⟶	He said (that) he **was working** hard.
(c) He said, "I **have worked** hard." ⟶	He said (that) he **had worked** hard.
(d) He said, "I **worked** hard." ⟶	He said (that) he **had worked** hard.
(e) He said, "I **am going to work** hard." ⟶	He said (that) he **was going to work** hard.
(f) He said, "I **will work** hard." ⟶	He said (that) he **would work** hard.
(g) He said, "I **can work** hard." ⟶	He said (that) he **could work** hard.
(h) He said, "I **may work** hard." ⟶	He said (that) he **might work** hard.
(i) He said, "I **have to work** hard." ⟶	He said (that) he **had to work** hard.
(j) He said, "I **must work** hard." ⟶	He said (that) he **had to work** hard.
(k) He said, "I **should work** hard." ⟶	He said (that) he **should work** hard. (*no change*)
(l) He said, "I **ought to work** hard." ⟶	He said (that) he **ought to work** hard. (*no change*)

*If the main verb of the sentence is in the present (e.g., *says*), no change is made in the verb tense or modal in the noun clause.

He says, "I **work** hard." ⟶	He says (that) he **works** hard.
He says, "I'm **working** hard." ⟶	He says (that) he's **working** hard.
He says, "I **worked** hard." ⟶	He says (that) he **worked** hard.
He says, "I **will work** hard." ⟶	He says (that) he **will work** hard.

INFORMAL:	Sometimes, especially in speaking, the verb in the noun clause is not changed if the speaker is reporting something *immediately or soon after* it was said.
(m) Immediate reporting:	A: What did Ann just say? I didn't hear her. B: She **said** (that) she **is** hungry.
(n) Later reporting:	A: What did Ann say when she got home last night? B: She **said** (that) she **was** hungry.

EXERCISE 4:   Change the quoted speech to reported speech. Change the verb in quoted speech to a past form in reported speech as appropriate.

1.   Jim said, "I am sleepy." _____ Jim said (that) he was sleepy. _____

2.   Sally said, "I don't like chocolate." _____

3.   Mary said, "I am planning to take a trip." _____

4.   Tom said, "I have already eaten lunch." _____

5.   Linda said, "I called my doctor." _____

6.   Mr. Rice said, "I'm going to go to Chicago." _____

7.   Fred said, "I will come to the meeting." _____

8.   Jean said, "I can't afford to buy a new car." _____

9.   Martha said, "I may go to the library." _____

10. Ted said, "I have to finish my work." _____

11. Sue said, "I must talk to Professor Reed." _____

12. Alice said, "I should visit my aunt and uncle." _____

13-4   USING *SAY* VS. *TELL*

(a) Ann said that she was hungry.	*Say* is followed immediately by a noun clause.*
(b) Ann **told me** that she was hungry. (c) Ann **told us** that she was hungry. (d) Ann **told John** that she was hungry. (e) Ann **told someone** that she was hungry.	*Tell* is <u>not</u> followed immediately by a noun clause. *Tell* is followed immediately by a (pro)noun object (e.g., *me*, *us*, *John*, *someone*) and then by a noun clause.

*Also possible: *Ann said to me that she was hungry.*

NOTE: In reported speech, it is often important to indicate who heard the speaker's words. In this case, **tell** is usually used instead of **say**. In other words, it is more common to say *Ann told me that she was hungry.* than *Ann said to me that she was hungry.*

EXERCISE 5—ORAL: Practice using *told (someone)* in reported speech.

STUDENT A: Look briefly at your book. Say the words in the book to Student B.
STUDENT B: Don't look at the book. Report Student A's words to the rest of the class. Use *told.*

Example: I need to talk to you.
Student A: I need to talk to you.
Student B: (Ali) told me that he needed to talk to me.*

1. I will call you tomorrow.
2. I know your cousin.
3. I have met your roommate.
4. I'll meet you after class for a cup of coffee.
5. I'm going to take a vacation in Hawaii.
6. I have to take another English course.
7. I won't be in class tomorrow.
8. I can't read your handwriting.
9. I think it's going to rain.
10. I may be absent from class tomorrow.
11. I walked to school this morning.
12. I like your shirt/blouse.
13. I think you speak English very well.
14. You should see (*title of a movie*).
15. I'm getting hungry.
16. I'm not married.
17. Your pronunciation is very good.
18. I've already seen (*title of a movie*).
19. I'm going to go to bed early tonight.
20. I don't like (*a kind of food*).

*In immediate reporting, it is not necessary to change the noun clause verb to a past form. You may wish to practice both forms:

Immediate reporting, informal: **(Ali) told me that he needs to talk to me.**
Formal sequence of tenses: **(Ali) told me that he needed to talk to me.**

NOTE: In spoken English and in informal written English, sometimes native speakers change noun clause verbs to past forms and sometimes they don't.

13-5   USING *ASK IF*

YES/NO QUESTION	NOUN CLAUSE	
(a) Bob said to me, **"Are you hungry?"**	(b) Bob asked me **if I was hungry.**	**Ask**, not **say** or **tell**, is used to report yes/no questions. Notice in the examples: the noun clause following **ask** begins with **if** (not **that**).
(c) Bob said to Jane, **"Are you hungry?"**	(d) Bob asked Jane **if she was hungry.**	

(e) Bob asked me **if** I was hungry. (f) Bob asked me **whether** I was hungry.	**Whether** has the same meaning as **if.** (e) and (f) have the same meaning.*
(g) Bob **asked if** I was hungry.	The (pro)noun object (e.g., **me**) may be omitted after **ask**.
(h) Bob **wanted to know if** I was hungry.	In addition to **ask**, **want to know** is frequently used to report yes/no questions.

*See 12–3 for the use of **or not** with **if** and **whether:** e.g., *Bob asked me whether or not I was hungry.*

> **EXERCISE 6—ORAL:** Practice using **asked if.**
>
> **STUDENT A:** Say the words in the book to Student B.
> **STUDENT B:** Don't look at your book. Report Student A's question. Use **asked**.
>
> > *Example:* Are you married?
> > *Student A:* Are you married?
> > *Student B:* (Ali) asked me if I am married. OR: (Ali) asked me if I was married.*
>
> 1. Do you know my cousin?
> 2. Are you hungry?
> 3. Can you speak French?
> 4. Did you enjoy your vacation?
> 5. Are you going to take another English course?
> 6. Will you be at home tonight?
> 7. Have you ever been in Mexico?
> 8. Can you hear me?
> 9. Are you listening to me?
> 10. Do you need any help?
> 11. Did you finish your homework?
> 12. Do you think it's going to rain?
> 13. Are you going to go downtown tomorrow?

Immediate reporting, informal: *(Ali) asked me if I'm married.*
Formal sequence of tenses: *(Ali) asked me if I was married.*

14. Do you know how to cook?
15. Do you know whether or not (*name of a classmate*) is married?
16. Can you come to my party?
17. Do you have a car?
18. Have you ever been in Russia?
19. Did you move into a new apartment?
20. Are you going to call me tonight?

EXERCISE 7—ORAL: Practice using noun clauses after *asked.**

STUDENT A: Say the words in the book to Student B.
STUDENT B: Don't look at your book. Report Student A's question. Use *asked.*

> *Example:* Where do you live?
> *Student A:* Where do you live?
> *Student B:* (Maria) asked me where I live. OR: (Maria) asked me where I lived.

1. Where is your apartment?
2. Is your apartment far from here?
3. What do you need?
4. Do you need a pen?
5. When does the semester end?
6. Does the semester end in December?
7. Why is (*name of a classmate*) absent?
8. Is (*name of a classmate*) absent?
9. How often do you go downtown?
10. Do you go downtown every week?

EXERCISE 8: Complete the sentences by changing the quoted speech to reported speech. Practice using the formal sequence of tenses.

1. Jane said, "Are you tired?"

   Jane asked me ___if I was tired._____

2. Bob said, "Where do you live?"

   Bob asked me _____

---

*See 12–2 for the use of question words in noun clauses.

3. He said, "Do you live in the dorm?"

   He asked me _____

4. I said, "I have my own apartment."

   I told him _____

5. He said, "I'm looking for a new apartment."

   He said _____

6. He said, "I don't like living in the dorm."

   He told me _____

7. I said, "Do you want to move in with me?"

   I asked him _____

8. He said, "Where is your apartment?"

   He asked me _____

9. I said, "I live on Seventh Avenue."

   I told him _____

10. He said, "I can't move until the end of the semester."

    He said _____

11. He said, "I will cancel my dorm contract at the end of the semester."

    He told me _____

12. He said, "Is that okay?"

    He asked me _____

13. I said, "I'm looking forward to having you as a roommate."

    I told him _____

EXERCISE 9:   Complete the sentences by changing the sentences in quotation marks to noun clauses. Practice using the formal sequence of tenses.

1. "Where do you live?"   Tom asked me _where I lived._____

2. "Do you live in the   He asked me _if I lived in the dorm.____
   dorm?"

3. "I stole the money."   The thief admitted

                              _that he had stolen the money._____

4. "Where is Gloria?"   Ed asked me _____

5. "I'm going to quit   Jessica announced _____
   school and find a job."

6. "Did you mail the letter?"   Tim asked me _____

7. "What are you thinking about?"   Karen asked me _____

8. "I have to go to the drug store."   Steve said _____

9. "I can't pick you up at the airport."   Alice told me _____

10. "I will take a taxi."   I told her _____

11. "You should speak English as much as possible."   My teacher told me _____

12. "Do you like spaghetti?"   Don asked me _____

13. "Have you already eaten dinner?"   Sue asked me _____

14. "Did you finish your work?"   Jackie asked me _____

15. "What time do you want to leave for the airport?"   Harry asked me _____

16. "I made a mistake."   Carol admitted _____

17. "The final exam will be on the 15th."   The teacher announced _____

18. "An earthquake occurred in Peru."   The newspaper reported _____

EXERCISE 10—WRITTEN: Complete the following. Use the formal sequence of tenses.

1. . . . asked me if . . . .
2. . . . asked me where . . . .
3. . . . told me that . . . .
4. . . . said that . . . .
5. . . . asked me when . . . .
6. . . . told my friend that . . . .
7. . . . asked my friend if . . . .
8. . . . asked my friend why . . . .

EXERCISE 11:   Read the dialogues and complete the sentences. Use the formal sequence of tenses.

1. *A: Oh no! I forgot my briefcase! What am I going to do?*
   B: I don't know.

   When Bill got on the bus, he realized that he ___had forgotten___ his briefcase.

2. *A: Where's your bicycle, Jimmy?*
   B: I sold it to a friend of mine.
   A: You what?

   Yesterday I asked my fourteen-year-old son where his bicycle _____

   _____ . He told me that he _____ it to a friend of his. I was flabbergasted.

3. *A: Look at this!*
   B: What?
   A: My test paper. I got an "F." I'm sorry I didn't study harder.

   When George got his test paper back, he was sorry that he _____ _____ harder.

4. *A: The bus is supposed to be here in three minutes. Hurry up! I'm afraid we'll miss it.*
   B: I'm ready. Let's go.

   I told my friend to hurry because I was afraid that we _____ the bus.

5. *A: Can you swim?*
   B: Yes.
   A: Thank heavens.

   When the canoe tipped over, I was glad that my friend _____

6. *A: Do you want to go downtown?*
   B: I can't. I have to study.

   When I asked Kathy if she _____ to go downtown, she said

   that she _____ because she _____

7 *A: Ow! My finger really hurts! I'm sure I broke it.*
   B: Let me see.

   When Nancy fell down, she was sure that she _____ her finger.

8. *A: Where's Jack? I'm surprised he isn't here.*
   B: He went to Chicago to visit his sister.

   When I got to the party, I asked my friend where Jack _____.

   I was surprised that he _____ there. My friend told me that

   Jack _____ to Chicago to visit his sister.

9. *A: Will you be home in time for dinner?*
   B: I'll be home around 5:30.

   My wife asked me if I _____ home in time for dinner. I told

   her that I _____ home around 5:30.

10. *A: Have you ever been in Mexico?*
    B: Yes, I have. Several times.

    I asked George if he _____ ever _____ in Mexico. He said that he

    _____ there several times.

13-6 USING VERB + INFINITIVE TO REPORT SPEECH

QUOTED SPEECH	REPORTED SPEECH
(a) Joe said, "Please come to my party."	
(b) Joe said, "Can you come to my party?"	(d) Joe **invited me to come to his party.**
(c) Joe said, "Would you like to come to my party?"	

S + V + O + INFINITIVE PHRASE	
(e) Joe | invited | me | to come to his party. (f) I told Ann to study harder.	Some verbs are followed immediately by a (pro)noun object and then an infinitive phrase. These verbs (see the list below) are often used to report speech.

REPORTING SPEECH: COMMON VERBS FOLLOWED BY A (PRO)NOUN OBJECT AND AN INFINITIVE*		
advise someone to	*invite someone to*	*remind someone to*
ask someone to	*order someone to*	*tell someone to*
encourage someone to	*permit someone to*	*warn someone to*

*Other common verbs followed by a (pro)noun object and an infinitive are:

allow	*convince*	*instruct*
beg	*direct*	*persuade*
challenge	*expect*	*urge*

EXERCISE 12: Complete each sentence with an infinitive phrase which, combined with the main verb (*invited, advised, etc.*), reports the idea of the speaker's words.

1. Joe said, "Please come to my party."

    Joe invited me ___to come to his party.___

2. My teacher said, "I think you should take another English course."

    My teacher advised me ___to take another English course.___

3. Mrs. Jacobson said, "You may use the phone."

    Mrs. Jacobson permitted me _____

4. The doctor said, "Take a deep breath."

    The doctor told the patient _____

5. My mother said, "Make an appointment with the dentist."

    My mother reminded me _____

6. My friend said, "I think you should take a long vacation."

    My friend encouraged me _____

7. The Smiths said, "Would you like to come to our house for dinner?"

    The Smiths invited us _____

8. My friend said, "You should see a doctor about the pain in your knee."

    My friend advised me _____

9. The judge said, "You must pay a fine of fifty dollars."

    The judge ordered Mr. Silverman _____

10. Bill said, "Don't touch that hot pot."

    Bill warned me ___not to touch that hot pot.*___

11. Sue said, "Don't buy a used car."

    Sue advised me _____

12. Mr. Gray said, "Don't play in the street."

    Mr. Gray warned the children _____

---

*To make an infinitive negative, put *not* in front of it.

EXERCISE 13: Following are some dialogues. Report *the first speaker's words.* Use the verb in parentheses and an infinitive phrase.

1.   *Joe:*   Would you like to go to a movie with me?
    Mary: Yes.

    (*invite*) _____ Joe invited Mary to go to a movie with him. _____

2.   *Dr. Miller:*   You should lose five pounds.
        Fred: I'll try.

    (*advise*) _____

3.   *Ms. Holt:*   Could you please open the door for me?
        Tom: I'd be happy to.

    (*ask*) _____

4.   *Nancy:*   Call me around nine.
        Me: Okay.

    (*tell*) _____

5.   *Mr. Ward:*   You may have a cookie and a glass of milk.
    The children: Thanks, Dad.

    (*permit*) _____

6.   *Prof. Larson:*   You should take a physics course.
            Me: Oh?

    (*encourage*) _____

7.   *The police officer:*   Put your hands on top of your head!
        The thief: Who? Me? I didn't do anything!

    (*order*) _____

8.   *Jack:*   Don't worry about me.
    His mother: I won't.

    (*tell*) _____

9. *Sue:* Don't forget to call me.
   Me: I won't.

   (*remind*)* _____

10.   *Alice:* Don't forget to lock the door.
    Her roommate: Okay.

    (*remind*) _____

11. *Mrs. Peterson:* Please don't slam the door.
    Her daughter: Okay, Mom.

    (*ask*) _____

12. *Prof. Roth:* Don't look directly at the sun during a solar eclipse.
          Us: Okay.

    (*warn*) _____

EXERCISE 14—ERROR ANALYSIS: All of the following sentences contain mistakes in grammar. Can you find the mistakes and correct them?

1. She asked me that I wanted to go to the zoo.
2. Tom said me that he was hungry.
3. Bob asked me where do you live.
4. Ann told that she had enjoyed the party.
5. Kathy asked me open the window.
6. My friend told to me that she understood my problem.
7. My mother asked me when am I coming home?

_____

*Two possible sentences: *Sue reminded me to call her.*
                       Sue reminded me not to forget to call her.

8. Do you know where is the nearest gas station?
9. David invited me for eating dinner with him.
10. I asked Tom that when will your plane arrive?
11. I told Bobby don't pull the cat's tail.
12. Ann said, Are you tired?

13-7 SOME TROUBLESOME VERBS: *ADVISE, SUGGEST,* **AND** *RECOMMEND*

(a) Tom **advised me to call** a doctor. (b) Tom **advised calling** a doctor.	(a) and (b) have the same meaning. In (a): When *advise* is followed by a (pro)noun object, an infinitive is used. In (b): When there is no (pro)noun object after *advise,* a gerund is used.
(c) Tom **suggested calling** a doctor. (d) Tom **recommended calling** a doctor.	*Suggest* and *recommend* can also be followed immediately by a gerund.
(e)　　CORRECT: Tom **suggested that I should call** a doctor. 　　INCORRECT: Tom suggested me to call a doctor. (f)　　CORRECT: Tom **recommended that I should call** a doctor. 　　INCORRECT: Tom recommended me to call a doctor.	*Suggest* and *recommend* cannot be followed by a (pro)noun object and an infinitive, but they can be followed by a "*that* clause" in which *should* is used.*

*The use of *should* in the noun clause is not necessary. However, if *should* is not used, the verb in the noun clause is always in the simple form after *suggest* and *recommend*:

Tom **suggested/recommended that**　$\begin{cases} \textbf{I call} \text{ a doctor. (not } \textit{called}) \\ \textbf{we call} \text{ a doctor. (not } \textit{called}) \\ \textbf{Ann call} \text{ a doctor. (not } \textit{calls} \text{ or } \textit{called}) \\ \textbf{he call} \text{ a doctor. (not } \textit{calls} \text{ or } \textit{called}) \end{cases}$

EXERCISE 15:　Complete the sentences. Give the idea of the speaker's words.

1. The doctor said, "You should lose weight."

(a) The doctor advised me _____ to lose weight. _____

(b) The doctor advised _____ losing weight. _____

(c) The doctor suggested _____

(d) The doctor recommended _____

(e) The doctor suggested that _____

(f) The doctor recommended that _____

2. My teacher said, "You should study harder."

    (a) My teacher suggested that _____

    (b) My teacher advised me _____

    (c) My teacher advised _____

    (d) My teacher recommended _____

3. Mr. Madison said, "Why don't you buy a Toyota?"

    Mr. Madison suggested _____

4. Don said, "I think you should see a doctor about that problem."

    Don recommended _____

5. Mary said, "Let's go to a movie."

    Mary suggested _____

6. Sharon said, "I think you should go to Iowa State University."

    Sharon advised _____

EXERCISE 16: Work in pairs. Each pair should create a short dialogue (five to ten sentences) based on one of the given situations. Each pair will then present their dialogue to the class. After the dialogue, the class will report what was said.*

SAMPLE SITUATION

Have a conversation about going to the zoo.

SAMPLE DIALOGUE

Ann: *Would you like to go to the zoo tomorrow?*

Bob: *I can't. I have to study.*

Ann: *That's too bad. Are you sure you can't go? It will take only a few hours.*

Bob: *Well, maybe I can study in the morning and then go to the zoo in the afternoon.*

Ann: *Great! What time do you want to go?*

Bob: *Let's go around two o'clock.*

To the teacher: The dialogues can be written either in class or out of class. They can be checked over by you prior to presentation if you wish. They can be dittoed or photocopied to ensure accurate reporting. The reports can be either oral or written, or both.

SAMPLE REPORT

Ann asked Bob if he wanted to go to the zoo tomorrow. Bob said that he could not go because he had to study. Ann finally persuaded him to go. She said that it would take only a few hours. Bob decided that he could study in the morning and go to the zoo in the afternoon. Ann asked Bob what time he wanted to go. He suggested going around two o'clock.

(Notice in the sample report: The writer gives the idea of the speakers' words without necessarily using the speakers' exact words.)

1. Have a conversation in which one of you invites the other one to a party.
2. One of you is a teenager and the other one is a parent. The teenager is having problems at school and is seeking advice and encouragement.
3. The two of you are a married couple. One of you is reminding the other one about the things s/he should or has to do today.
4. Have a conversation in which one of you persuades the other one to begin a health program by taking up a new kind of exercise (jogging, walking, tennis, etc.). Beginning of the dialogue:

   A: I need to get some physical exercise.
   B: Why don't you take up. . .?
   A: No, I don't want to do that.
5. One of you is fourteen years old and the other is the parent. The fourteen-year-old wants to stay out late tonight. What will the parent say?
6. One of you is a store detective and the other is a shoplifter. The store detective has just seen the shoplifter take something.
7. One of you is a stubborn, old-fashioned, uneducated person who thinks the world is flat. The other one convinces the stubborn one that the world is round.

chapter *14*

Using *Wish*; Using *If*

14-1 EXPRESSING WISHES ABOUT THE PRESENT/FUTURE

THE TRUE SITUATION	EXPRESSING A WISH ABOUT THAT SITUATION	People often make wishes when they want reality to be different, to be exactly the opposite of (contrary to) the true situation.
I don't know how to dance.	(a) *I wish* (that) **I knew** how to dance.	
I don't have a bicycle.	(b) *I wish* **I had** a bicycle.	A noun clause* usually follows **wish**. Special verb forms are used in the noun clause. When a speaker expresses a wish about a present situation, s/he uses *a past verb form.*
Ron has to work tonight.	(c) *Ron wishes* **he didn't have to work** tonight.	
I can't speak Chinese.	(d) *I wish* **I could speak** Chinese.	
I'm not home in bed. **Ann isn't** home in bed. **It's cold** today. **We aren't** in Hawaii.	(e) *I wish* **I were** home in bed. (f) *Ann wishes* **she were** home in bed. (g) *I wish* **it weren't** cold today. (h) *We wish* **we were** in Hawaii.	Notice in (e), (f), (g), and (h): **were** is used for all subjects: *I wish* { *I / you / he / she / it / we / they* } *were* ....

*For more information about noun clauses which begin with **that**, see Chapter 12.

EXERCISE 1:   Use the given information to complete the sentences.

THE TRUE SITUATION	EXPRESSING A WISH
1. I don't have a car.	I wish __(that) I had a car.__
2. Alice doesn't have a car.	Alice wishes __(that) she had a car.__
3. I have a cold.	I wish _____
4. I don't have a tape recorder.	I wish _____
5. I don't know how to swim.	I wish _____
6. Bill doesn't have a good job.	Bill wishes _____
7. I live in the dorm.	I wish _____
8. I don't live in an apartment.	I wish _____
9. I can't speak French.	I wish _____
10. Sue can't find a good job.	Sue wishes _____
11. My friend can't come to my party.	I wish _____
12. I'm not at home right now.	I wish _____
13. Mary isn't here.	I wish _____
14. Jim isn't here.	I wish _____
15. It isn't Saturday.	I wish _____
16. My friends aren't here.	I wish _____
17. I have to study for a test.	I wish _____
18. I have to write a composition.	I wish _____
19. Dick has to get up at 6:00 a.m.	Dick wishes _____

EXERCISE 2—ORAL (BOOKS CLOSED):   Make sentences beginning with "*I wish. . . .*"

Example: You don't have a bicycle.
Response: I wish (that) I had a bicycle.

1. You don't have a car.
2. You don't have a color TV.
3. You don't have a window fan.
4. You have a headache.

5. You don't know how to dance.

6. You don't know how to play chess.

7. You have to study tonight.

8. You have to go to the dentist.

9. You can't speak (*language*).

10. You can't go to (*place*).

11. You can't whistle.

12. You're not in (*country*) right now.

13. (. . .) isn't here today.

14. It isn't Sunday.

15. It's hot/cold today.

16. You don't have enough money to buy a car.

17. You have to work tonight.

18. You can't go to the zoo today.

19. You're not rich.

20. You're sleepy.

EXERCISE 3:   Study the examples and then complete the sentences with auxiliary verbs.

1. I don't have a car, but I wish I _____did_____ .

2. I have to study tonight, but I wish I _____didn't_____ .

3. I can't speak Italian, but I wish I _____could_____ .

4. I'm not tall, but I wish I _____were_____ .

5. Bob is tall, but he wishes he _____weren't_____ .

6. I don't know Mary Smith, but I wish I _____ .

7. I have to take a history course, but I wish I _____ .

8. I can't dance very well, but I wish I _____ .

9. I'm not a good cook, but I wish I _____ .

10. Linda isn't a good writer, but she wishes she _____ .

11. Jack has to go to the laundromat, but he wishes he _____ .

12. Carol doesn't live in the same city as her boyfriend, but she wishes she

    _____ .

13. It's too cold to go swimming today, but I wish it _____ .

14. Sally can't afford to take a vacation in Hawaii, but she wishes she

    _____ .

15. I have to clean my apartment, but I wish I _____ .

16. I don't remember that man's name, but I wish I _____ .

EXERCISE 4: Complete the following conversations. Use auxiliary verbs in the completions.

1. A: Can you go to Jim's party tonight?

   B: No, _____I can't_____ , but I wish _____I could_____ .

2. A: Are you a good musician?

   B: No, _____ , but I wish _____ .

3. A: Do you smoke?

   B: Yes, _____ , but I wish _____ .

4. A: Does your son know how to play a musical instrument?

   B: No, _____ , but I wish _____ .

5. A: Can you play a musical instrument?

   B: No, _____ , but I wish _____ .

6. A: Do you have to take the bus to work?

   B: Yes, _____ , but I wish _____ .

7. A: Is Maria in your class?

   B: No, _____ , but I wish _____ .

8. A: Do you understand what Professor Martin is talking about?

   B: No, _____ , but I wish _____ .

9. A: Do you know the people who live in the apartment next to yours?

   B: No, _____ , but I wish _____ .

10. A: Is your roommate neat?

    B: No, _____ , but I wish _____ .

11. A: Are the students always on time for class?

    B: No, _____ , but I wish _____ .

12. A: Do you have enough time to drink a cup of coffee between classes?

    B: No, _____ , but I wish _____ .

13. A: Can you come over to my house for dinner tomorrow night?

    B: I'm sorry, but I _____ . I wish _____ .

14. A: Is there a grocery store near your apartment?

    B: No, _____ , but I wish _____ .

15. A: Is there an art museum in this town?

    B: No, _____ , but I wish _____ .

14-2 EXPRESSING WISHES ABOUT THE PAST

THE TRUE SITUATION	MAKING A WISH ABOUT THE PAST	
I didn't study for the test.	(a) **I wish** (that) **I had studied** for the test.	The past perfect* is used after *wish* when people make wishes about a past situation.
Jim didn't finish his work.	(b) Jim **wishes he had finished** his work.	
I went to the meeting.	(c) **I wish I hadn't gone** to the meeting.	

*See 6–9 for the forms of the past perfect.

EXERCISE 5: Use the given information to make sentences with *wish*.

THE TRUE SITUATION	MAKING A WISH
1. Bobby didn't tell me the truth.	I wish <u>(that) Bobby had told me the truth.</u>
2. I didn't call my friend last night.	I wish _____
3. I didn't cash a check yesterday.	I wish _____
4. Tom spent all of his money yesterday.	Tom wishes _____
5. I didn't go to class yesterday.	I wish _____
6. Ann didn't finish high school.	Ann wishes _____
7. Jerry wasn't at the meeting last week.	I wish _____
8. Jerry isn't here today.	I wish _____
9. Fred doesn't understand my problem.	I wish _____
10. Fred didn't help me.	I wish _____

EXERCISE 6:   Complete the sentences with the correct form of the words in parentheses.

1. It took me three days to get to Chicago by bus. I wish I (*fly*)

    _____ there instead of taking the bus.

2. I miss my family. I wish they (*be*) _____ here now.

3. The kitchen is a mess this morning. I wish I (*wash*) _____
    the dishes last night.

4. I'd like to wear my black suit to the meeting today, but it's wrinkled and

    dirty. I wish I (*take*) _____ it to the cleaner's last week.

5. I have to walk up three flights of stairs to get to my apartment. I wish my

    apartment building (*have*) _____ an elevator.

6. I wish I (*can remember*) _____ where I put the pliers. I can't
    find them anywhere.

7. I wish I (*know*) _____ more English.

8. Sue bought a used car a couple of months ago. It's given her nothing but

    trouble. She wishes she (*buy, not*) _____ it.

9. I'm tired today. I wish I (*stay up, not*) _____ late last night.

10. I'd like to go camping this weekend. I wish the weather (*be, not*)

    _____ so cold.

11. You told me to save a little money out of each of my pay checks, but I

    didn't. I wish I (*take*) _____ your advice.

12. My brother goes to school in another city. He came here last Friday to spend a few days with me. I've enjoyed having him here. I wish he (*have to, not*) _____ leave today. I wish he (*can spend*) _____ a few more days here.

EXERCISE 7: Complete the sentences with auxiliary verbs.

1. Bobby didn't tell me the truth, but I wish he _____had_____ .

2. I don't know Carol Jones, but I wish I _____did_____ .

3. I can't move into a new apartment, but I wish I _____ .

4. I didn't finish my homework last night, but I wish I _____ .

5. Sally didn't come to the party last night, but I wish she

   _____ .

6. I don't have enough money to buy that coat, but I wish I

   _____ .

7. I'm too tired to go for a walk, but I wish I _____ .

8. I didn't study any English before I came here, but I wish I

   _____ .

9. Dick doesn't live close to school, but he wishes he _____ .

10. Jane can't speak French, but she wishes she _____ .

EXERCISE 8: Complete the following conversations. Use auxiliary verbs in the completions.

1. A: Did you go to the party last night?
   B: Yes, _____I did_____ , but I wish _____I hadn't_____ . It was boring.

2. A: Did you eat breakfast this morning?
   B: No, _____ , but I wish _____ . I'm hungry. My stomach is growling.

3. A: Do you exercise regularly?

   B: No, _____ , but I wish _____ . I always feel better when I exercise regularly.

4. A: Did you study for the test?

   B: No, _____ , but I wish _____ . I got an "F" on it.

5. A: Are you a good artist?

   B: No, _____ , but I wish _____ . I'd like to be able to draw.

6. A: Did you go to the movie last night?

   B: Yes, _____ , but I wish _____ . It was a waste of time and money.

7. A: Do you have to eat at the student cafeteria?

   B: Yes, _____ , but I wish _____ . The food is lousy.

8. A: Can you speak Chinese?

   B: No, _____ , but I wish _____ .

9. A: Is it hard to learn a second language?

   B: Yes, _____ , but I wish _____ .

10. A: Did you go to the meeting last night?

    B: No, _____ , but I wish _____ .

EXERCISE 9—ORAL (BOOKS CLOSED):   Answer *no*. Use *wish*.

Example: Can you speak Arabic?
Response: No, I can't, but I wish I could.

1. Did you study last night?
2. Did you go to bed early last night?
3. Do you have a car?
4. Are you rich?
5. Can you speak (*language*)?
6. Did you eat breakfast?
7. Is (. . .) here today?
8. Do you know how to dance?
9. Did (. . .) help you with your homework?
10. Can you play (*a musical instrument*)?
11. Did you finish your homework before you went to bed last night?
12. Are you full of energy today?
13. Do you live in an apartment?

14. Is the weather nice today?
15. Did (. . .) call you last night?
16. Is your family here?
17. Do you have to go to class tomorrow?
18. Can you buy (*a Rolls Royce*)?
19. Did you bring your dictionary to class?
20. Do you know how to type?

EXERCISE 10—ORAL: Make wishes based on the given situations. Try to think of as many possible wishes as you can for each situation.

    Example: I'm hungry. I wish . . . .
    Responses: I wish I'd eaten breakfast.
               I wish I had a candy bar.
               I wish I could go to (*name of a place*) and get a hamburger.
               I wish I weren't in class right now.
               I wish I didn't have to go to another class after this one.
               I wish the classroom were a restaurant and I had a steak in front of me instead of my grammar book.
               Etc.

1. I'm tired. I wish . . . .
2. I'm broke. I wish . . . .
3. The weather is . . . today. I wish . . . .
4. I live in (*kind of residence*). I wish . . . .
5. I don't have many talents. I wish . . . .
6. This is a nice classroom, but I wish . . . .
7. I'm very busy. I have a lot of things to do today. I wish . . . .
8. There are some things about myself and my life that I would like to change. I wish . . . .

EXERCISE 11—ORAL (BOOKS CLOSED): Use *wish*.

(To the teacher: Have the students tell you things that are not perfect in their lives and then ask them to make wishes. You may wish to introduce a "fairy godmother" into the discussion.)

    Example: Not everything in your life is perfect. Tell me something that makes you unhappy about your life.
    Response: My classes begin at 8 o'clock in the morning.
    Teacher: Pretend you have a fairy godmother and make a wish.

Response: I wish my classes didn't begin at eight.
I wish my classes began at ten.
I wish I didn't have to get up so early.

(You may wish to expand the exercise to include an introduction to conditional sentences with if.)

Teacher: What would you do if your classes didn't begin at eight?
Response: If my classes didn't begin at eight, I would sleep until
the middle of the morning.

14-3   USING *IF*: CONTRARY-TO-FACT IN THE PRESENT/FUTURE

TRUE SITUATION: MAKING A WISH: USING **IF**:	(a) I don't have enough money. (b) I wish I had enough money. (c) **If** I **had** enough money, I **would buy** a car. (d) **If** I **had** enough money, I **could buy** a car.	**If** is often used to talk about situations that are contrary to fact. In (c) and (d): In truth, I don't have enough money. In (g) and (h): In truth, the weather isn't nice today.
TRUE SITUATION: MAKING A WISH: USING **IF**:	(e) The weather isn't nice today. (f) I wish the weather were nice today. (g) **If** the weather **were** nice today, I **would go** to the zoo. (h) **If** the weather **were** nice today, I **could go** to the zoo.	

	IF *CLAUSE*	RESULT *CLAUSE*	VERB FORM USAGE: CONTRARY-TO-FACT (PRESENT/FUTURE)*
(i)	If I **had** enough money,	I $\begin{Bmatrix} \text{would} \\ \text{could} \end{Bmatrix}$ buy a car.	*IF CLAUSE* — **simple past** / *RESULT CLAUSE* — **would / could** + **simple form**
(j) (k)	If the weather **were** nice, I **would go** to the zoo. *(The speaker wants to go to the zoo.)* If the weather **were** nice, I **could go** to the zoo. *(The speaker is expressing an option, a possibility.)*		*Would* expresses intended or definite results. *Could* expresses possible options. *Could = would be able to.*
(l) (m) (n)	**If the weather were** nice, I would go swimming. **If Mary were** here, she would help us. **If I were** you, I wouldn't accept their invitation.		Notice in (l), (m), and (n): *were* is used for all subjects in an "*if* clause."
(o)	If the weather were nice, **I'd** go to the beach.		Contractions of *would* with pronouns: ***I'd, you'd, he'd, she'd, it'd, we'd, they'd.***

*Sentences with an "*if* clause" and a "result clause" are called *conditional sentences.*

EXERCISE 12:   Complete the sentences with words in parentheses.

1.   TRUE SITUATION: I don't have enough time.

     I wish I (*have*) _____ enough time.

     If I (*have*) _____ enough time, I (*go*) _____ to
     the park.

2.   TRUE SITUATION: I don't have enough money.

     I wish I (*have*) _____ enough money.

     If I (*have*) _____ enough money, I (*fly*) _____
     home this weekend.

3.   TRUE SITUATION: It's cold today.

     I wish it (*be, not*) _____ cold today.

     If it (*be, not*) _____ cold today, I (*go*) _____
     swimming.

4.   TRUE SITUATION: I don't know how to swim.

     I wish I (*know*) _____ how to swim.

     If I (*know*) _____ how to swim, I (*go*) _____
     to the beach with you.

5.   TRUE SITUATION: I don't understand that sentence.

     I wish I (*understand*) _____ that sentence.

     If I (*understand*) _____ that sentence, I (*explain*)

     _____ it to you.

6.   TRUE SITUATION: I have to go to class today.

     I wish I (*have to go, not*) _____ to class today.

     If I (*have to go, not*) _____ to class today, I (*go*)

     _____ shopping, or I (*visit*) _____ my friends.

7.   TRUE SITUATION: It isn't Saturday.

     I wish it (*be*) _____ Saturday.

     If it (*be*) _____ Saturday, I (*go*) _____ to the
     beach.

8.   TRUE SITUATION: I'm not rich.

     I wish I (*be*) _____ rich.

     If I (*be*) _____ rich, I (*live*) _____ on a farm

     and (*raise*) _____ horses.

EXERCISE 13: Complete the sentences with the words in parentheses.

1. Jim doesn't study hard. If he (*study*)_____studied_____ harder, he (*get*) _____would get_____ better grades.

2. The weather isn't nice. I (*take*) _____ a walk if the weather (*be*) _____ nice.*

3. My wife and I want to buy a house, but houses are too expensive. We (*buy*) _____ a house if we (*have*) _____ enough money for a downpayment.

4. If money (*grow*) _____ on trees, all of us (*be*) _____ rich.

5. Life (*be*) _____ boring if everyone (*have*) _____ the same opinions about everything.

6. If I (*be*) _____ you, I (*tell*) _____ Jim the truth.

7. Airplane tickets are expensive. If they (*be*) _____ cheap, I (*fly*) _____ to Paris for the weekend.

_____

*An "*if* clause" can come (a) before a result clause, or (b) after a result clause:

   (a) **If I had enough money,** *I would buy a car.*
   (b) *I would buy a car* **if I had enough money.**

NOTICE: When an "*if* clause" comes first, a comma is used after the "*if* clause."

8. I wish I (*have*) _____ a camera. I (*take*) _____

    a picture of the sunset tonight if I (*have*) _____ a camera.

9. The student cafeteria is relatively inexpensive, but the food isn't very good.

    I (*eat*) _____ there all the time if the food (*be*)

    _____ better.

10. Sometimes our teacher gives surprise quizzes. If I (*teach*)

    _____ this English class, I (*give, not*) _____

    surprise quizzes.

11. I wish I (*have*) _____ a car. If I (*have*) _____

    a car, I (*drive*) _____ to school.

12. I'm very tired tonight. If I (*be, not*) _____ tired, I (*go*)

    _____ to the movie with you.

EXERCISE 14—ORAL (BOOKS CLOSED):   **What would you do if you were. . .?** Practice using verb forms in contrary-to-fact sentences with *if.*

> *Example:* (What would you do if you were) a house painter?
> *Response:* If I were a house painter, I would (paint houses, paint your house, etc.).
> *Example:* a cat
> *Response:* If I were a cat, I would (chase mice, jump into your lap, etc.)*

1. a bird	10. hungry
2. a mountain climber	11. sleepy
3. an artist	12. at home
4. a secretary	13. (. . .)
5. a dog	14. (*name of a famous person*)
6. a good cook	15. a professional athlete
7. a teacher	16. a surgeon
8. a police officer	17. a musician
9. a parent	18. a mouse

To the teacher: Include a Student B if you wish.

> *Example:*   a cat
> *Student A:*   If I were a cat, I would chase mice.
> *Sudent B:*   If (. . .) were a cat, s/he would chase mice.

19. the (*President of the United States/the Prime Minister of Canada/etc.*)
20. the leader of your country
21. a magician
22. an astronaut
23. ninety years old
24. at/in (*a particular place*)
25. a genius
26. a billionaire
27. the captain of a ship
28. ambitious

14-4   USING *IF*: TRUE VS. CONTRARY-TO-FACT IN THE PRESENT/FUTURE

TRUE SITUATION:	(a) **If** you **need** some money, I (*simple present*)	{ will can } **lend** you some.	In (a): Perhaps you need some money. If that is true, I will (or can) lend you some. Reminder: Do not use **will** in an "**if** clause." (See 3-2.)
CONTRARY-TO-FACT SITUATION:	(b) **If** you **needed** some money, I some. (*simple past*)	{ would could } **lend** you	In (b): In truth, you don't need any money. But if the opposite were true, I would (or could) lend you some.

VERB FORM USAGE SUMMARY (PRESENT/FUTURE)

SITUATION	*IF* CLAUSE	RESULT CLAUSE
TRUE	simple present	will can } + simple form
CONTRARY-TO-FACT	simple past	would could } + simple form

EXERCISE 15:   Complete the sentences with the words in parentheses. Some of the sentences express true situations, and some of the sentences express contrary-to-fact situations.

1. Maybe I will have enough time tonight. If I (*have*) _____ enough time, I (*write*) _____ a letter to my cousin.

2. I won't have enough time tonight. But if I (*have*) _____
   enough time, I (*write*) _____ a letter to my cousin.

3. Maybe I will have enough money. If I (*have*) _____ enough
   money, I (*buy*) _____ a ticket to the rock concert.

4. Unfortunately, I don't have enough money. But if I (*have*)
   _____ enough money, I (*buy*) _____ a ticket to
   the rock concert.

5. Maybe I will buy a car. If I (*buy*) _____ a car, I (*drive*)
   _____ to Springfield next month to visit my friend.

6. I'm not going to buy a car. But if I (*buy*) _____ a car, I
   (*drive*) _____ to Springfield next month to visit my friend.

7. The weather is terrible today. But if the weather (*be*) _____
   good, I (*go*) _____ for a five-mile walk.

8. Maybe the weather will be nice tomorrow. If the weather (*be*)
   _____ nice, I (*go*) _____ for a long walk.

9. I know that you don't want to go to a movie tonight. But if you (*want*)
   _____ to go to a movie, I (*go*) _____ with you.

10. What would you like to do tonight? Do you want to go to a movie? If you
    (*want*) _____ to go to a movie, I (*go*) _____
    with you.

EXERCISE 16: Complete the following with your own words.

1. If I have enough money, _____

2. If I had enough money, _____

3. If I have enough time, _____

4. If I had enough time, _____

5. If the weather is nice tomorrow, _____

6. If the weather were nice today, _____

7. If you studied hard, _____

8. If you study hard, _____

9. If my uncle comes to visit me, _____

10. If my uncle were here, _____

11. I would fly to London if _____

12. I will fly to London if _____

13. I would get fat if _____

14. You will lose weight if _____

15. I won't be in class tomorrow if _____

16. If I didn't have to go to class tomorrow, _____

14-5 USING *IF*: CONTRARY-TO-FACT IN THE PAST

TRUE SITUATION:	(a) I didn't have enough money. *(last year, yesterday, etc.)*		Notice in (c) and (f): When the speaker is talking about past time, the past perfect is used in an "*if* clause." *Would have* + *past participle* or *could have* + *past participle* is used in a result clause.
MAKING A WISH:	(b) I wish I had had enough money.		
	IF **CLAUSE**	**RESULT CLAUSE**	
USING *IF*:	(c) If I **had had** enough money,	I { **would have bought** / **could have bought** } a car.	
TRUE SITUATION:	(d) The weather wasn't nice. *(yesterday, last week, etc.)*		
MAKING A WISH:	(e) I wish the weather had been nice.		
	IF **CLAUSE**	**RESULT CLAUSE**	
USING *IF*:	(f) If the weather **had been** nice,	I { **would have gone** / **could have gone** } to the zoo.	

EXERCISE 17: Complete the sentences with the words in parentheses.

1. TRUE SITUATION: I didn't have enough time yesterday.

    I wish I (*have*) _____ enough time yesterday.

If I (*have*) _____ enough time yesterday. I (*go*)

_____ to the park.

2.   TRUE SITUATION: I didn't have enough money last night.

I wish I (*have*) _____ enough money last night.

If I (*have*) _____ enough money last night, I (*go*)

_____ to a show.

3.   TRUE SITUATION: Mary didn't come to my party last week.

I wish she (*come*) _____ to my party.

If she (*come*) _____ to my party, she (*meet*)

_____ my fiancé.

4.   TRUE SITUATION: It was cold yesterday.

I wish it (*be, not*) _____ cold yesterday.

If it (*be, not*) _____ cold yesterday, I (*go*) _____
swimming.

5.   TRUE SITUATION: Jack didn't study for the test.

Jack wishes he (*study*) _____ for the test.

If he (*study*) _____ for the test, he (*pass*) _____
it.

14-6 SUMMARY: VERB FORMS IN SENTENCES WITH *IF* (CONDITIONAL SENTENCES)

SITUATION	IF CLAUSE	RESULT CLAUSE	EXAMPLES
TRUE IN THE PRESENT/FUTURE	simple present	*will* *can* } + simple form	(a) If I **have** enough money, I { **will buy** **can buy** } a ticket.
CONTRARY-TO-FACT IN THE PRESENT/FUTURE	simple past	*would* *could* } + simple form	(b) If I **had** enough money, I { **would buy** **could buy** } a ticket.
CONTRARY-TO-FACT IN THE PAST	past perfect	*would have* *could have* } + past participle	(c) If I **had had** enough money, I { **would have bought** **could have bought** } a ticket.

EXERCISE 18:   Complete the sentences with the words in parentheses.

1. I didn't feel good yesterday. If I (*feel*) _____ better, I (*come*)

   _____ to class yesterday.

2. I don't feel good today. If I (*feel*) _____ better, I (*take*)

   _____ a walk in the park today.

3. I have a cold today, but I will probably feel better tomorrow. If I (*feel*)

   _____ better tomorrow, I (*go*) _____ to class.

4. I'm sorry that you didn't come to the party. If you (*come*)

   _____ , you (*have*) _____ a good time.

5. I didn't know that Bob was sick. If I (*know*) _____ that he

   was sick, I (*take*) _____ him some chicken soup.

6. I'm tired. If I (*be, not*) _____ tired, I (*help*)

   _____ you.

7. Snow is predicted for tomorrow. If it (*snow*) _____

   tomorrow, I (*stay*) _____ home.

8. I may have a dollar. Let me look in my wallet. If I (*have*)

   _____ a dollar, I (*lend*) _____ it to you.

9. I don't have any money. If I (*have*) _____ a dollar, I (*lend*)

   _____ it to you.

10. I didn't have a dollar yesterday. If I (*have*)_____ a dollar

    yesterday, I (*lend*) _____ it to you.

11. I didn't know it was your birthday yesterday. I wish you (*tell*)

    _____ me. I (*get*) _____ you a present if I

    (*know*) _____ it was your birthday yesterday.

12. Why didn't you tell me when your plane was supposed to arrive? If you

    (*tell*) _____ me, I (*pick*) _____ you up at the
    airport.

EXERCISE 19—ORAL: Make sentences with *wish* and *if*. Follow the patterns in the examples.

> *Example:*   I don't have enough time.
> *Response:*   I wish I had enough time. If I had enough time, I (would/could go shopping this afternoon, etc.).
> *Example:*   I didn't have enough time.
> *Response:*   I wish I had had enough time. If I'd had enough time, I (would have/could have gone shopping yesterday afternoon, etc.)

1. I don't have enough money.
2. I didn't have enough money.
3. I don't have enough time.
4. I didn't have enough time.
5. The weather isn't nice.
6. The weather wasn't nice.
7. I'm in class right now.
8. I came to class yesterday.
9. My friend isn't at home.
10. My friend wasn't at home.
11. I don't know how to play the guitar.
12. I didn't know that my uncle was in the hospital.

EXERCISE 20—ORAL: Make sentences with *if*. Follow the patterns in the examples.

> *Example:*   If I have enough money. . . .
> *Student A:*   If I have enough money, I'll buy (can buy) a car.
> *Student B:*   If I buy a car, I'll drive (can drive) to Florida.
> *Student C:*   If I drive to Florida, I'll go (can go) to Miami.
> *Student D:*   If I go to Miami, I. . . .
>
> *Example:*   If I had enough money. . . .
> *Student A:*   If I had enough money, I would buy (could buy) a car.
> *Student B:*   If I bought a car, I would drive (could drive) to Florida.
> *Student C:*   If I drove to Florida, I would go (could go) to Miami.
> *Student D:*   If I went to Miami, I. . . .
>
> *Example:*   If I had had enough money. . . .
> *Student A:*   If I had had enough money, I would have bought (could have bought) a car.
> *Student B:*   If I had bought a car, I would have driven (could have driven) to Florida.

Student C: If I had driven to Florida, I would have gone (could
           have gone) to Miami.
Student D: If I had gone to Miami, I. . . .

1. If I have enough money. . . .
2. If I had enough money. . . .
3. If I had had enough money. . . .
4. If I have enough time. . . .
5. If I had enough time. . . .
6. If I had had enough time. . . .

7. If the weather is hot/cold tomorrow. . . .
8. If the weather were hot/cold. . . .
9. If the weather had been hot/cold yesterday. . . .
10. If I had a million dollars. . . .

EXERCISE 21—ORAL (BOOKS CLOSED): Answer the questions in complete sentences.

1. Where would you be right now if you weren't in class?
2. What would you have done yesterday if you hadn't come to class?
3. What would you do today if you had enough time?
4. What would you have done yesterday if you had had enough time?
5. What would you buy if you had enough money?
6. What would you have bought yesterday if you had had enough money?
7. What would you do if there were a fire in this building?
8. If you had your own private plane, where would you go for dinner tonight?
9. (. . .) is tired today. Give him/her some advice. What would you do if you were (. . .)?
10. (. . .) wants to learn English as quickly as possible. What would you do if you were (. . .)?
11. Could ships sail around the world if the earth were flat?
12. What would happen if there were a nuclear war?
13. What would you do if you were the teacher of this class?
14. Tell me one thing that you did yesterday. What would have happened if you had not (done that)?
15. What would you do tonight if you didn't have to study?
16. What do you wish were different about the world we live in?

EXERCISE 22—WRITTEN: Write on the following topic.

In what ways do you wish the world were different? Why do you wish these things? What would be the results?

appendix 1

Irregular Verbs

	SIMPLE FORM	SIMPLE PAST	PAST PARTICIPLE		SIMPLE FORM	SIMPLE PAST	PAST PARTICIPLE
B	be	was, were	been	**E**	eat	ate	eaten
	become	became	become	**F**	fall	fell	fallen
	begin	began	begun		feed	fed	fed
	bend	bent	bent		feel	felt	felt
	bite	bit	bitten		fight	fought	fought
	blow	blew	blown		find	found	found
	break	broke	broken		fit	fit	fit
	bring	brought	brought		fly	flew	flown
	broadcast	broadcast	broadcast		forget	forgot	forgotten
	build	built	built		forgive	forgave	forgiven
	buy	bought	bought		freeze	froze	frozen
C	catch	caught	caught	**G**	get	got	gotten (got)
	choose	chose	chosen		give	gave	given
	come	came	come		go	went	gone
	cost	cost	cost		grow	grew	grown
	cut	cut	cut	**H**	hang	hung	hung
D	dig	dug	dug		have	had	had
	do	did	done		hear	heard	heard
	draw	drew	drawn		hide	hid	hidden
	drink	drank	drunk		hit	hit	hit
	drive	drove	driven		hold	held	held
					hurt	hurt	hurt

	SIMPLE FORM	SIMPLE PAST	PAST PARTICIPLE		SIMPLE FORM	SIMPLE PAST	PAST PARTICIPLE
K	keep	kept	kept		shut	shut	shut
	know	knew	known		sing	sang	sung
L	lay	laid	laid		sit	sat	sat
	lead	led	led		sleep	slept	slept
	leave	left	left		slide	slid	slid
	lend	lent	lent		speak	spoke	spoken
	let	let	let		spend	spent	spent
	lie *poler*	lay	lain		spread	spread	spread
	light	lit (lighted)	lit (lighted)		stand	stood	stood
	lose	lost	lost		steal	stole	stolen
M	make	made	made		stick	stuck	stuck
	mean	meant	meant		strike	struck	struck
	meet	met	met		swear	swore	sworn
P	pay	paid	paid		sweep	swept	swept
	put	put	put		swim	swam	swum
Q	quit	quit	quit	**T**	take	took	taken
R	read	read	read		teach	taught	taught
	ride	rode	ridden		tear	tore	torn
	ring	rang	rung		tell	told	told
	rise	rose	risen		think	thought	thought
	run	ran	run		throw	threw	thrown
S	say	said	said	**U**	understand	understood	understood
	see	saw	seen		upset	upset	upset
	sell	sold	sold	**W**	wake	woke	waked (woken)
	send	sent	sent		wear	wore	worn
	set	set	set		win	won	won
	shake	shook	shaken		withdraw	withdrew	withdrawn
	shoot	shot	shot		write	wrote	written

appendix 2

Spelling of *-ing* and *-ed* Forms

END OF VERB	DOUBLE THE CONSONANT?	SIMPLE FORM	*-ING*	*-ED*	
-e	NO	(a) **smile** **hope**	**smiling** **hoping**	**smiled** **hoped**	*-Ing* form: Drop the **-e,** add **-ing.** *-Ed* form: Just add **-d.**
Two Consonants	NO	(b) **help** **learn**	**helping** **learning**	**helped** **learned**	If the verb ends in two consonants, just add **-ing** or **-ed.**
Two Vowels + One Consonant	NO	(c) **rain** **heat**	**raining** **heating**	**rained** **heated**	If the verb ends in two vowels + a consonant, just add **-ing** or **-ed.**
One Vowel + One Consonant	YES	ONE-SYLLABLE VERBS (d) **stop** **plan**	**stopping** **planning**	**stopped** **planned**	If the verb has one syllable and ends in one vowel + one consonant, double the consonant to make the **-ing** or **-ed** form.*

*Exceptions: Do not double **w** or **x**: *snow, snowing, snowed*
fix, fixing, fixed

		TWO-SYLLABLE VERBS			
	NO	(e)	visit offer	visiting offering	visited offered	If the first syllable of a two-syllable verb is stressed, do not double the consonant.
	YES	(f)	prefér admit	preferring admitting	preferred admitted	If the second syllable of a two-syllable verb is stressed, double the consonant.
-y	NO	(g)	play enjoy	playing enjoying	played enjoyed	If the verb ends in a vowel + **y,** keep the **-y.** Do not change it to **-i.**
		(h)	worry study	worrying studying	worried studied	If the verb ends in a consonant + **-y,** keep the **-y** for the **-ing** form, but change the **-y** to **-i** to make the **-ed** form.
-ie	N/A	(i)	die tie	dying tying	died tied	**-Ing** form: Change **-ie** to **-y** and add **-ing**. **-Ed** form: Just add **-d**.

EXERCISE 1: Write the **-ing** and **-ed** forms of the following verbs. (The simple past/past participle of irregular verbs is given in parentheses.)

	-ING	-ED
1. start	starting	started
2. wait		
3. quit		(quit)
4. write		(wrote/written)
5. shout		
6. cut		(cut)
7. meet		(met)
8. hope		
9. hop		

10. help _____ _____

11. sleep _____ _____ (slept) _____

12. step _____ _____

13. tape _____ _____

14. tap _____ _____

15. rain _____ _____

16. run _____ _____ (ran/run) _____

17. whine _____ _____

18. win _____ _____ (won) _____

19. explain _____ _____

20. burn _____ _____

21. swim _____ _____ (swam/swum) _____

22. aim _____ _____

23. charm _____ _____

24. cram _____ _____

25. tame _____ _____

EXERCISE 2:   Write the *-ing* and *-ed* forms of the following verbs.

	-ING	-ED
1. open	_____	_____
2. begin	_____	(began/begun)
3. occur	_____	_____
4. happen	_____	_____
5. refer	_____	_____

  6. offer   _____   _____

  7. listen   _____   _____

  8. admit   _____   _____

  9. visit   _____   _____

10. omit   _____   _____

11. hurry   _____   _____

12. study   _____   _____

13. enjoy   _____   _____

14. reply   _____   _____

15. stay   _____   _____

16. buy   _____   _____ (bought) _____

17. try   _____   _____

18. tie   _____   _____

19. die   _____   _____

20. lie*   _____   _____

EXERCISE 3: Write the **-ing** and **-ed** forms of the following verbs.

	-ING	-ED
1. lift	_____	_____
2. promise	_____	_____
3. slap	_____	_____
4. wave	_____	_____
5. carry	_____	_____
6. happen	_____	_____

Lie is a regular verb when it means "not tell the truth." *Lie* is an irregular verb when it means "put one's body flat on a bed or another surface": *lie, lay, lain.*

7. choose   _____   _____(chose/chosen)_____

8. ride   _____   _____(rode/ridden)_____

9. mop   _____   _____

10. mope   _____   _____

11. smile   _____   _____

12. fail   _____   _____

13. file   _____   _____

14. drag   _____   _____

15. use   _____   _____

16. prefer   _____   _____

17. pray   _____   _____

18. point   _____   _____

19. appear   _____   _____

20. relax   _____   _____

21. borrow   _____   _____

22. cry   _____   _____

23. eat   _____   _____(ate/eaten)_____

24. remind   _____   _____

25. tip   _____   _____

appendix 3

Capitalization

CAPITALIZE THE FOLLOWING:		
1. The first word of a sentence	(a) **W**e saw a movie last night. **I**t was very good.	*Capitalize* = use a big letter, not a small letter.
2. The names of people	(b) I met **G**eorge **A**dams yesterday.	
3. Titles used with the names of people	(c) I saw **D**octor (**D**r.) Smith. Do you know **P**rofessor (**P**rof.) Alston?	*Compare:* I saw a doctor. I saw Doctor Wilson.
4. Months, days, holidays	(d) I was born in **A**pril. Bob arrived last **M**onday. It snowed on **T**hanksgiving **D**ay.	NOTE: Seasons are not capitalized: *spring, summer, fall/autumn, winter*
5. The names of places: city state/province country continent ocean lake river desert	(e) He lives in **C**hicago. She was born in **C**alifornia. They are from **M**exico. **T**ibet is in **A**sia. They crossed the **A**tlantic **O**cean. Chicago is on **L**ake **M**ichigan. The **M**ississippi **R**iver flows south. The **S**ahara **D**esert is in Africa.	*Compare:* She lives in a city. She lives in New York City. *Compare:* They crossed a river. They crossed the Yellow River.

mountain school business street, etc. building park, zoo	We visited the **Rocky Mountains.** I go to the **University of Florida.** I work for the **General Electric Company.** He lives on **Grand Avenue.** We have class in **Ritter Hall.** I went jogging in **Forest Park.**	*Compare:* I go to a university. I go to the University of Texas. *Compare:* We went to a park. We went to Central Park.
6. The names of courses	(f) I'm taking **Chemistry 101** this term.	*Compare:* I'm reading a book about psychology. I'm taking Psychology 101 this term.
7. The names of languages and nationalities	(g) She speaks **Spanish.** We discussed **Japanese** customs.	Words that refer to the names of nations, nationalities, and languages are always capitalized.
8. The names of religions	(h) **Buddhism, Christianity, Hinduism, Islam,** and **Judaism** are major religions in the world. Talal is a **Moslem.**	Words that refer to the names of religions are always capitalized.

EXERCISE I: Add capital letters where necessary.

    W   T

1. we're going to have a test next tuesday.
2. do you know richard smith? he is a professor at this university.
3. professor smith teaches at the university of arizona.
4. the nile river flows into the mediterranean sea.
5. john is a catholic. ali is a moslem.
6. anna speaks french. she studied in france for two years.
7. i'm taking a history course this semester.
8. i'm taking modern european history 101 this semester.
9. we went to vancouver, british columbia, for our vacation last summer.
10. venezuela is a spanish-speaking country.
11. canada is in north america.*

---

*When *north*, *south*, *east*, and *west* refer to the direction on a compass, they are not capitalized: *Japan is east of China.*
When they are part of a geographical name, they are capitalized: *Japan is in the Far East.*

12. canada is north of the united states.
13. the sun rises in the east.
14. the mississippi river flows south.

EXERCISE 2:   Add capital letters where necessary.

1. We don't have class on saturday.
2. I'm taking biology 101 this semester.
3. I'm taking history, biology, english, and calculus this semester.
4. We went to a zoo. We went to brookfield zoo in chicago.
5. I live on a nice street. I live at 2358 olive street.
6. We went to canada last summer. We went to montreal in july.
7. I like vietnamese food.
8. The religion of saudi arabia is islam.
9. She works for the xerox corporation. It is a very large corporation.
10. Pedro is from latin america.
11. My uncle lives in st. louis. I'm going to visit uncle bill next spring.
12. On valentine's day (february 14), sweethearts give each other presents.
13. We went to a park. We went to woodland park.
14. Are you going to go to the university of oregon or oregon state university?
15. Alice goes to a university in oregon.
16. I voted for senator jones. A senator is an important person.

appendix **4**

Preposition Combinations

I. PREPOSITION COMBINATIONS WITH VERBS AND ADJECTIVES

This list contains only those preposition combinations used in exercises in the text.

A *be* absent from
 be accustomed to
 be acquainted with
      admire (someone) for (something)
 be afraid of
      agree with (someone) about (something)
 be angry at/with
      apologize to (someone) for (something)
      apply to (a place) for (something)
      approve of
      argue with (someone) about (something)
      arrive at (a building, a room)
      arrive in (a city, a country)
      ask (someone) about (something)
      ask (someone) for (something)

B *be* bad for
      believe in
      belong to
 be bored with/by
      borrow (something) from (someone)

335

C *be* clear to
        compare (X) to/with (Y)
        complain to (someone) about (something)
        consist of
    be crowded with

D   depend on/upon (someone) for (something)
    be different from
    be disappointed in   *defraudado*
    be divorced from
    be done with
        dream about/of
    be drunk on

E *be* engaged to
    be equal to
    be excited about
        excuse (someone) for (something)
    (*be*) exhausted from   *vaciar*

F *be* familiar with
    be famous for
    be finished with
        forgive (someone) for (something)
    be friendly to/with
    be frightened of/by
    be full of

G   get rid of
    be gone from
    be good for
        graduate from

H   happen to
        hear about/of
        hear from
        help (someone) with (something)
        hope for
    be hungry for

I   insist on
    be interested in
        introduce (someone) to (someone)
        invite (someone) to (something)
    be involved in

K *be* kind to
        know about

L   laugh at
listen to
look at
look for
look forward to

M *be* mad at
be married to
matter to
be the matter with

N *be* nice to

O *be* opposed to

P   pay for
be polite to
be prepared for
protect (X) from (Y)
be proud of

Q *be* qualified for

R *be* ready for
be related to
rely on/upon
be responsible for

S *be* satisfied with
be scared of/by *Temor a*
search for   *enbascade*
separate (X) from (Y)
be similar to
speak to/with (someone) about (something)
stare at

T   talk to/with (someone) about (something)
be terrified of/by
thank (someone) for (something)
be thirsty for
be tired from
be tired of
travel to

W   wait for
wait on
be worried about

II. TWO-WORD VERBS

This list contains only those two-word verbs used in the exercises in the text.
The verbs with an asterisk (*) are nonseparable. The others are separable, See 8–4
and 8–5 for a discussion of separable and nonseparable two-word verbs.

A ask out . . . .*ask someone to go on a date*

C call back . . . .*return a telephone call*
    call off . . . .*cancel*
  *call on . . . .*ask to speak in class*
    call up . . . .*make a telephone call*
    cross out . . . .*draw a line through*

D do over . . . .*do again*
  *drop in (on) . . . .*visit without calling first or without an invitation*
  *drop out (of) . . . .*stop attending school*

F figure out . . . .*find the solution to a problem*
    fill in . . . .*complete a sentence by writing in a blank*
    fill out . . . .*write information in a form (e.g., an application form)* '
    fill up . . . .*fill completely with gas, water, coffee, etc.*
    find out . . . .*discover information*
  *fool around (with) . . . . .*have fun while wasting time*

G *get along (with) . . . .*have a good relationship with*
  *get back (from) . . . .*return from a trip*
  *get in(to) . . . .*enter a car, a taxi*
  *get off . . . .*leave a bus, an airplane, a train, a subway, a bicycle*
  *get on . . . .*enter a bus, an airplane, a train, a subway, a bicycle*
  *get out (of) . . . .*leave a car, a taxi*
  *get over . . . .*recover from an illness*
  *get through (with) . . . . .*finish*
    give back . . . .*return something to someone*
    give up . . . .*quit doing something or quit trying*
  *grow up (in) . . . .*become an adult*

H hand in . . . .*give homework, tests papers, etc., to a teacher*
    hand out . . . .*give something to this person, then that person, then another person, etc.*
    hang up . . . .*(1) hang on a hanger or a hook; (2) end a telephone call*

K *keep on . . . .*continue*

L leave out . . . .*omit*
  *look out (for) . . . .*be careful*
    look up . . . .*look for information in a reference book*

M make up . . . .*invent*

P pay back . . . .*return money to someone*
    pick up . . . .*lift*

	put away	. . . .	*put something in its usual or proper place*
	put back	. . . .	*return something to its original place*
	put down	. . . .	*stop holding or carrying*
	put off	. . . .	*postpone*
	put on	. . . .	*put clothes on one's body*
	put out	. . . .	*extinguish (stop) a fire, a cigarette, a cigar*
R	*run into	. . . .	*meet by chance*
	*run out (of)	. . . .	*finish the supply of something*
S	shut off	. . . .	*stop a machine or light, turn off*
	start over	. . . .	*start again*
T	take off	. . . .	*remove clothes from one's body*
	tear down	. . . .	*destroy a building*
	tear off	. . . .	*detach, tear along a dotted or perforated line*
	tear out (of)	. . . .	*remove a piece of paper from a book or notebook*
	tear up	. . . .	*tear into small pieces*
	throw away/out	. . . .	*put in the trash, discard*
	try on	. . . .	*put on clothing to see if it fits*
	turn down	. . . .	*decrease the volume* *desminuir*
	turn off	. . . .	*stop a machine or a light, shut off*
	turn on	. . . .	*begin a machine or a light*
	turn up	. . . .	*increase the volume*
W	wake up	. . . .	*stop sleeping*
	*watch out (for)	. . . .	*be careful*
	write down	. . . .	*write a note on a piece of paper*

appendix 5

Guide to Correcting Compositions

To the student: Each number represents an area of usage. Your teacher will use these numbers when marking your writing to indicate that you have made an error. Refer to this list to find out what kind of error you have made and then make the necessary correction.

1	SINGULAR-PLURAL	He have(1) been here for six month(1). *He has been here for six months.*
2	WORD FORM	I saw a beauty(2) picture. *I saw a beautiful picture.*
3	WORD CHOICE	She got on(3) the taxi. *She got into the taxi.*
4	VERB TENSE	He is(4) here since June. *He has been here since June.*
5+	ADD A WORD	I want ‸(5+) go to the zoo. *I want to go to the zoo.*
5−	OMIT A WORD	She entered to(5−) the university *She entered the university.*

6   WORD ORDER

⑥

I saw five times that movie.
I saw that movie five times.

7   INCOMPLETE SENTENCE

⑦

I went to bed. Because I was tired.
I went to bed because I was tired.

8   SPELLING

⑧

An accident occured.
An accident occurred.

9   PUNCTUATION

⑨

What did he say.
What did he say?

10   CAPITALIZATION

⑩

I am studying english.
I am studying English.

11   ARTICLE

⑪

I had a accident.
I had an accident.

12?   MEANING NOT CLEAR

⑫?

He borrowed some smoke.
(???)

13   RUN-ON SENTENCE*

⑬

My roommate was sleeping, we didn't want to wake her up.
My roommate was sleeping. We didn't want to wake her up.

---

*A run-on sentence occurs when two sentences are incorrectly connected: the end of one sentence and the beginning of the next sentence are not properly marked by a period and a capital letter.

Index